ANSWERING
A GODSLAYER

ANSWERING A GODSLAYER

THOMAS CLOTHIER

TATE PUBLISHING
AND ENTERPRISES, LLC

Published by Tate Publishing & Enterprises, LLC
127 E. Trade Center Terrace | Mustang, Oklahoma 73064 USA
1.888.361.9473 | www.tatepublishing.com

Tate Publishing is committed to excellence in the publishing industry. The company reflects the philosophy established by the founders, based on Psalm 68:11,
"The Lord gave the word and great was the company of those who published it."

Book design copyright © 2016 by Tate Publishing, LLC. All rights reserved.
Cover design by Joshua Rafols
Interior design by Gram Telen

Published in the United States of America

ISBN: 978-1-68319-787-4
1. Religion / General
2. Religion / Religious Intolerance, Persecution & Conflict
16.09.08

Now who is there to harm you if you are zealous for what is good? But even if you should suffer for righteousness' sake, you will be blessed. Have no fear of them, nor be troubled, but in your hearts honor Christ the Lord as holy, always being prepared to make a defense to anyone who asks you for a reason for the hope that is in you; yet do it with gentleness and respect, having a good conscience, so that, when you are slandered, those who revile your good behavior in Christ may be put to shame. For it is better to suffer for doing good, if that should be God's will, than for doing evil.

—1 Peter 3:13–17 (ESV)

Soli Deo Gloria!

Acknowledgments

This work is the result of many individuals whose love an encouragement have been an expression of God's work in their lives as I trust this is an expression of God's work in mine.

I am grateful to the staff at Tate publishing. Jim, Michelle, and others have proven to be a great source of knowledge and insight. Thank you!

I am grateful to the staff at First Christian Church: Bob, Michael, Jon, and Linda. They are a joy in which to serve the Lord together.

I am grateful to the elders of First Christian Church and their constant support and laughter. Thanks for keeping me grounded.

I am grateful to the congregation of First Christian Church and their insatiable desire to grow in the grace and knowledge of the Lord Jesus Christ. They have patiently waited for this work to be completed so that they may become more fully prepared to defend the faith.

I am grateful to my family. My wife Diana, my children Timothy and Carrie, along with Elizabeth and Dylan. I am also grateful for the greatest name I have, and hear, from Allegra, Adelaide, Toban, and Tucker: Papa.

Finally, I am most grateful to the Lord who saved me by grace alone, through faith alone in Christ alone to the glory of God alone. Soli deo Gloria!

Contents

Preface

There are no coincidences. A coincidence is a situation or encounter that supposedly happens by accident, chance, luck, or a simple twist of fate. Life and living is viewed as a series of unrelated incidents, which have no relationship to each other.

However, the more I study God's Word and walk with God in a covenant relationship through faith in Jesus Christ, so-called coincidences of life are really recognized as divine appointments that God sovereignly orchestrates. These engagements provide teachable moments and opportunities for worship and service for the follower of Jesus.

The writer of Proverbs states, "Commit your work to the LORD, and your plans will be established. The LORD has made everything for its purpose, even the wicked for the day of trouble. The heart of man plans his way, but the LORD establishes his steps" (Prov. 16:3–4, 9; ESV).[1]

Rather than be taken by surprise by such God-purposed occurrences, the follower of Jesus must learn that God uses these events to strengthen our trust in Him as One who uses us for His glory and who is actively involved in our lives. What I would previously take little notice of, or simply ignore, I now consciously thank and praise God for.

Such is the purpose for this book. It began with an offer from my community's local newspaper several years ago. They contacted the church office and wondered if any of us on the pastoral staff would be interested in writing for and contributing to the paper's Professional Advice Column. The column is a monthly collection of articles featuring various professionals from the community, such as podiatrists, optometrists, dentists, lawyers, golf pro's, pastors, etc. These experts offer advice and insight from their respective professions to the interested reader. The columns' emphasis is on the practical.

Upon agreeing to participate, I submitted a series of articles. I began with the *Evidences for the Bible being the Word of God.* I then submitted a second series on the *Reality and Purpose of Suffering and Evil in the World.* Admittedly brief in scope and length, I endeavored to touch upon key elements of both subjects. The purpose of this was to explain to readers the reasonableness of, and the evidences for, the Bible being the trustworthy and inerrant Word of God. This assertion would be especially significant as it related to the subject of suffering and evil in the world: historically and currently.

What I did not anticipate, but what was no coincidence, were a series of responses from an apparent reader of my column. I received a letter following the publication of each one of my articles. The letters contained no return address and no identification as to their author except for the cryptic name: the godslayer.

When the first letter arrived in the church mail, my secretary was more than a bit concerned. In fact, she approached one of the church elders, who "coincidently" happened to be in the building at the time, to see whether he thought I should even see and read the letter's contents. He stated that I should.

Each one of the letters I received, coinciding with each column I wrote, were antagonistic in tone and content. The author consistently took issue with what I had written. He expressed a deep hated for God, and not surprisingly me. He expressed that God was either a nonexistent figment of my imagination, a monster, and/or just plain evil.

You may be wondering how I know the godslayer is a man. Through the letters, I made several observations based on his writings. The godslayer has a wife and presents himself as an intelligent individual. He is a self-described atheist and strives to be a logician. He is also a bad speller.

I have encountered three kinds of atheists as a Christian and as a pastor. The first type of atheist is the practical or practicing atheist. This is the individual we probably all know. It is the person who may attend church, seeks to live by a moral code, is respected within the community, and even may express a belief in God's existence. However, they live their life as if God does not exist. Life's decisions are made, things are said and done, and situations encountered with little or no thought as to God's perspective. What eventually matters is not what God thinks or wants, but what they think and want.

The second kind is what I'll call the "gentle" atheist. This is the individual who wants to know what I believe, why I believe it, and who engages in polite and respectful conversation. They may not accept what I believe as true, but they respect my right to believe what I believe to be true.

I once had a student, when I taught freshmen English composition at a local state university, who fit this description. He wanted to know why I believed in the existence of God. He acknowledged that he was an agnostic, if not an atheist during our first class. When we met to discuss this issue, our meeting was pleasant and respectful.

One of the most telling moments in our conversation was when this young man acknowledged that he wished there was a God. This was because he admitted he was afraid to die. In response, I shared the gospel with him. He even let me pray with him and for him.

The third type of atheist is the "angry" atheist. This is the individual who is not interested in holding a polite conversation. Rather, this person is on the attack. In their mind, there is no redeemable reason to believe in the existence of the God of the Bible. They may respect world religions but are particularly antagonistic toward biblical Christianity. They state that the God of the Bible is nonexistent.

However, if the God of the Bible is as they say, nonexistent, then why do they hate even the very idea of this so-called nonexistent God? Their anger is so intense in what they say about Him and toward those who believe in Him that it borders on an obsession. Based upon the content of his letters, the godslayer fits into this final category.

If God does not exist, why not just acknowledge that those who believe in His existence are either delusional or naive. Why such anger? Why such hatred and angst? This is why I suspect, from the expressed anger and tone of his letters, that someone or something hurt the godslayer and he blames God for that pain.

The godslayer's questions and objections concerning God must be answered. Whether they are gentle, practical or angry, logical, wise, gentle, and coherent, answers must be given to atheists.

The godslayer made a variety of assertions and challenges in his letters. It will be my goal to answer these assertions and challenges and to articulate the reasonableness and rationale for the Christian faith. While I remain skeptical as to his acceptance of my answers, I want any atheist to know there are answers to their questions and objections about God.

Ministering to such individuals must not be conducted with a sense of pride or arrogance in asserting a biblical point of view. That type of attitude will not go over well with any audience; especially a person who is antagonistic to biblical truth. What I hope to accomplish the Apostle Peter expressed quite well:

> Now who is there to harm you if you are zealous for what is good? But even if you should suffer for righteousness' sake, you will be blessed. Have no fear of them, nor be troubled, but in your hearts honor Christ the Lord as holy, always being prepared to make a defense to anyone who asks you for a reason for the hope that is in you; yet do it with gentleness and respect, having a good conscience, so that, when you are slandered, those who revile your good behavior in Christ may be put to shame. For it is better to suffer for doing good, if that should be God's will, than for doing evil. (1 Pet. 3:13–17, ESV).[2]

Peter acknowledges to his readers then, and believers today, how the follower of Christ should live. The believer should be zealous for what is good. Peter explains this through the literary device of cause and effect. He mentions the effect first and the corresponding cause second.

He asks the believer, "Who is it who is going to harm you?" This refers to someone who seeks to render evil upon a Christian because of their faith in Christ. Peter says that in most situations that the believer in Christ, who seeks to be joyful, honorable, and upright, will not encounter harm from other people.

Yet, Peter is not so naive to believe that even when believers do good, harm will not befall them. He says that even if the disciple of Jesus should suffer and be afflicted for righteousness' sake, the disciple should be happy and blessed.

Additionally, the apostle strongly commands that we should neither fear our outward circumstances nor be troubled by any inner commotion within our souls. On the contrary, we should acknowledge, in our thinking, feeling, and decisions the Lord Jesus Christ as holy. Instead of being awed by our circumstances, we are to regard Christ with awe and wonder.

The believer should also be prepared to defend their faith in Christ. In the Greek New Testament, the word for defend is *apologia*. It means to make a verbal and reasoned defense or argument. Our English word *apologetics* comes from this Greek word. Within this context, the believer's calling is to defend the gospel. The believer should always be prepared to make such a defense to anyone who asks the reason for the hope in Christ for eternal life.

However, the believer should not defend the gospel arrogantly or angrily but rather with gentleness of disposition and spirit, with respect for the questioner, and with a clear conscience. This is so that if anyone should slander the believer in question, they would be ashamed. Peter concludes that it is better to suffer, if it is God's will, for doing good than to suffer for doing evil.

This then is the perspective in approaching any response to the questions posed by the godslayers in our lives.

We launch this quest of answering an atheist's objections by reproducing my initial articles, which prompted the godslayer's responses to me. These articles will form the initial chapters. We will begin with the biblical and philosophical evidences for God's existence. Since the godslayer continually attacks the reality of the God's existence and holiness, exploring evidence to the contrary is where we must begin.

We will then follow this by examining the evidences that the Bible is the Word of God. This will be proposed not only by examining internal evidence within the Scriptures, but also by viewing the external evidence and arguments outside of the Scriptures. We will also examine the problem of evil.

The second portion of the book will involve reproducing each of the letters the godslayer mailed to me and then answer each objection he raises in each letter, point by point. It is imperative and important to not let any atheist and opponent to biblical truth assume there are no answers to their questions. Many may be intimidated by atheists who have practiced taking the offense in conversations with Christians. It is time for believers in Christ to graciously and gently stop being intimidated by those opposed to the gospel.

As J. Mack Styles writes, "Defending the faith is a fine thing to do, but it is easy to give apologetics for Christianity without explaining the gospel—and we cannot evangelize without the gospel".[3] What then is the gospel?

The gospel is the good news of salvation in Jesus Christ as Savior and Lord. The major components of the gospel message are as follows:

God exists. Genesis 1:1; John 1:1–2. A thorough examination of God's existence will be offered in a later chapter, but this is where the gospel begins: with the reality of God's existence. Among all of His many other attributes, we fundamentally acknowledge that God is Creator, He is love (1 John 4:7–11), He is just (1 John 1:8–10), and most importantly, He is holy (Isa. 6:1–7).

Sin exists. Genesis 3; Romans 1–3; Ephesians 2:1–10. Sin is any lack of obedience, active or passive, to the revealed and moral will of God. Sin occurs not only in our actions, but also in an individual's speech and thought life. Fallen man is a sinner by nature (Eph. 2:1–3). He does not become a sinner when he sins, rather he sins because he is by nature a sinner.

A Savior exists. Isaiah 52:13–53:12; Romans 3:21–26; Acts 4:12; Colossians 1:15–20. Through the person and work of Jesus Christ, sinners are delivered from not only the penalty of sin (justification), but also from the power of sin (sanctification) and ultimately the presence of sin (glorification).

Salvation exists. Ephesians 2:1–10; Colossians 1:21–26. God's deliverance of the sinner from the penalty, power, and eventual presence of sin is by grace alone, through faith alone in the person, and work of Jesus Christ alone. God enables the sinner, on the basis of God's grace, to not only repent of his sin (Mark 1:15; Luke 24:47; Acts 2:38, 3:19, 5:31, 20:21; 2 Tim. 2:25), but also to place their faith in Jesus Christ as Savior and Lord (Eph. 2:8–9; Acts 13:48; Phil. 1:29; 2 Pet. 1:1–2). This results in conversion.

Conversion must involve the sinner's knowledge of his sinful condition (Rom. 3:20; Ps. 51:1–4; Ezek. 36:25–32), along with knowing the divine remedy (Rom. 10:13–17; Ps. 91:1–10).

Conversion must also involve an acceptance or agreement of the aforementioned truths. This is demonstrated by a broken and contrite heart (2 Sam. 12; Ps. 51:17; 2 Cor. 7:1–10). Sinful man must also feel the conviction to be drawn to Jesus Christ (John 4:1–43; 1 Thess. 2:13).

Finally, conversion must involve the sinner actively turning from sin, which is repentance (Acts 26:12–18; Ezek. 14; 2 Cor. 7:1–11). It also involves the sinner turning by faith in Christ alone and relying solely upon Him for salvation (Mark 1:14–15; Acts 15:6–11, 16:25–34; Phil. 3:1–9).

Should believers assume that by answering every question raised by an atheist that this will convince the unbeliever of their need for Christ? On the contrary! You may correctly and thoroughly address every objection an atheist may have toward the Bible, but only the Holy

Spirit can quicken their soul and enable them to believe in the gospel of Jesus Christ. Our task is to sow and water the seeds of biblical truth. It is God's work to bring that watered seed to germination, growth, and fruition. As the Apostle Paul writes in 1 Corinthians 3:5–9,

> What then is Apollos? What is Paul? Servants through whom you believed, as the Lord assigned to each. I planted, Apollos watered, but God gave the growth. So neither he who plants nor he who waters is anything, but only God who gives the growth. He who plants and he who waters are one and each will receive his wages according to his labor. For we are God's fellow workers. You are God's field, God's building. (1 Cor. 3:5–9, ESV).[4]

So let us begin sowing the seeds of biblical truth. Soli Deo gloria!

The Biblical Evidences for God's Existence

What does the Bible teach about God's existence? Joe Boot writes, in his article *Broader Cultural and Philosophical Challenges*, that "We must begin any pursuit of knowledge (of God) with confident submission to God in his Word."[1] Nowhere does Scripture argue for God's reality. On the contrary, the very first verse in the Bible sets forth the doctrine of God. "In the beginning, God created the heavens and the earth" (Gen. 1:1, ESV).[2]

There are two basic philosophies in the world. Call them worldviews. These worldviews form the basis of how people live and think about life. However, these two worldviews are diametrically opposed to each other. They always have been and always will be. They represent the ongoing conflict between truth and deception, between what is real and what is unreal.

The first basic worldview is known as creationism. Creationism is the religious belief that humanity, life, the

Earth, and the universe are the creation of a supernatural being. As we will see, the proposition of creationism begins at the very outset of God's revealed truth, the Bible. The consequence of creationism is that the God of the Bible is the One True Creator, and creation is therefore accountable to Him. The purpose of life therefore is to glorify the One True Creator by loving Him and loving others by being obedient to His revealed truth contained in the Holy Scriptures, the Bible.

The second basic worldview is known as naturalism. Naturalism commonly refers to the philosophical belief that only natural laws and forces (as opposed to supernatural ones) operate in the world and that nothing exists beyond the natural world. Natural laws are the rules that govern the structure and behavior of the natural world. The goal of science is to discover and publish these laws.

Philosopher Paul Kurtz argues that nature is best accounted for by reference to material principles. These principles include mass, energy, and other physical and chemical properties accepted by the scientific community. Further, this sense of naturalism holds that spirits, deities, and ghosts are not real and that there is no "purpose" in nature. The conclusion of naturalism is that there is no God to whom the natural world is accountable. There is no ultimate and singular purpose to life and living. Therefore, the natural world does whatever it desires in order to establish some reason for life and living.

Examples of these desires to find purpose within the natural realm, void of a personal creator God, include but are not limited to the following:

- Rationalism. In epistemology (the study of knowledge and understanding) and in its modern sense, rationalism is the worldview that appeals to reason as a source of knowledge.

- Hedonism. It is a school of thought that argues that pleasure is the only intrinsic good. In very simple terms, a hedonist strives to maximize net pleasure (pleasure minus pain).

- Epicureanism. In the Epicurean view, the highest pleasure (tranquility and freedom from fear) was obtained by knowledge, friendship, and living a virtuous and temperate life. He lauded the simple life, and advocated reducing one's desires, verging on asceticism. He argued that when eating, one should not eat too richly, for it could lead to dissatisfaction later, such as the grim realization that one could not afford such delicacies in the future.

- Stoicism. It teaches the development of self-control and fortitude as a means of overcoming destructive emotions.

- Materialism. In philosophy, the theory of materialism holds that the only thing that exists is matter.

- Pessimistic existentialism. Useless passions are passions that are futile. They have no meaning. Philosopher Jean Paul Sartre's grim conclusion is that all of our caring, our concerns, and our deepest aspirations are empty of significance. Human life is meaningless. It is a cosmic joke and the cold, impersonal, indifferent universe is the comedian. It would be better for us if the universe were hostile. At least we could be involved with an enemy that might possibly be vanquished or persuaded to be friendly. But an indifferent universe is a universe that doesn't care. It doesn't care, because it cannot care; it is impersonal.

- Secularism. It is the separation of a government, organization, or institution from religion and/or religious beliefs.

- Sentimental humanism is a secular ideology, which espouses reason, ethics, and justice, while also rejecting supernatural and religious doctrine and teachings as a basis of reason, ethics, justice, morality, and decision-making.

- Pragmatism. Whatever works is good. The ends justify the means.

- Moralism. In our own context, one of the most seductive false gospels is moralism. This false gospel can take many forms and can emerge from any number of political and cultural impulses. Nevertheless, the basic structure of moralism comes down to this—the belief that the Gospel can be reduced to improvements in man's behavior.

As one author has written, "Naturalism has now replaced Christianity as the main religion of the Western world and evolution has become naturalism's principle dogma."[3] Naturalism is appropriately described by the Apostle Paul in Romans 1:18–22 where he writes:

> For the wrath of God is revealed from heaven against all ungodliness and unrighteousness of men, who by their unrighteousness suppress the truth. For what can be known about God is plain to them, because God has shown it to them. For his invisible attributes, namely, his eternal power and divine nature, have been clearly perceived, ever since the creation of the world, in the things that have been made. So they are without excuse. For although they knew God, they did not honor him as God or give thanks to him, but they became futile in their thinking, and their foolish hearts were darkened. Claiming to be wise, they became fools. (Rom. 1:18–22, ESV).[4]

The basis for the propositional truth for creationism, and its consequential implications, including being accountable to God, stems from the very first verse from the first book of the Bible: Genesis 1:1. Rather than view this verse as an archaic, ancient, or outdated text having no application to lives today, the text establishes the foundation, source, and starting point for all the Christian Creationist believes and consequentially does in knowing and living for God the Creator.

To begin with we observe the event of creation! "In the beginning" (Gen. 1:1, ESV).[5] The phrase is one word in the Hebrew (רֵאשִׁית / rēʾšît). It refers to the point in time, which is the beginning: the beginning of time at the point of the initiation of life that God created. The word appears fifty times in nearly all parts of the Old Testament (OT). The primary meaning is "first" or "beginning" of a series.

This term may refer to the initiation of a series of historical events (Gen. 10:10; Jer. 26:1), but it also refers to a foundational or necessary condition as the reverence or fear of God (Ps. 111:10; Prov. 1:7) and the initiation, as opposed to the results, of a life (Job 8:7, 42:12). It is used frequently in the special sense of the choicest or best of a group or class of things, particularly in reference to items to be set aside for God's service or sacrifice. The "first fruits" (Lev. 2:12, 23:10; Neh. 12:44)[6] and "choicest" (Num. 18:12)[7] fruits are so distinguished. Difficult uses of the term occur in several passages. In Deuteronomy 33:21 the King James Version reads "first part."[8] While in Daniel 11:41, the text reads "chief of the children of Ammon."[9]

The most important use of *rēšît* in the Old Testament occurs in Genesis 1:1. There has been a great deal of debate over the use of *rēšît*. Many commentators, both ancient and modern, have tried to read the phrase as "when" rather than "in the beginning" as do several modern translations. John 1:1 translates the Hebrew and follows the Greek Old Testament Translation (the Septuagint) precisely in its reading of Genesis 1:1.

The use of this root leaves no doubt that Genesis 1:1 opens with the very first and initial act of the creation of the cosmos. However, the naturalist (e.g. Carl Sagan) believes that the cosmos is all there ever was, all there ever is, and all there ever will be. Yet the Bible sets forth the propositional truth that the created universe results from the creative act of the One True Eternal God.

Secondly, we observe the person responsible for creation: God. The word for God is אֱלֹהִים / 'ĕlohîm. This refers to the One True God. We should note that though the form is a grammatical plural, the meaning is singular, and many sources believe this implies a plurality of majesty or stateliness. When indicating the true God, Elōhîm functions as the subject of all divine activity revealed to man and as the object of all true reverence and fear from men. Often Elōhîm is accompanied by the most personal name of God, Yahweh or as translated, LORD (Gen. 2:4–5; Gen. 24:12; Exod. 34:23; Ps. 68:18).

There are several descriptive words attached to the noun Elōhîm. These words serve as titles by which God reveals himself to his people. Several examples are as follows:

- *hāēl bêt-ēl* "the El of Bethel" (Gen. 31:13, 35:7).[10]
- *ēl saḥ* "El my rock" (Ps. 42:9).[11]
- *ēl yĕšûˀātı* "El my Savior" (Isa. 12:2).[12]
- *ˀēl ḥayyāy* "El of my life" (Ps. 42:8).[13]
- *ˀēl gōmēr ˀālāy* "El the performer on me" (Ps. 57:3).[14]
- "the El of … " (Gen. 49:25).[15]
- *ēlı* "My El" (Ps. 89:26, 102:24, 118:28).[16]
- *hāˀēl māˀûzzı* "El my fortress" (2 Sam. 22:33).[17]
- *hāˀēl hamˀazĕrēnı ḥāyil* "El the girder of me with strength" (Ps. 18:32).[18]
- *hāˀēl hannōtēn nĕqāmôt lı* "the El giving me vengeance" (Ps. 18:47; 2 Sam. 22:48).[19]

While the word *Elōhım* may refer to God's work in creation (Gen. 1:1; Isa. 45:18; Jonah 1:9), it also focuses on His sovereignty, which is evident in Isaiah 54:5, ("God of All the Earth")[20]; 1 Kings 20:28, ("God of the Hills")[21]; and Jer. 32:27, ("God of All Flesh")[22].

Additional phrases emphasizing God's sovereign rule include "The God of All the Kingdoms of the Earth" (Isa. 37:16)[23]; "God of Heaven" (Neh. 2:4, 20)[24]; "Yahweh God of the Heaven" (Gen. 24:7; 2 Chron. 36:23)[25]; "God in the Heaven" (2 Chron. 20:6)[26]; "The Lord God of the Heaven and God of the Earth" (Gen. 24:3; Deut. 4:39; Josh. 2:11)[27]; and "God of gods and Lord of Lords, the Great, the Mighty, and the Terrible Who Does Not Regard Favorites and Does Not Take Bribes" (Deut. 10:17)[28]. An all-inclusive title is "God Most High" (Ps. 57:2).[29]

Elōhım also speaks of God's majesty and glory. He is the "God of Eternity" (Isa. 40:28)[30]; "God of Justice" (Isa. 30:18)[31]; "God of Certainty" (Isa. 65:16)[32]; "Living God" (Jer. 10:10)[33]; and "This Holy God" (1 Sam. 6:20).[34]

Elōhım focuses on God's actions on behalf of His people in the past. He is known as "The Living God, Speaker from the Midst of the Fire" (Deut. 5:23; 1 Kings 18:24)[35]; "God, the Bringer of Prisoners into Prosperity" (Ps. 68:7)[36]; "God ... the Bringer out to you Water from the Flinty Rock" (Deut. 8:15)[37]; and "Your God Who Separated You from the Peoples" (Lev. 20:24).[38]

One of the most far reaching group of titles for *Elōhım* are those relevant to the Savior God. These include "Their God" (Gen. 17:8)[39]; "The God of Abraham" (Gen. 26:24)[40]; "The God of Abraham ... and the God of Isaac" (Gen. 28:13)[41]; "The God of Abraham, the God of Isaac, and the God of Jacob" (Exod. 3:6).[42] It is estimated that more than one hundred such titles are found in the Old Testament. Sometimes to these titles is added the personal name, "Yahweh" (Gen. 24:12).[43]

Finally, *Elōhîm* expresses intimacy with God. These include "The God of Nearness" (Jer. 23:23)[44]; "Your God in Whom you Trust" (2 Kings 19:10)[45]; "God Your Chastener" (Deut. 8:5)[46]; "The God Feeding Me My Life Long Until

Now" (Gen. 48:15)[47]; "God of My Righteousness" (Ps. 4:1)[48]; "God of My Mercy (Ps. 59:17)[49]; "God of My Strength" (Ps. 43:2)[50]; and "Our God Being Merciful" (Ps. 116:5).[51]

It is this all supreme creator God who created (ברא; ברא; ברא / *bara', bara', bara'*). It was He who fashioned and shaped that which had not been in existence prior to His command for it to come into being. He created the universe at a particular point in time and space, which He also created, and the impact of the act continues to the present day. The root *bārā'* means "to create" something from nothing.

Bārā also means to initiate something new and to bring into existence that which did not exist before (Isa. 43:1; Ezek. 21:30, 28:13–15). The word also possesses the meaning of "bringing into existence" in several passages (Isa. 43:1; Ezek. 21:30 [H 35]; 28:13, 15).[52] God's actions indicate that He is sovereign (Ps. 89:11–12; Isa. 40:21–26), purposeful (Isa. 42:1–5; 45:12), majestic (Amos 4:13) and orderly (Isa. 45:18).

We also observe the extent of creation. God created the heavens *(שָׁמַ֫יִם / šamayim) and the earth (אות, אֵת / 'owt, 'ēt /אֶ֫רֶץ / 'eres)*. The heavens refer to the sky (Ps. 18:10), the universe (1 Kings 18:45) and the abode of God (Deut. 14:10). The earth refers to the ground, the whole earth as opposed to a part, countries, regions, districts and the specifically nations, such as the Land of Israel or the Promised Land. The word *earth* occurs 2,400 times in the Old Testament.

From the starting point of Genesis 1:1, the Scriptures articulate a wealth of additional information or revelation concerning God.

God is Spirit (John 4:24; 2 Cor. 3:17). He is declared to be light (Isa. 60:1–19; James 1:17; 1 John 1:5), love (1 John 4:7–11,16), invisible (Job 23:8,9; John 1:18; 5:37; Col. 1:15; 1 Tim. 1:17), unsearchable (Job 11:7; 37:23; Ps. 145:3; Isa. 40:28; Rom. 11:33), incorruptible (Rom. 1:23), eternal (Deut. 33:27; Ps. 90:2; Rev. 4:8–10), and immortal (1 Tim. 1:17; 6:16).

God is omnipotent (Gen. 17:1; Exod. 6:1–3), omniscient (Psalm 139:1–6; Proverbs 5:21), omnipresent (Ps. 139:7; Jer. 23:23), and immutable (Ps. 102:26–27; James 1:17). He is the only-wise God (Rom. 16:27; 1 Tim. 1:17), who is glorious (Exod. 15:11; Ps. 145:5), and the most high (Ps. 83:18; Acts 7:48).

God is perfect (Matt. 5:48), holy (Ps. 99:9; Isa. 5:16, 6:1–7), just (Deut. 32:4; Isa. 45:21), true (Jer. 10:10; John 17:3), and upright (Ps. 25:8, 92:15). He is also righteous (Ezra 9:15; Ps. 145:17), good (Ps. 25:8; 119:68), great (2 Chron. 2:5; Ps. 86:10), gracious (Exod. 34:6; Ps. 116:5), faithful (1 Cor. 10:13; 1 Pet. 4:19), merciful (Exod. 34:6–7; Ps. 86:5, 103:8–17), and long-suffering (Num. 14:18; Micah 7:1).

Additionally, God is a jealous God (Josh. 24:19; Nahum 1:2), but also compassionate (2 Kings 13:23). The Scriptures describe Him as a consuming fire (Heb. 12:29). There is none beside Him (Deut. 4:35; Isa. 44:6), none before Him

(Isa. 43:10), none like to Him (Exod. 9:14; Deut. 33:26; 2 Sam. 7:22; Isa. 46:5–9; Jer. 10:6), and none good but Him (Matt. 19:17). He fills heaven and earth (1 Kings 8:27; Jer. 23:24) and should alone be worshipped in spirit and in truth (John 4:24).

Moreover, God is self-existent (Exod. 3:1–4), self-sufficient (Ps. 50:11–12), and infinite (1 Kings 8:22–27; Jer. 23:24). God is wise (Prov. 3:19; 1 Tim. 1:17). He is also sovereign (Isa. 46:1–11).

Without divine assistance by the Holy Spirit, God is incomprehensible (Job 11:17–19; Rom. 11:33; 1 Cor. 1:18–2:16). He is also faithful (Deut. 7:1–9; Ps. 89:1–2), good (Ps. 107:8), and gracious (Ps. 111:4; 1 Pet. 5:10). He is one (Deut. 6:1–5; Isa. 44:6–8) but also subsists as three persons (Matt. 29:19–20; 2 Cor. 13:14).

The practical implications are as follows:

- As creator, we see that God is sovereign, majestic, and intimately involved in creation. This includes when tragedy strikes in this fallen and sinful world. E.g. 9/11.

- Has God brought sinners into a covenant relationship with Him through the finished work, the subsitutionary death, burial, and resurrection, of Jesus Christ? This is the beginning point of possessing and living eternally in light of God the Creator who is also Savior and Lord.

- It would be logically reasonable to assume that Christians, in light of their commitment to the Bible's teachings of creationism, would therefore live their lives accountable to God and His Word and seek to bring Him glory by submission and obedience to His Word and will.

- However, a tension increasingly exists where Christians affirm creationism in principle by what they say but reject creationism in what they do in practice by rebelliously rejecting God's Word as it pertains to salvation and consequentially ethical living. In other words, believers cannot truly affirm creationism on the one hand while at the same time rejecting salvation solely in Jesus Christ and living lives, which are more in keeping with naturalism on the other. It is contradictory or hypocritical to affirm the existence of a personal creator God who is also Savior and Lord but at the same time live in rebellion to the ethical teachings and commands of that very same personal creator God, Savior and Lord.

- Therefore, believers in Christ must examine their lives and lifestyle, their ethical choices to see if they are living consistently to their commitment to the personal Creator and Savior of the Bible (God) or if their life, lifestyle, and ethical choices are consistent with naturalism's rejection of the personal creator of the Bible (God). The believer who is truly committed to biblical truth will repent of the latter and renew their commitment to the former.

- Jesus says in Matthew 5:13–16, "You are the salt of the earth, but if salt has lost its taste, how shall its saltiness be restored? It is no longer good for anything except to be thrown out and trampled under people's feet. You are the light of the world. A city set on a hill cannot be hidden. Nor do people light a lamp and put it under a basket, but on a stand, and it gives light to all in the house. In the same way, let your light shine before others, so that they may see your good works and give glory to your Father who is in heaven.[53]

- Ephesians 2:8–10 says, "For by grace you have been saved through faith. And this is not your own doing; it is the gift of God, not a result of works, so that no one may boast. For we are his workmanship, created in Christ Jesus for good works, which God prepared beforehand, that we should walk in them".[54]

Having established the biblical evidence for God's existence, what are the philosophical arguments supporting the idea of God's existence? Both will prove helpful in establishing a balance between revelation and reasoning in addressing the concept of the reality of God.

The Philosophical Arguments for God's Existence

Balancing the evidence for God's existence from the information in the Scriptures are the philosophical arguments supporting the idea of God's existence. Admittedly, these arguments may not convince those antagonistic to the Christian faith of its validity. However, they do provide a thought-provoking response to those who contend that Christianity does not contain any assemblage of reasoning or logical thought. What we witness between chapter one and chapter two is the balance between revelation and reasoning in addressing the concept of God.

What then are the philosophical arguments for God's existence? They include the ontological argument, the cosmological argument, the teleological argument, the moral argument, the anthropological argument, the religious experience argument, and the argument from the existence of miracles: most notably Jesus Christ's resurrection from the dead.

The ontological argument is an argument that attempts to prove the existence of God through abstract reasoning alone. The argument begins with an explanation of the concept of God. Part of what we mean when we speak of God is a "perfect being"; that is what the word *God* means. The reasoning is that a God that exists, of course, is better than a God that doesn't.

Additionally, to speak of God as a perfect being is therefore to imply that He exists. Where does the idea of "God" originate? There is a sense of man's need to worship something, or someone, greater than himself. Man, in whatever culture he exists, is inwardly driven to honor and praise an object—even if that object is himself.

If God's perfection is a part of the concept of God, and if God's perfection implies God's existence, then God's existence is implied by the idea of God. When we speak of "God," we cannot but speak of a being that exists. To say that God does not exist is to contradict ourselves; it is literally to speak nonsense. The argument is saying that the very idea of God, and the corresponding idea that God does not exist, implies that He does indeed exist; otherwise if God did not exist, we would never think of the concept of God. Since we do think of the concept of God, even in a person's denial, this implies God's very existence.

The Bible gives credibility to the ontological argument. I refer again to Romans 1:18–23:

For the wrath of God is revealed from heaven against all ungodliness and unrighteousness of men, who by their unrighteousness suppress the truth. For what can be known about God is plain to them, because God has shown it to them. For his invisible attributes, namely, his eternal power and divine nature, have been clearly perceived, ever since the creation of the world, in the things that have been made. So they are without excuse. For although they knew God, they did not honor him as God or give thanks to him, but they became futile in their thinking, and their foolish hearts were darkened. Claiming to be wise, they became fools, and exchanged the glory of the immortal God for images resembling mortal man and birds and animals and creeping things.[1]

God has revealed himself and his existence to every human being. This awareness is not only within the visible creation, but also within each and every individual. This awareness extends to possessing a concept of God's invisible attributes, His eternal power and His divine nature. Therefore, man is without excuse in saying there is no God and denying he knew God's existence.

The cosmological argument is the argument from the existence of the world or universe to the existence of a God that brought it into being and keeps it in existence. It comes in two forms, one modal (having to do with possibility) and the other temporal (having to do with time).

The modal cosmological argument, the argument from contingency, suggests that because the universe might not have existed (i.e. is contingent), we need some explanation of why it does. This is the argument of cause and effect. Wherever there is cause and effect possibilities, the argument suggests something must determine not only the reality of the effect, but also offer an explanation for the cause of said effect. As the universe is conditional to some cause for its existence, what that cause may be, there must be some reason for its existence; it must have a cause. In fact, the only kind of being whose existence requires no cause is a necessary being, a being that could not have failed to exist. The ultimate cause of everything must therefore be a necessary being: God. God is the only uncaused cause. The Bible sets forth this doctrine.

- Psalm 89:11—"The heavens are yours; the earth also is yours; the world and all that is in it, you have founded them."[2]

- Psalm 90:1–2—"Lord, you have been our dwelling place in all generations. Before the mountains were brought forth, or ever you had formed the earth and the world, from everlasting to everlasting you are God.[3]

- Psalm 104:5–9—"He set the earth on its foundations, so that it should never be moved. You covered it with the deep as with a garment; the waters stood above the mountains. At your rebuke they fled; at the sound of your thunder they took to flight. The mountains rose, the valleys sank down to the place that you appointed for them. You set a boundary that they may not pass, so that they might not again cover the earth."[4]

- Acts 17:22–24—"So Paul, standing in the midst of the Areopagus, said: 'Men of Athens, I perceive that in every way you are very religious. For as I passed along and observed the objects of your worship, I found also an altar with this inscription, "To the unknown god." What therefore you worship as unknown, this I proclaim to you. The God who made the world and everything in it, being Lord of heaven and earth, does not live in temples made by man.'"[5]

- Hebrews 11:1–3—"Now faith is the assurance of things hoped for, the conviction of things not seen. For by it the people of old received their commendation. By faith we understand that the universe was created by the word of God, so that what is seen was not made out of things that are visible."[6]

The temporal cosmological argument argues that the past is finite. The idea that the universe has an infinite past stretching back in time into infinity is, the argument notes, both philosophically and scientifically problematic. All indications are that there is a point in time at which the universe began to exist. This beginning must either have been caused or uncaused. It cannot have been uncaused for the idea of an uncaused event is absurd; nothing comes from nothing. The universe must therefore have been brought into existence by something outside of itself. The temporal argument thus confirms one element of Christianity, the doctrine of creation.

The teleological argument is the argument from the order in the world to the existence of a being that created it with a specific purpose in mind. The universe is a highly complex system. The universe evidences design. This implies a designer. The scale of the universe alone is astounding, and the natural laws that govern it perplex scientists still after generations and centuries of study. It is a highly ordered system. It serves a purpose. It possesses design. This is in alignment with Scripture.

> You make springs gush forth in the valleys; they flow between the hills; they give drink to every beast of the field; the wild donkeys quench their thirst. Beside them the birds of the heavens dwell; they sing among the branches. From your lofty abode you water the mountains; the earth is satisfied with the fruit of your work. You cause the grass to grow for the livestock and plants for man to cultivate, that he may bring forth food from the earth and wine to gladden the heart of man, oil to make his face shine, and bread

to strengthen man's heart. The trees of the LORD are watered abundantly, the cedars of Lebanon that he planted. In them the birds build their nests; the stork has her home in the fir trees. The high mountains are for the wild goats; the rocks are a refuge for the rock badgers. He made the moon to mark the seasons; the sun knows its time for setting. You make darkness, and it is night, when all the beasts of the forest creep about. The young lions roar for their prey, seeking their food from God. When the sun rises, they steal away and lie down in their dens. And goes out to his work and to his labor until the evening. O LORD, how manifold are your works! In wisdom have you made them all; the earth is full of your creatures.[7]

God provides exactly the right conditions for the development and sustenance of life, and life is a valuable thing. That this is so is remarkable. There are numerous ways in which the universe might have been different, but the vast majority of possible universes would not have supported life.

To say that the universe is so ordered by chance is therefore unsatisfactory as an explanation of the appearance of design around us. It is far more plausible, and far more probable, that the universe is the way it is because it was created by a designer with life in mind. The Bible contends that this designer, who created this world evidencing design, is God. The psalmist articulates this argument in Psalm 19.

The moral argument is the argument from the existence or nature of morality to the existence of God. Two forms of moral argument are distinguished: formal and perfectionist.

The formal moral argument takes the form of morality to imply that it has a divine origin: morality consists of an ultimately authoritative set of commands. Where can these commands have come from but from a commander that has ultimate authority?

The perfectionist moral argument sets up a problem: how can it be that morality requires perfection of us, that morality cannot require of us more than we can give, but that we cannot be perfect? The only way to resolve this paradox, the argument suggests, is to conceive the existence of God. The Bible sets forth this truth in succinctly in Micah 6:6–8:

> "With what shall I come before the Lord, and bow myself before God on high? Shall I come before him with burnt offerings, with calves a year old? Will the Lord be pleased with thousands of rams, with ten thousands of rivers of oil? Shall I give my firstborn for my transgression, the fruit of my body for the sin of my soul?" He has told you, O man, what is good; and what does the Lord require of you but to do justice, and to love kindness, and to walk humbly with your God?[8]

The moral argument is perhaps unconsciously set forth by the so-called mainstream media each and every time a random shooting occurs at a school or other social setting. Especially when children are victims of violence, media commentators will state that the actions of the perpetrator were evil. The question then is how can anything be called evil if there is no contrasting standard, which we recognize as the ultimate good, right or non-evil? In order to call anything evil implies a righteous standard by which any act can be defined as evil. The righteous standard that defines and is in contrast to evil is God and His righteousness. Therefore, whenever society calls something good or evil, it implies an object standard that can define something as either good or evil. This inherent sense of right and wrong comes from God. Scripture sets forth this truth.

- Exodus 9:27: "Then Pharaoh sent and called Moses and Aaron and said to them, "This time I have sinned; the Lord is in the right, and I and my people are in the wrong."[9]

- 2 Chronicles 12:6: "Then the princes of Israel and the king humbled themselves and said, 'The Lord is righteous.'"[10]

- Psalm 7:9–11: "The Lord judges the peoples; judge me, O Lord, according to my righteousness and according to the integrity that is in me. Oh, let the evil of the wicked come to an end, and may you establish the righteous—you who test the minds and hearts, O righteous God! My shield is with

God, who saves the upright in heart. God is a righteous judge, and a God who feels indignation every day."[11]

- Psalm 116:5: "Gracious is the LORD, and righteous; our God is merciful."[12]

- Psalm 129:4: "The LORD is righteous; he has cut the cords of the wicked."[13]

- Psalm 145:17: "The LORD is righteous in all his ways and kind in all his works."[14]

- Lamentations 1:18: "The LORD is in the right, for I have rebelled against his word; but hear, all you peoples, and see my suffering; my young women and my young men have gone into captivity."[15]

- Daniel 9:7: "To you, O Lord, belongs righteousness, but to us open shame, as at this day, to the men of Judah, to the inhabitants of Jerusalem, and to all Israel, those who are near and those who are far away, in all the lands to which you have driven them, because of the treachery that they have committed against you."[16]

- Daniel 9:14: "Therefore the LORD has kept ready the calamity and has brought it upon us, for the LORD our God is righteous in all the works that he has done, and we have not obeyed his voice."[17]

The anthropological argument indicates that man is a unique creation by God. The Scriptures claim that man is created in the image of God (Gen. 1:26–27). The doctrine of God's image in man is interpreted in the Scriptures as the spiritual image, not the physical image. Most interpret this as referring to man's ability to think, feel, and make conscious and rational decisions. David speaks eloquently of his own creation in Psalm 139:13–16:

> For you formed my inward parts; you knitted me together in my mother's womb. I praise you, for I am fearfully and wonderfully made. Wonderful are your works; my soul knows it very well. My frame was not hidden from you, when I was being made in secret, intricately woven in the depths of the earth. Your eyes saw my unformed substance; in your book were written, every one of them, the days that were formed for me, when as yet there was none of them.[18]

To a great extent, man's behavior is learned while animals are bound by instinct. Characteristic of man alone is that he is a creature of reasoning intelligence who has the capacity of adapting means to an end, along with having a moral and spiritual consciousness.

The argument from religious experience is the argument that personal religious experiences can prove God's existence to those that have them. One can only perceive that which exists, and so God must exist because there are those that have experienced Him.

While religious experiences themselves can only constitute direct evidence of God's existence for those fortunate enough to have them, the fact that there are many people who testify to having had such experiences constitutes indirect evidence of God's existence even to those who have not had such experiences themselves. The prophet Isaiah faithfully served the LORD, based upon his religious experience recorded in Isaiah 6:1–8:

> In the year that King Uzziah died I saw the Lord sitting upon a throne, high and lifted up; and the train of his robe filled the temple. Above him stood the seraphim. Each had six wings: with two he covered his face, and with two he covered his feet, and with two he flew. And one called to another and said: "Holy, holy, holy is the LORD of hosts; the whole earth is full of his glory!" And the foundations of the thresholds shook at the voice of him who called, and the house was filled with smoke. And I said: "Woe is me! For I am lost; for I am a man of unclean lips, and I dwell in the midst of a people of unclean lips; for my eyes have seen the King, the LORD of hosts!" Then one of the seraphim flew to me, having in his hand a burning coal that he had taken with tongs from the altar. And he touched my mouth and said: "Behold, this has touched your lips; your guilt is taken away, and your sin atoned for." And I heard the voice of the Lord saying, "Whom shall I send, and who will go for us?" Then I said, "Here I am! Send me."[19]

The argument from miracles is the argument that the occurrence of miracles demonstrates both the existence of God and the truth of Christianity. If the Bible is to be believed, then Jesus's ministry was substantiated and proven by frequent miraculous signs that his claims and his teachings were endorsed by God the Father.

His resurrection from the dead was, of course, the greatest of these miracles. It is still taken by followers of Jesus today to be the solid foundation for their faith. Miracles typically involve the suspension of the natural operation of the universe as some supernatural event occurs. That can only happen, of course, given the existence of some supernatural being.

Did Jesus really rise from the dead? Why is the resurrection so critical to the Christian faith? What evidences do we have that supports the idea of Jesus's resurrection? Are there any other plausible theories to explain what happened, other than a bodily resurrection? These are the serious questions we address and seek to answer to see whether the miraculous argument for God's existence is valid.

As Dr. Irwin Lutzer explains, "We cannot give our religious convictions a privileged position that is closed to rational investigation or else we have to regulate our beliefs to private opinions and personal preferences. Unless we can point to evidence outside of ourselves, evidence accessible to everyone, we have no reason to say our beliefs are true for us and for others."[20]

This is a fundamental question to our study. As the late apologist Paul Little wrote in his book *Know Why You Believe*, "Both friends and enemies of the Christian faith have recognized the resurrection of Christ to be the foundation stone of the Christian Faith. The attack on Christianity by its enemies has most often concentrated on the resurrection because it has been correctly seen that this event is the crux of the matter."[21]

Why is the resurrection of Jesus Christ so critical and foundational to the Christian faith? There are several reasons to consider. To begin with, the resurrection fulfills Jesus Christ's prediction and claims that this event (the resurrection) is the final sign He would give to the world. In Matthew 12:38–40 Jesus said,

> Then some of the scribes and Pharisees answered him, saying, "Teacher, we wish to see a sign from you." But he answered them, "An evil and adulterous generation seeks for a sign, but no sign will be given to it except the sign of the prophet Jonah. For just as Jonah was three days and three nights in the belly of the great fish, so will the Son of Man be three days and three nights in the heart of the earth.[22]

Following Peter's great confession of Christ, Matthew 16:21 records, "From that time Jesus began to show His disciples that He must go to Jerusalem…and be killed and be raised on the third day." Please also take note of Matthew 20:17; Mark 8:31; 9:31; Luke 9:22; 18:31; 24:26; John 10:11, 15, 17–18.[23]

If Jesus did not rise from the grave, then His words were not fulfilled. If His words were not fulfilled, then He is either a liar or deceived. Either way, He cannot be trusted and certainly He cannot be worshipped. Therefore, what other observations can be made regarding the truth of Jesus Christ's resurrection?

The resurrection was predicted throughout the Old Testament.

- Psalm 2:1–12—"Why do the nations rage and the peoples plot in vain? The kings of the earth set themselves, and the rulers take counsel together, against the LORD and against his Anointed, saying, 'Let us burst their bonds apart and cast away their cords from us.' He who sits in the heavens laughs; the Lord holds them in derision. Then he will speak to them in his wrath, and terrify them in his fury, saying, 'As for me, I have set my King on Zion, my holy hill.' I will tell of the decree: The LORD said to me, 'You are my Son; today I have begotten you. Ask of me, and I will make the nations your heritage, and the ends of the earth your possession. You shall break them with a rod of iron and dash them in pieces like a potter's vessel.' Now therefore, O kings, be wise; be warned, O rulers of the earth. Serve the

Lᴏʀᴅ with fear, and rejoice with trembling. Kiss the Son, lest he be angry, and you perish in the way, for his wrath is quickly kindled. Blessed are all who take refuge in him."[24]

- Psalm 16:8–11—"I have set the Lᴏʀᴅ always before me; because he is at my right hand, I shall not be shaken. Therefore my heart is glad, and my whole being rejoices; my flesh also dwells secure. For you will not abandon my soul to Sheol, or let your holy one see corruption. You make known to me the path of life; in your presence there is fullness of joy; at your right hand are pleasures forevermore."[25]

- Isaiah 26:19 – "Your dead shall live; their bodies shall rise. You who dwell in the dust, awake and sing for joy! For your dew is a dew of light, and the earth will give birth to the dead."[26]

- Isaiah 52:13—"Behold, my servant shall act wisely; he shall be high and lifted up, and shall be exalted."[27]

- Isaiah 53:12—"Therefore I will divide him a portion with the many, and he shall divide the spoil with the strong, because he poured out his soul to death and was numbered with the transgressors; yet he bore the sin of many, and makes intercession for the transgressors."[28]

The resurrection is the foundation stone of the biblical theology of the church. It is the primary message the church must communicate to lost sinners. It is also the primary message the church must continue to communicate to the redeemed. I refer to three significant texts concerning the resurrection of Jesus Christ.

- Acts 2:22–24—"Men of Israel, hear these words: Jesus of Nazareth, a man attested to you by God with mighty works and wonders and signs that God did through him in your midst, as you yourselves know—this Jesus, delivered up according to the definite plan and foreknowledge of God, you crucified and killed by the hands of lawless men. God raised him up, loosing the pangs of death, because it was not possible for him to be held by it."[29]

- Acts 2:29–36—"Brothers, I may say to you with confidence about the patriarch David that he both died and was buried, and his tomb is with us to this day. Being therefore a prophet, and knowing that God had sworn with an oath to him that he would set one of his descendants on his throne, he foresaw and spoke about the resurrection of the Christ, that he was not abandoned to Hades, nor did his flesh see corruption. This Jesus God raised up, and of that we all are witnesses. Being therefore exalted at the right hand of God, and having received from the Father the promise of the Holy Spirit, he has poured out this that you yourselves are seeing and hearing. For David did not ascend into the heavens, but he himself says, 'The Lord said to my Lord, Sit at my right hand, until I make your enemies your footstool.' Let all the house of Israel therefore know for certain that God has made him both Lord and Christ, this Jesus whom you crucified."[30]

- 1 Corinthians 15:12–19—"Now if Christ is proclaimed as raised from the dead, how can some of you say that there is no resurrection of the dead? But if there is no resurrection of the dead, then not even Christ has been raised. And if Christ has not been raised, then our preaching is in vain and your faith is in vain. We are even found to be misrepresenting God, because we testified about God that he raised Christ, whom he did not raise if it is true that the dead are not raised. For if the dead are not raised, not even Christ has been raised. And if Christ has not been raised, your faith is futile and you are still in your sins. Then those also who have fallen asleep in Christ have perished. If in this life only we have hoped in Christ, we are of all people most to be pitied."[31]

The Apostle Paul places great importance on the resurrection. He makes eight observations in 1 Corinthians 15. In a series of eight conditional statements, Paul sets forth the importance of the resurrection for the believer.

- vs. 13—if no resurrection … then Christ is not raised.[32]

- vs. 14—if no resurrection …then our preaching is empty.[33]

- vs. 14b—if no resurrection … then our faith is empty.[34]

- vs. 15—if no resurrection …then we are false witnesses.[35]

- vs. 17—if no resurrection …then our faith is futile.[36]

- vs. 17b—if no resurrection …then we are still in our sins.[37]

- vs. 18—if no resurrection …then those who have died in Christ have perished.[38]

- vs. 19—if no resurrection …then we are of all men the most pitiable.[39]

  (See also Acts 4:2; 13:35; 17:18; 24:15; Philippians 1:21–23; 3:10–11; 2 Corinthians 5:1–8; Revelation 20:6).[40]

Beyond what Scripture explicitly says, what other evidence is there that supports the doctrine of Jesus's resurrection from the dead? The following must be considered.

First, there is the bibliographical test. This refers to the eyewitness accounts of the resurrection: Matthew, Mark, Luke, and John. Are these witnesses credible? There is substantial evidence that the gospels, and for that matter the entire New Testament, is indeed credible and truthful regarding what they teach, especially as it pertains to the resurrection.

Second, the existence of the church. It is worldwide in scope and significant in its depth of influence. Its history can be traced to AD 32. The early church constantly referred to the resurrection as the basis for their teaching, preaching, living, and most significantly, dying (Acts 2, 4, and 7).

Third, the change in the day for worship. Sunday is the day of worship for Christians. This can be traced back to AD 32. There must have been something truly remarkable to change the day of worship from the Jewish Sabbath. In fact the Christians celebrated Sunday in recognition of the resurrection. This is all the more significant when you realize the first Christians were in fact Jews. See Acts 2.

Fourth, the change within the disciples. Where once they had been a band of frightened cowards they became disciples of courage and conviction in Jesus Christ. These same men who fled for fear when Jesus was arrested (Matt. 26:31, 56; Mark 14:27, 53–54; Luke 22:54–62; John 18:15–27) and who would deny Him became bold and were willing to die if necessary for their faith (Acts 4:1–22; 5:21–32; Phil. 1:21). In fact, one of the most strident persecutors of the early church (Saul of Tarsus) was himself converted (Acts 9:1–9, 22:1–22, 26:9–20) and endured much persecution. See 2 Corinthians 6:1–10, 11:21–33. What could have happened to so change these men? The Bible submits that the only plausible answer is the resurrection of Jesus Christ.

Finally, the appearances of Christ. There were some ten appearances Jesus made after His resurrection. They occurred over a period of 40 days. These appearances represented a great variety with respect to time, place, and location, to particular individuals and to large crowds. They include the following:

- To Mary Magdalene—John 20:11–18.
- To the other women—Matthew 28:1–10; Mark 16:1–8; Luke 24:1–11. These include (1) Mary the mother of James and Joseph, (2) Salome, (3) Joanna, and (4) other unidentified women.
- To Peter—Luke 24:34.
- To the ten disciples (minus Thomas)—Luke 24:36–43; John 20:19–25.
- To the eleven disciples (including Thomas)—John 20:26–29.
- To the Emmaus disciples–Luke 24:13–35.
- To the disciples in Galilee—Matthew 28:16–20; John 21:1–24.
- To the five hundred brethren—1 Corinthians 15:6.
- To James and the apostles—1 Corinthians 15:7.
- At the ascension—Luke 24:50–53; Acts 1:4–12.

Please note the resurrection appearance, which the Apostle Paul encountered on the Road to Damascus (Acts 9:1–6, 18:9–10, 22:1–8, 23:11, 26:12–18; 1 Cor. 15:8). With the evidence presented, it is beyond a reasonable doubt that Jesus Christ indeed rose from the dead. This is the only plausible explanation. Dr. Don Carson, professor of New Testament at Trinity Evangelical Divinity School, explains:

> As important as the cross is, it is not the end of the story, for all of the New Testament writers focus equally on the resurrection of the Lord Jesus. The resurrection accounts are rich and diverse. There is no way they can be reduced to mass hallucination. Jesus appeared to too many people many times over a period of forty days or so. He appeared to ones and twos; he appeared to as many as five hundred at a time; he appeared to the apostles more than once; he appeared in locked rooms; he appeared on the seashore and ate some fish that he was cooking for them. The witnesses multiply. He shows up when they are not expecting him, and he shows up when they are. He cannot be categorized or dismissed or domesticated. The resurrection appearances are simply too frequent, too diverse, and supported by too many witnesses. What do you do with them?[41]

What are the alternative arguments for the resurrection of Jesus Christ, and how are believers to respond? It remains ironical that those dismissing and rejecting the evidence regarding the bodily resurrection of Jesus Christ go to such ridiculously, great lengths to support their contention that Jesus did not rise from the dead. In effect, it takes more faith to believe and ascribe to the following alternative views than the factual biblical account.

First of all, there is the swoon theory. This point of view teaches that Jesus didn't die but simply fainted. The cool air of the tomb later revived him. He then lived many years thereafter and died a natural death. This is refuted …

- By the soldiers. In John 19:31–37 the soldiers broke the legs of both of the criminals crucified on either side of Jesus for the purpose of hastening their death so their bodies would not remain on the cross during the Sabbath. However, when they got to Jesus, they saw that He was already dead, so they did not break His legs. They also stabbed Him in the side just to make sure that He was indeed deceased.

- By Joseph of Arimathea. All four gospels (Matt. 27:57–61; Mark 15:42–47; Luke 23:50–55; John 19:38–42) record Joseph of Arimathea, along with Nicodemas and other women, carefully anointed Jesus's body for burial, bound it in strips of linen with spices, and laid Him in a new tomb. Surely they would have noticed if He was still breathing.

- By Nicodemas. (See previous point).

- By Pilate. Mark 14:42–47 reports that Pilate was surprised to hear that Jesus had already died after only being on the cross for six hours. Sometimes death by crucifixion could take up to six days. Therefore Pilate had the centurion in charge of the execution verify that Jesus was indeed dead. The centurion did so.

- By Jesus. If Jesus had simply fainted, to regain consciousness later, this would mean that Jesus would have been a part of a fragrant lie by pretending to have risen from the grave when He would have known that He had not. He would therefore neither be good nor a moral teacher who should be followed.

As Paul Little writes, "It is impossible that One who had just come forth from the grave half dead, who crept about weak and ill, who stood in need of medical treatment, of bandaging, strengthening, and tender care and who at last succumbed to such great suffering on the cross could ever have given the disciples the impression that He was the conqueror over death and the grave; that He was the Prince of Life."[42]

Second is the stolen body theory. This theory argues that Christ didn't rise from the dead but that His disciples stole the body and pretended to everyone that Christ had risen. This is refuted…

- By the actions of the chief priests. When the chief priests heard that the tomb of Jesus was empty and His body gone, they bribed the soldiers to say that Jesus's disciples had stolen the body. This would protect the soldiers from punishment. Why would the chief priest bribe the soldiers to say that Jesus's disciples had stolen Christ's body if the disciples had indeed stolen the body of the Lord? See Matthew 28:11–15.

- The presence of the Roman guards. In Matthew 27:57–65 we see that the chief priests and the Pharisees came to Pilate and requested that the tomb be made secure so that the disciples couldn't steal His body. They even had guards posted. They anticipated such a theft taking place.

- The sealing of the tomb. Again in Matthew 27:65–66 we see that the utmost caution was made to ensure that the tomb couldn't be breached. Is it possible that the disciples got past the guards, unsealed the tomb, and took the body of Jesus without being detected?

- The fear of the disciples. In Mark 14:50 along with Matthew 26:56, we see the disciples having fled in fear following the arrest of Jesus. With the exception of John (John 19:25–27) and maybe Peter (1 Pet. 2:21–25) none were present at the crucifixion. In John 20:19 we see them huddled in the upper room with the doors shut and locked for fear of the Jews. The disciples believed that as the enemies of Jesus had executed Him, they would soon be next. Is it plausible that these fearful men would seek out Jesus's body and try to steal it?

- The orderly condition of the grave clothes. In Luke 24:1–12 along with John 20:3–7, we see the burial clothes Jesus wore lying in the tomb. The handkerchief that had been wrapped around His head was not lying with the linen clothes but folded together in a place by itself. Does it make sense that had the disciples stolen the body they would have taken the time to neatly fold the strips of Jesus's burial linen before they left the tomb?

- The preaching of the Gospel. If the disciples had stolen the body, they would have known that the resurrection story was a lie. Why then would they preach a lie and in some cases die for a lie, knowing it was a lie? See Acts 4:8–12. While it makes sense to suffer persecution for something you believe is true, even if it is not, it makes no sense to be persecuted for something you know not to be true. The only logical explanation is that the disciples were willing to suffer and die for the gospel because they knew that Jesus had indeed risen from the dead.

Third is the hallucination theory. This theory states that the disciples so wanted to believe that Jesus rose from the dead that they hallucinated and actually believed He had risen. This is refuted...

- By Jesus's appearances. Too many people saw Christ after His death for his resurrection to be anything else than what it was (1 Corinthians 15:1–8). When He appeared to the disciples they thought He was a ghost. He finally had to tell them to touch and handle Him. He even asked them for some fish (Luke 24:36–43).

- The skepticism of the disciples. The disciples didn't believe at first that Jesus had risen from the dead. They were skeptical (Mark 16:9–11; Luke 24:1–12; John 20:1–25). Thomas flat out refused to believe it was true unless he placed his hands in Jesus's wounds. They thought words of His resurrection were "idle tales."

- The behavior by the women. If Mary, and the other women, were so convinced that He would rise, then why did they go to the tomb on first day of week to anoint His body? They obviously weren't expecting Him to be alive (John 20:1–10). In fact, Mary didn't recognize Jesus but thought He was a gardener (John 20:11–18).

Fourth is the wrong tomb theory. This perspective states that the reason there wasn't a body in the tomb is because everyone went to the wrong tomb. This is refuted by

- The women who took such special care to note where Jesus's body had been laid (Matt. 27:61; Mark 15:47; Luke 23:55).

- Peter and John also knew exactly where the tomb was even though they arrived separately (John 20:2–8).

- The Roman guards. How could they have been mistaken when such specific plans and procedures had been carefully thought out by the chief priests to guard the tomb so Jesus's body would not be stolen? (Matt. 27:62–66; Matt. 28:1–4, 11).

- Why were the guards bribed to lie about the empty tomb if they had been at the wrong tomb? (Matt. 28:12–15).

- If it was the wrong tomb, then why didn't the chief priests, the Sanhedrin, the Roman soldiers, Joseph of Arimathea, or even Pilate himself go to the right tomb and produce the body? The conclusion is simple. They were at the right tomb and it was empty because Jesus had risen from the dead.

Finally, there is the body was moved theory. Perhaps, as some speculate, Jewish or Roman authorities moved the body. This is refuted by the following:

- The lack of reasoning behind it. Having placed guards at the tomb to insure no one would tamper with the body of Jesus, what would be the reason for moving the body? Certainly, it could be argued that the Jewish and/or Roman authorities did so to prevent the disciples from doing the very thing they suspected they would do: steal the body of Jesus. Therefore, by moving the body they would hide Christ's body and therefore prevent the disciples from achieving their intended goal. But this leads us to a second point, which is…

- The apostles preaching. In the face of such boldness on the part of the disciples, as documented in the Book of Acts, why wouldn't the authorities simply produce the body of Jesus if it indeed had only been moved? The Jewish leaders were enraged at Peter and John in Acts 4 and 5 but did nothing to neither prevent the message of the gospel nor suppress it. They also did nothing to produce the body of Jesus if indeed it had only been moved by the religious leaders.

The conclusion is that the external evidence resoundingly affirms, beyond a reasonable doubt, that Jesus Christ is indeed the eternal God/Man, that the Scriptures can be trusted, and the reason why Christianity flourishes after two thousand years is because it is the truth of Almighty God.

As Paul Little concludes, "Finally there is the evidence for the resurrection which is contemporary and personal. If Jesus Christ rose from the dead He is alive today. Powerful enough to invade and change those who invite Him into their lives. Thousands now living bear uniform testimony that their lives have been revolutionized by Jesus Christ."[43]

The evidences for the resurrection of Jesus Christ are just one example regarding the validity of the Bible. There are many other evidences that the Bible is the Word of God. These facts are contained not only within the Scriptures, but also from without. Both lines of reasoning are necessary to understand the authority of the biblical text as the Word of God. It is to this subject that is addressed in the next chapter.

The Evidences the Bible Is the Word of God

As with the evidences for the resurrection of Jesus Christ, there are also many compelling evidences that the Bible is the Word of God. These facts are contained not only within the Scriptures, but also from outside the biblical text. Both are necessary lines of evidence to understand the validity of the biblical text as the Word of God.

To begin with, there is the Bible's amazing unity. The Bible was written over a period of two thousand years with four hundred years between the Old Testament and the New Testament. Over forty writers, some anonymous, contributed to its content. It also was written from over eleven geographical locations. Additionally, the biblical writers came from various backgrounds, economic levels, and occupations.

What is amazing concerning the overall unity of the Bible's content is that it was additionally written with several different styles of writing. These various genres include history, prophecy, biography, autobiography, poetry, law, letters, proverbs, wisdom, symbolic, and doctrinal. Yet in spite of these various styles of writing, there remains one overall theme: God is holy and man is not. Man's only hope is in the mercy of God and that mercy culminated at the cross.

Secondly, there is confirmation of the Bible's trustworthiness by its historical reliability. This is true not only by the Old Testament but also by the New Testament text.

The reader of the Old Testament can be confident that what is within the text is faithful to the original writings. This is supported not only by the amazing discovery of the Dead Sea Scrolls in 1947, but also by the relatively few textual variants in the text, the consistency between the Hebrew text and its Greek translation (the Septuagint), the meticulous practice and rules of the Old Testament scribes, the similarity of parallel passages and consistent archaeological confirmation of the Old Testament's accuracy.

The student of the New Testament can also approach its twenty-seven books with the same degree of confidence as with the Old Testament. This is based upon the factual evidence of over five thousand existing Greek manuscripts, which are consistent not only with each other but also available for examination by New Testament scholars. Additionally, the vast number of existing Greek manuscripts of the New Testament (5,000) is comparatively larger than with other ancient and classical works such as Homer's *Iliad* (643), Caesar's *Gallic Wars* (10), and Livy's *History of Rome* (20).

Also, most of the New Testament manuscripts are within 100–200 years of the original documents. This is in contrast with other ancient works, which manuscript evidence dates between 900–1,300 years from their respective, original writings.

There is also the widespread support by the early church fathers to the reliability and authenticity of the twenty-seven New Testament books. The church fathers quoted so frequently from the New Testament that scholars attest they could reconstruct the entire New Testament Scriptures just from the writings of the church fathers alone. Harold Greenlee writes that "These quotations are so extensive that the New Testament could virtually be reconstructed from them without the use of New Testament Manuscripts."[1]

Third, there is the Bible's indestructibility. For anything to be indestructible, including the Scriptures, it must be permanent, unyielding, durable, everlasting, imperishable, and eternal. The Bible proves that it is all these things by its resiliency. This is in spite of political persecution (Ancient Rome; Hitler's Nazism; Communism), religious persecution (the Roman Catholic Church; Jehovah's Witness; Mormonism; Islam), and philosophical persecution. The various worldviews, which place themselves against God's

Word, thereby embodying philosophical persecution, include the following:

1. Secularism—meaning world. The secular refers to this world in this time. Its point of focus is here and now. "The accent of the secular is on the present time rather than on eternity" (R. C. Sproul). The secularist flatly denies or remains utterly skeptical about the eternal. He either says there is no eternal, or if there is, we can know nothing about it. What matters is now and only now. E.g. "Seize the day!"

2. Pessimistic existentialism—Man is not viewed or evaluated by his thoughts or his soul but rather his feelings. The mantra today is "How do you feel?" "Man cannot be understood simply by intellectual activity. It is his passion that makes him a man." The question is no longer "What do you think about that?" The result is that life is meaningless and you try the best you can in a life that makes no sense. Angst! E.g. Trent Reznor; Nirvana; M*A*S*H.

3. Sentimental humanism—Man is the measure of all things. Man, in himself, is the ultimate norm by which values are determined. He is the ultimate being and the ultimate authority; all reality and life center upon him. It is interesting to note how this perspective has infected our understanding of

Scripture, especially pertaining to the sovereignty of God in salvation and life.

4. Pragmatism—If it works, then it must be good. The end justifies the means. "Modern man looks to the scientific community to solve his problems. Cancer, heart disease, arms control, war, and a sound economy are the issues with which mankind is concerned. People don't look to God to solve their problems. Rather, they look to science or government to come up with the solutions" (Sproul).

5. Moralism—Attempting to solve spiritual problems and sin problems by moralistic and social programs. While these attempts may be noble in design, e.g. Moral Majority, they fail to accomplish mankind's root problem; a fallen sinful nature that needs to be redeemed. Abortion is a blight upon our society, but the overturning of *Roe v. Wade* will not stop abortions.

6. Atheism—The belief that God does not exist was fervently taught by the philosopher Voltaire who said, "Another century and there will be not a Bible on the earth." After he died, his old printing press and the very house where he lived was purchased by the Geneva Bible Society and made a depot for Bibles. Atheist Thomas Paine wrote, "I have gone through the Bible as a man would go through a

forest with an axe to fell trees. I have cut down tree after tree; here they lie. They will never grow again."

Fourth, there is the Bible's historical accuracy (continually supported through archaeology). Sir William Ramsey, who was professor of humanity at the University of Aberdeen, Scotland, was an unbeliever who initially sought to disprove the Bible's accuracy. He eventually became a staunch defender of the Word of God and its accuracy, even in the most intimate of details.

Halley's Bible Handbook lists some 112 examples of archaeological finds authenticating the Bible. Unger's Bible Handbook lists ninety-six examples.

Fifth is the Bible's scientific accuracy. The following references are cited as supporting this point.

The earth is a sphere.

1. Isaiah 40:18–31 (vs. 22)—"It is He who sits above the circle of the earth, and its inhabitants are like grasshoppers, Who stretches out the heavens like a curtain and spreads them out like a tent to dwell in."[2]

2. Job 26:10—"He has inscribed a circle on the surface of the waters at the boundary of light and darkness."[3]

3. Proverbs 8:27—"When He (God) established the heavens I was there, When He inscribed a circle on the face of the deep."[4] The word for circle indicates the earth is a globe.

4. In Job 26:10 the Creator has "compassed the waters with bounds" (KJV), or according to the more literal rendering of the RSV, "He has described a circle upon the face of the waters."[5] This may mean the establishment of a boundary in the distance as the NEB, "He has fixed the horizon," or at the shore (cf. Job 38:8, 11).[6] This is also the thought found in the use of the noun in Proverbs 8:27, "He set a compass upon the face of the depth" (KJV), which the NEB renders, "He girdled the ocean with the horizon."[7]

5. Job 22:14 (KJV) declares that God walketh in the circuit of heaven": the "vault" of heaven is the expression used by the RSV, NAB, and NEB. The JB translates, "He prowls on the rim of the heavens."[8]

6. Isaiah 40:22 (KJV) asserts that the Creator sits upon the "circle of the earth," a rendering retained by the ASV, RSV, and JB. The nabhas, "He sits enthroned above the vault of the earth," which the NEB amplifies as the "vaulted roof of the earth." NIV: "He sits enthroned above the circle of the earth."[9] The poets of the OT describe their universe phenomenological, i.e. as it appears to them standing on the earth and looking above and about. This perspective differs from that of modern scientific thought, which assumes a perspective beyond the earth. Both are accurate and useful according to their own perspectives.

7. Some have held that Isaiah 40:22 implies the sphericity of the earth. It may, but it may refer only to the Lord enthroned above the earth with its obviously circular horizon. Note the remarkable concept given in Job 26:7.

The earth is suspended in space. Job 26:7—"He stretches out the north over empty space and hangs the earth on nothing."[10] This statement is accurate, meaning it corresponds to reality, and was given in ancient times before scientific verification.

The mountains and canyons in the sea.

1. 2 Samuel 22:16—"Then the channels of the sea appeared."[11]

2. Jonah 2:6—"I descended to the roots of the mountains (within the depths of the sea)."[12]

The stars are innumerable.

1. Genesis 15:5—"And He [God] took him [Abram] outside and said, 'Now look toward the heavens, and count the stars, if you are able to count them.' And He said to him, 'So shall your descendants be.'"[13]

2. Genesis 22:17—"Indeed I will greatly bless you, and I will greatly multiply your seed as the stars of the heavens and as the sand which is on the seashore."[14]

3. Genesis 26:4—"I will multiply your descendants as the stars of heaven."[15]

4. Genesis 32:12—But you said, 'I will surely do you good, and make your offspring as the sand of the sea, which cannot be numbered for multitude.'"[16]

5. Deuteronomy 1:10—"The LORD your God has multiplied you, and behold, you are this day like the stars of heaven in number."[17]

6. Isaiah 40:12—"Who has measured the waters in the hollow of his hand and marked off the heavens with a span, enclosed the dust of the earth in a measure and weighed the mountains in scales and the hills in a balance."[18]

7. Jeremiah 33:22—"As the host of heaven cannot be counted and the sand of the sea cannot be measured, so I will multiply the descendants of David My servant."[19]

8. Jeremiah 31:37–Thus says the LORD: "If the heavens above can be measured, and the foundations of the earth below can be explored, then I will cast off all the offspring of Israel for all that they have done, declares the LORD."[20]

9. Hebrews 11:12—"As the stars of heaven in number, and innumerable as the sand which is by the seashore."[21]

The springs and fountains in the sea

1. Genesis 7:11—"In the six hundredth year of Noah's life, in the second month, on the seventeenth day of the month, on that day all the fountains of the great deep burst forth, and the windows of the heavens were opened."[22]

2. Genesis 8:2—"The fountains of the deep and the windows of the heavens were closed, the rain from the heavens was restrained."[23]

3. Proverbs 8:28—"When He made from the skies above, when the springs of the deep became fixed, when He set for the sea its boundary so that the water would not transgress His command, when He marked out the foundations of the earth."[24]

The hydrologic cycle/weather patterns.

1. Job 26:8—"He wraps up the waters in His clouds, and the cloud does not burst under them."[25]

2. Job 36:27–29—"For He draws up the drops of water; they distill rain from the mist. Which the clouds pour down. They drip upon man abundantly. Can anyone understand the spreading of the clouds, the thundering of His pavilion."[26]

3. Job 37:16—"Do you know about the layers of the thick clouds? The wonders of One perfect in knowledge."[27]

4. Job 38:25–27—"Who has cleft a channel for the flood, or a way for the thunderbolt. To bring rain on the land without people, on a desert without a man in it. To satisfy the waste and desolate land and to make the seeds of grass to sprout."[28]

5. Psalm 135:7—"He causes the vapors to ascend from the ends of the earth; Who makes lightening for the rains. Who brings forth the wind from His treasures."[29]

6. Ecclesiastes 1:6–7—"The wind goes toward the south, and turns around to the north; the wind whirls about continually, and comes again on its circuit. All the rivers run into the sea, yet the sea *is* not full; to the place from which the rivers come, there they return again."[30]

7. The ocean currents. Psalm 8:8—"The birds of the heavens and the fish of the sea, whatever passes through the paths of the sea."[31]

Living things that produce after their kind.

1. Genesis 1:20–31—"And God said, 'Let the waters swarm with swarms of living creatures, and let birds fly above the earth across the expanse of the

heavens.' So God created the great sea creatures and every living creature that moves, with which the waters swarm, according to their kinds, and every winged bird according to its kind. And God saw that it was good. And God blessed them, saying, 'Be fruitful and multiply and fill the waters in the seas, and let birds multiply on the earth.' And there was evening and there was morning, the fifth day. And God said, 'Let the earth bring forth living creatures according to their kinds—livestock and creeping things and beasts of the earth according to their kinds.' And it was so. And God made the beasts of the earth according to their kinds and the livestock according to their kinds, and everything that creeps on the ground according to its kind. And God saw that it was good. Then God said, 'Let us make man in our image, after our likeness. And let them have dominion over the fish of the sea and over the birds of the heavens and over the livestock and over all the earth and over every creeping thing that creeps on the earth.' So God created man in his own image, in the image of God he created him; male and female he created them. And God blessed them. And God said to them, 'Be fruitful and multiply and fill the earth and subdue it, and have dominion over the fish of the sea and over the birds of the heavens and over every living thing that moves on the earth.' And God said, 'Behold, I have given you every plant yielding seed that is on the face of all the earth, and every tree with seed in its fruit. You shall have them for food. And to every beast of the earth and to every bird of the heavens and to everything that creeps on the earth, everything that has the breath of life, I have given every green plant for food.' And it was so. And God saw everything that he had made, and behold, it was very good. And there was evening and there was morning, the sixth day. [32]

2. Genesis 6:19—"But *I* will establish my covenant with you, and you shall come into the ark, you, your sons, your wife, and your sons' wives with you." [33]

The need for health and sanitation.

1. Concerning sickness—Numbers 5–6.

2. Concerning sanitation—Deuteronomy 23:12–13. "You shall have a place outside the camp, and you shall go out to it. And you shall have a trowel with your tools, and when you sit down outside, you shall dig a hole with it and turn back and cover up your excrement. Because the LORD your God walks in the midst of your camp, to deliver you and to give up your enemies before you, therefore your camp must be holy, so that he may not see anything indecent among you and turn away from you."[34]

3. Concerning circumcision—Genesis 17:9–14. "And God said to Abraham, 'As for you, you shall keep my covenant, you and your offspring after you throughout their generations. This is my covenant, which you shall keep, between me and you and your offspring after you: Every male among you shall be circumcised. You shall be circumcised in the flesh of your foreskins, and it shall be a sign of the covenant between me and you. He who is eight days old among you shall be circumcised. Every male throughout your generations, whether born in your house or bought with your money from any foreigner who is not of your offspring, both he who is born in your house and he who is bought with your money, shall surely be circumcised. So shall my covenant be in your flesh an everlasting covenant. Any uncircumcised male who is not circumcised in the flesh of his foreskin shall be cut off from his people; he has broken my covenant.'"[35]

4. The human bloodstream. Leviticus 17:11—"For the life of the flesh is in the blood…for it is the blood by reason of the life that makes atonement."[36]

The two laws of thermodynamics. The first being that energy cannot be created or destroyed.

1. Genesis 2:1–3—"Thus the heavens and the earth were finished, and all the host of them. And on

the seventh day God finished his work that he had done, and he rested on the seventh day from all his work that he had done. So God blessed the seventh day and made it holy, because on it God rested from all his work that he had done in creation."[37]

2. Psalm 33:6–9—"By the word of the LORD the heavens were made, and by the breath of his mouth all their host. He gathers the waters of the sea as a heap; he puts the deeps in storehouses. Let all the earth fear the LORD; let all the inhabitants of the world stand in awe of him! For he spoke, and it came to be; he commanded, and it stood firm."[38]

3. Psalm 102:25—"Of old you laid the foundation of the earth, and the heavens are the work of your hands. They will perish, but you will remain; they will all wear out like a garment. You will change them like a robe, and they will pass away, but you are the same, and your years have no end. The children of your servants shall dwell secure; their offspring shall be established before you."[39]

The second law of thermodynamics is the reality of energy deterioration; the Earth is winding down.

1. Romans 8:18–25—"For I consider that the sufferings of this present time are not worth comparing with the glory that is to be revealed to us. For the creation waits with eager longing for the revealing of the sons

of God. For the creation was subjected to futility, not willingly, but because of him who subjected it, in hope that the creation itself will be set free from its bondage to corruption and obtain the freedom of the glory of the children of God. For we know that the whole creation has been groaning together in the pains of childbirth until now. And not only the creation, but we ourselves, who have the first fruits of the Spirit, groan inwardly as we wait eagerly for adoption as sons, the redemption of our bodies. For in this hope we were saved. Now hope that is seen is not hope. For who hopes for what he sees? But if we hope for what we do not see, we wait for it with patience."[40]

2. Hebrews 1:10–12–And, "You, Lord, laid the foundation of the earth in the beginning, and the heavens are the work of your hands; they will perish, but you remain; they will all wear out like a garment, like a robe you will roll them up, like a garment they will be changed. But you are the same, and your years will have no end."[41]

Sixth, the occurrences of fulfilled prophecy. The Bible contains remarkable prophetic accuracy. Some examples include prophecies regarding Israel. These include that Israel would become a great nation (Gen. 12:1–3), Israel would spend seventy years in Babylon (Jer. 25:11; 29:10),

Israel would be hounded and persecuted (Deut. 28:65–67), would reject her Messiah (Isa. 53), and Jerusalem would be destroyed (Luke 19:41–44; 21:20). This occurred in 70 AD. Additionally, that Israel would endure (Gen. 17:7; Isa. 66:22; Jer. 31:35–36; Matt. 24:34), and that it would return to Palestine in the latter days prior to the Second Coming of Christ (Deut. 30:1–3; Ezek. 36:24, 37:1–14, 38:1–39:29). This occurred in 1948.

Other biblical examples of fulfilled prophecy involve Gentile nations. These include Babylon (present day Iraq; Dan. 2; Isa. 13), Medo-Persia (present day Iran; Dan. 8:1–7, 20–21), Greece (Dan. 7–8), Rome (Dan. 2), and Egypt (Ezek. 29–39).

Other prophecies concern specific cities. These include Tyre (Ezek. 26), Jericho (Josh. 6), Nineveh (Nahum 1–3), and Jerusalem (Matt. 24:1–2; Luke 19:41–44, 21:2–24). Even still, there are prophecies concerning specific individuals. These include but are not limited to the following: Josiah (1 Kings 13:1–2; 2 Kings 23:15–16), Cyrus (Jer. 25:12, 29:10), Alexander the Great (Dan. 8:1–8), Antiochus Epiphanies IV (Dan. 8:9–14), and John the Baptist (Isa. 40:1–5).

Most notably, there are prophecies fulfilled by Jesus Christ at His first advent. There are some thirty-seven prophecies alone concerning the earthly ministry of Jesus Christ, which He fulfilled from His virgin birth (Isa. 7:14; Matt. 1:22–23) to His ascension (Ps. 24:7–10; Mark 16:19; Luke 24:50).

Seventh, there is the Bible's universal influence upon the world. Western civilization was founded directly upon the Bible and its teachings. The world's calendar and most holidays stem from the Bible. The Bible's influence can be directly seen in literature, art, and music. The Bible has also produced the law of the Western world; what is called the Judeo-Christian ethic.

Eighth, there is its incredible care and copy. No book has been copied and translated into more languages as the Bible. The care concerning the Bible's copying is meticulous. As previously mentioned, there are over five thousand ancient Greek manuscripts of the New Testament. This is in vast contrast to the limited, if not scarce, number of copies of other ancient works by Plato, Euripides, Cicero, and even Shakespeare.

Ninth, there is its amazing circulation. Statistics show that only one percent of all books published survive even seven years. Eighty percent of books published are largely forgotten after one year. No other ancient book, 2,000–4,000 years old, is as widely read and circulated than the Bible.

Tenth, there is its absolute honesty regarding the human condition. Within the biblical record we witness that God is holy (Isa. 6) and man is sinful (Gen. 3; Rom. 1–8; Eph. 1–2; Col. 1–2; Titus 3; John 3). The Bible's human characters are flawed and sinful. Examples include Noah who became drunk (Gen. 9:20–24), Moses who committed murder (Exod. 1–2), King David who committed adultery and murder (2 Sam. 11–12), Elijah who feared Jezebel the Queen (1 Kings 18), and Peter who denied the Lord after boasting that he would not (Matt. 26).

The Bible's integrity regarding the human condition extends to its teachings. This includes the existence of an eternal hell (Rev. 14:1–10) unsaved man's total depravity and total helplessness before God (John 6; Rom. 3; Eph. 2:1–10), the exclusivity of Jesus Christ as the only Savior of sinful mankind (Acts 4:12; John 14:1–6) and the absolute sovereignty of God (Job 38–42; Jer. 18; Rom. 9–11).

Finally, there is the Bible's life transforming power. This is the effective power to transform the life of a sinner into one who lives life for the glory of God. This transformation does not occur exclusively in the behavior of an individual, but also occurs inwardly in the very nature of the person in question. It is this change in the essential nature that results in the corresponding behavior. This is what the Apostle Paul means in 2 Cor. 5:17: "Therefore, if anyone is in Christ, he is a new creation. The old has passed away; behold, the new has come."[42]

With this basis, we now turn our attention to the essential evidences that the God of the Bible is indeed the One True God of the universe.

The Evidences the God of the Bible is the One True God

In discussing the subject of God's existence, an atheist may ask the believing Christian how they can know for certain that the God of the Bible is indeed the One True God of the universe. Other religions claim to worship the only true God. How can Christians be so certain they alone are right? Within a pluralistic society in which all religions are regarded as equal are Christians guilty of being naive at best and arrogantly proud at worst? Therefore, the Christian's confidence that the God of the Bible is the One True God of the universe is submitted for the following reasons.

First, the God of the Bible is explicitly identified as the One True God of the universe. This is taught not only in the Old Testament but also in the New Testament Scriptures.

1. Exodus 20:1–6—"And God spoke all these words, saying, 'I am the LORD your God, who brought you out of the land of Egypt, out of the house of

slavery. You shall have no other gods before me. You shall not make for yourself a carved image, or any likeness of anything that is in heaven above, or that is in the earth beneath, or that is in the water under the earth. You shall not bow down to them or serve them, for I the Lord your God am a jealous God, visiting the iniquity of the fathers on the children to the third and the fourth generation of those who hate me, but showing steadfast love to thousands of those who love me and keep my commandments.'"[1]

2. Leviticus 19:1–4—"And the Lord spoke to Moses, saying, 'Speak to all the congregation of the people of Israel and say to them, You shall be holy, for I the Lord your God am holy. Every one of you shall revere his mother and his father, and you shall keep my Sabbaths: I am the Lord your God. Do not turn to idols or make for yourselves any gods of cast metal: I am the Lord your God.'"[2]

3. Psalm 31:5—"Into your hand I commit my spirit; you have redeemed me, O Lord, faithful God."[3]

4. Psalm 96:1– 5—"Oh sing to the Lord a new song; sing to the Lord, all the earth! Sing to the Lord, bless his name; tell of his salvation from day to day. Declare his glory among the nations, his marvelous works among all the peoples! For great is the Lord, and greatly to be praised; he is to be feared above all

gods. For all the gods of the peoples are worthless idols, but the LORD made the heavens. Splendor and majesty are before him; strength and beauty are in his sanctuary."[4]

5. Isaiah 45:5—"I am the LORD, and there is no other; Besides Me there is no God."[5] (See also Isa. 45:6; 18; 21–22).

6. Isaiah 46:9–11—"Remember the former things long past, for I am God, and there is no other; I am God, and there is no one like Me, declaring the end from the beginning, and from the ancient times things which have not been done, saying, 'My purpose will be established, and I will accomplish all My good pleasure'; …truly I have spoken; truly I will bring it to pass. I have planned it, surely I will do it."[6]

7. Isaiah 65:16—"Because he who is blessed in the earth will be blessed by the God of truth; and he who swears in the earth will swear by the God of truth."[7]

8. Jeremiah 10:10—"But the LORD is the true God. He is the living God and the everlasting King."[8]

9. John 3:33—"He who has received His [Jesus's] testimony has set his seal to this, that God is true."[9]

10. John 7:18—"He who speaks from himself seeks his own glory; by the One who is seeking the glory of

the One who sent Him, He is true, and there is no unrighteousness in Him."[10]

11. John 7:28—"Then Jesus cried out in the temple, teaching and saying, 'You both know Me and know where I am from; and I have not come of Myself, but He who sent Me is true, whom you do not know.'"[11]

12. John 8:26—"But He who sent Me is true;"[12]

13. John 17:3—"This is eternal life that they may know You, the only true God, and Jesus Christ whom You have sent."[13]

14. Romans 3:4—"Let God be found true, though every man be found a liar."[14]

15. 1 Thessalonians 1:9—"For they themselves report to us what kind of a reception we had with you, and how you turned to God from idols to serve a living and true God, and to wait for His Son from heaven, whom He raised from the dead, that is Jesus, who rescues us from the wrath to come."[15]

16. 1 John 5:20—"And we know that the Son of God has come, and has given us understanding so that we may know Him who is true and we are in Him who is true, in His Son Jesus Christ. This is the true God and eternal life."[16]

17. Revelation 3:7—"He who is holy and true."[17]

18. Revelation 3:14—"The Amen, the faithful and true Witness, the Beginning of the creation of God, says this."[18]

19. Revelation 6:10—"They cried out with a loud voice, 'O Sovereign Lord, holy and true, how long before you will judge and avenge our blood on those who dwell on the earth?'"[19]

20. Revelation 15:3—[1] "Great and amazing are your deeds, O Lord God the Almighty! Just and true are your ways, O King of the nations."[20]

21. Revelation 16:5–7—"'Just are you, O Holy One, who is and who was, for you brought these judgments. For they have shed the blood of saints and prophets, and you have given them blood to drink. It is what they deserve!' And I heard the altar saying, 'Yes, Lord God the Almighty.'"[21]

22. Revelation 19:11—"Then I saw heaven opened, and behold, a white horse! The one sitting on it is called Faithful and True, and in righteousness he judges and makes war."[22]

Second, the God of the Bible is a personal God who has chosen to reveal Himself to His creation. This He has done in order for His Creation to know Him personally. God does this by two definitive ways and methods: general and specific revelation. Psalm 19 speaks of both.

As previously noted in chapter two, God's general revelation is He disclosing Himself through creation. As the psalmist David writes,

> The heavens declare the glory of God, and the sky above proclaims his handiwork. Day to day pours out speech, and night to night reveals knowledge. There is no speech, nor are there words, whose voice is not heard. Their voice goes out through all the earth, and their words to the end of the world. In them he has set a tent for the sun, which comes out like a bridegroom leaving his chamber, and, like a strong man, runs its course with joy. Its rising is from the end of the heavens, and its circuit to the end of them, and there is nothing hidden from its heat.[23]

David continues his considerations about God's revelation in the latter portion of his song. It is here that the "man after God's own heart" specifically speaks about God's particular, written revelation and its impact upon the individual.

> The law of the LORD is perfect, reviving the soul; the testimony of the LORD is sure, making wise the simple; the precepts of the LORD are right, rejoicing the heart; the commandment of the LORD is pure, enlightening the eyes; the fear of the LORD is clean, enduring forever; the rules of the LORD are true, and righteous altogether. More to be desired are they than gold, even much fine gold; sweeter also than

honey and drippings of the honeycomb. Moreover, by them is your servant warned; in keeping them there is great reward. Who can discern his errors? Declare me innocent from hidden faults. Keep back your servant also from presumptuous sins; let them not have dominion over me! Then I shall be blameless, and innocent of great transgression. Let the words of my mouth and the meditation of my heart be acceptable in your sight, O LORD, my rock and my redeemer.[24]

Other verses pertinent to God's biblical revelation include 1 Corinthians 2:6–16.

Yet among the mature we do impart wisdom, although it is not a wisdom of this age or of the rulers of this age, who are doomed to pass away. But we impart a secret and hidden wisdom of God, which God decreed before the ages for our glory. None of the rulers of this age understood this, for if they had, they would not have crucified the Lord of glory. But, as it is written, "What no eye has seen, nor ear heard, nor the heart of man imagined, what God has prepared for those who love him"—these things God has revealed to us through the Spirit. For the Spirit searches everything, even the depths of God. For who knows a person's thoughts except the spirit of that person, which is in him? So also no one comprehends the thoughts of God except the Spirit of God. Now we have received not the spirit of the world, but the Spirit who is from God, that we might understand the things freely given us by God. And we impart this in words not taught by human wisdom but taught by the Spirit, interpreting spiritual truths to those who are spiritual.

The natural person does not accept the things of the Spirit of God, for they are folly to him, and he is not able to understand them because they are spiritually discerned. The spiritual person judges all things but is himself to be judged by no one. "For who has understood the mind of the Lord so as to instruct him?" But we have the mind of Christ.[25]

This is also the case in Hebrews 1:1–4 where it states,

God, who at various times and in various ways spoke in time past to the fathers by the prophets, has in these last days spoken to us by His Son, whom He has appointed heir of all things, through whom also He made the worlds; who being the brightness of His glory and the express image of His person, and upholding all things by the word of His power, when He had by Himself purged our sins, sat down at the right hand of the Majesty on high, having become so much better than the angels, as He has by inheritance obtained a more excellent name than they.[26]

Additional verses addressing the subject include Exodus 7:17; Exodus 8:10; 22; Exodus 9:14; Psalm 46:10; Psalm 100:3; Psalm 139; Jeremiah 31:34; Ezekiel 6:7; Hosea 8:2; Joel 2:27; Malachi 2:4; John 6:69; Acts 2:36; Philippians

3:10; 2 Timothy 3:16–17; 2 Peter 1:19–20; 1 John 2:3–29; 1 John 4:7.

Third, there is the comparison of the biblical God to false gods and religions. When one compares the God of the Bible to other world religions, many of them in contrast speak of a god who cannot be known personally. Their god is one who is impersonal and unknowable, even in the midst of mankind's attempts to know him or her.

It is estimated that there are approximately 2,300 religions in existence. This does not take in consideration many sub-religious systems that arise from the aforementioned 2,300 figure. There is no conceivable way to document every world religion and its perspective on God within the limited confines of this book. Therefore, the following religions and cults and their doctrine regarding God are highlighted.

Hinduism! Hinduism's supreme being is the indefinable, impersonal Brahman, a philosophical absolute. The Hindu views man as a manifestation of the impersonal Brahman without individual self or self-worth (value).

Jainism is a legalistic religion where salvation is through rigid self-denial. There is no concept of God in a personal sense. Jainism, and its founder Mahavira, rejected the idea of the existence of a supreme being.

Buddhism! The existence of a personal creator and Lord is denied.

Confucianism! Its ethical self-effort leaves no room for a personal, or a need of, God.

Taoism denies the existence of a personal and responsible Supreme Being or god.

The Shinto religion features many, impersonal gods.

Zoroastrianism does believe in a personal god but also believes that a person earns favor with God by his good works.

Judaism believes in the personal God of the Old Testament. However, salvation, or atonement, is accomplished through sacrifices, penitence, good deeds, and a little of God's grace.

Islam teaches an impersonal God who is so powerful and transcendent that he acts impersonally. Both good and evil come from the Islamic god Allah.

Din-Sikhism believes in an impersonal god who is equated with truth and reality.

Regarding various cults, Hare Krishna practices monotheism, but Krishna inhabits everything that is. The religion is pantheistic. Additionally, salvation is obtained by performing a series of works.

The Jehovah's Witnesses deny the Trinity but believe in a personal god. However, their doctrine of salvation is by works.

Mormonism! The Mormons believe in many gods and that God himself was once a man.

Transcendental Meditation denies a personal, infinite god.

Theosophy and the Unification Church reject the idea of a personal God.

The fourth evidence that the God of the Bible is the One True God is because He is hated by sinful mankind. Because of this animosity toward the Scriptures, the fallen world endeavors to create a god(s) in its own image. In explaining this, let us reexamine Romans 1:18–32.

> For the wrath of God is revealed from heaven against all ungodliness and unrighteousness of men, who by their unrighteousness suppress the truth. For what can be known about God is plain to them, because God has shown it to them. For his invisible attributes, namely, his eternal power and divine nature, have been clearly perceived, ever since the creation of the world, in the things that have been made. So they are without excuse. For although they knew God, they did not honor him as God or give thanks to him, but they became futile in their thinking, and their foolish hearts were darkened. Claiming to be wise, they became fools, and exchanged the glory of the immortal God for images resembling mortal man and birds and animals and creeping things.
>
> Therefore God gave them up in the lusts of their hearts to impurity, to the dishonoring of their bodies among themselves, because they exchanged the truth about God for a lie and worshiped and served the creature rather than the Creator, who is blessed forever! Amen.
> For this reason God gave them up to dishonorable passions. For their women exchanged natural relations

for those that are contrary to nature; and the men likewise gave up natural relations with women and were consumed with passion for one another, men committing shameless acts with men and receiving in themselves the due penalty for their error.

And since they did not see fit to acknowledge God, God gave them up to a debased mind to do what ought not to be done. They were filled with all manner of unrighteousness, evil, covetousness, malice. They are full of envy, murder, strife, deceit, maliciousness. They are gossips, slanderers, haters of God, insolent, haughty, boastful, inventors of evil, disobedient to parents, foolish, faithless, heartless, ruthless. Though they know God's righteous decree that those who practice such things deserve to die, they not only do them but give approval to those who practice them.[27]

In this brief treatment of this text, there are two main points to observe: (1) God's overall and general condemnation of the world and (2) God's specific charges of which the world is guilty as charged.

The general condemnation Paul speaks of is found in vs. 1:18–19. God reveals His wrath against sinful mankind's ungodliness, unrighteousness, and its suppression of the truth by their unrighteousness. This verdict is universal and applies to all the ungodly without Christ.

The reason for God's judgment is because the fallen world is without excuse for their sinful behavior. God consistently reveals Himself to the fallen world and it continues to ignore Him. This knowledge of God in creation is not sufficient to save the sinner but it is sufficient to condemn him.

The specific charges against man are now itemized. They are God's indictments.

The first indictment is inexcusable ignorance. "For since the creation of the world His invisible attributes, His eternal power and divine nature, have been clearly seen, being understood through what has been made, so that they are without excuse."[28]

The second indictment is ingratitude. "For even though they knew God, they did not honor Him as God or give thanks, but they became futile in their speculations, and their foolish heart was darkened."[29]

The third indictment is insolence. This is an attitude of disrespect and impertinence. "Professing to be wise, they became fools."[30]

The fourth indictment is idolatry. "And exchanged the glory of the incorruptible God for an image the form of corruptible man and of birds and four-footed animals and crawling creatures."[31]

The fifth indictment is immorality. "Therefore God gave them over in the lusts of their hearts to impurity, so that their bodies would be dishonored among them. For they exchanged the truth of God for a lie, and worshiped and served the creature rather than the Creator, who is blessed forever. Amen. For this reason God gave them over to degrading passions; for their women exchanged the natural function for that which is unnatural, and in the same way also the man abandoned the natural function of the woman and burned in their desire toward one another, men with men committing indecent acts and receiving in their own persons the due penalty of their error."[32]

The sixth indictment is incorrigibility. This is sin that becomes habitual and persistent. It is continual.

> "And just as they did not like to retain God in *their* knowledge, God gave them over to a debased mind, to do those things which are not fitting; being filled with all unrighteousness, sexual immorality, wickedness, covetousness, maliciousness; full of envy, murder, strife, deceit, evil-mindedness; *they are* whisperers, backbiters, haters of God, violent, proud, boasters, inventors of evil things, disobedient to parents, undiscerning, untrustworthy, unloving, unforgiving, unmerciful; who, knowing the righteous judgment of God, that those who practice such things are deserving of death, not only do the same but also approve of those who practice them."[33]

The fifth reason why the God of the Bible is the One True God is because the Bible presents God as the eternal and only Savior. Finite mankind is sinful and in need of a Savior. Man is totally depraved by his sin. Sin has permeated every part of his being; nothing less, nothing more, nothing else. Man is in need of a Savior, and the God of the Bible indicates that He and He alone is that Savior and the imputer of the righteousness sinful man needs, but does not possess in and of himself.

The Bible describes God's nature as sovereign (Rom. 9–11), holy (Isa. 6), eternal (John 1:1–2), immutable (Heb. 6:17), omnipresent (Acts 17:28), omnipotent (Luke 1:37), omniscient (1 John 3:20), just/righteous (Isa. 45:21), loving (1 John 4:8), good (Nahum 1:7), glorious (Eph. 1:11), creator (Gen. 1:1–31), truth (Isa. 65:16), unique (Isa. 45:21b–22; 46:9), comforting (2 Cor. 1:3–4), revealer of truth (Matt. 16:15), giver of life (John 5:21).

The Bible is equally clear as to the nature of man and why man needs God and salvation. Man is in need of God (John 3, 9, 10, 11, 14). Fallen man is sinful (Rom. 1–5), spiritually dead (Eph. 1:1–2:10), needing to be justified (Gal. 1–2), needing fellowship with God (1 John), needing righteousness from God (Phil. 1–3), totally depraved (Ps. 14), deceived (Jer. 17).

The sixth reason why the God of the Bible is the One True God is because the God of the Bible ordained Jesus Christ's death upon the cross as the only means to atone for sin. In Matthew 7:13–14 Jesus pointed out that the way to destruction is broad, and no one has any trouble finding that road, while the way to life is exceedingly narrow, and those who find it are few. The narrow way Jesus was speaking of was the narrow way of His own death. Man would not seek this way on his own, much less find it.

Jesus Christ's substitutionary atonement on the cross was a means to an end and not the end in and of itself. It was the only way in which Jesus would receive the curse for our sin (Gal. 3:1–14), to be the means of redemption (Rom. 3:21–31; 1 Pet. 1:18–19), the means of forgiveness (Col. 2:1–15), the only means by which sinners may receive the righteousness of God (Phil. 3:9; 2 Cor. 5:21), and the means for substitutionary atonement (Isa. 52:13–53:12).

Finally, the God of the Bible is the One True God because the God of the Bible is the God of grace. Sinful mankind cannot earn salvation or appease God by good works. However, the God of the Bible reaches down to sinful man by grace alone, through faith alone, in Christ alone providing regeneration, justification, sanctification, and ultimately glorification.

The sufficiency of God's grace is explicitly set forth in the following texts:

1. Acts 15:11—"But we believe that we will be saved through the grace of the Lord Jesus, just as they will."[34]

2. Romans 3:21–28—"But now the righteousness of God has been manifested apart from the law, although the Law and the Prophets bear witness to it— the righteousness of God through faith in Jesus Christ for all who believe. For there is no distinction: for all have sinned and fall short of the glory of God,

and are justified by his grace as a gift, through the redemption that is in Christ Jesus, whom God put forward as a propitiation by his blood, to be received by faith. This was to show God's righteousness, because in his divine forbearance he had passed over former sins. It was to show his righteousness at the present time, so that he might be just and the justifier of the one who has faith in Jesus."[35]

3. Romans 5:15—"But the free gift is not like the trespass. For if many died through one man's trespass, much more have the grace of God and the free gift by the grace of that one man Jesus Christ abounded for many."[36]

4. Romans 8:28–30—"And we know that for those who love God all things work together for good for those who are called according to his purpose. For those whom he foreknew he also predestined to be conformed to the image of his Son, in order that he might be the firstborn among many brothers. And those whom he predestined he also called, and those whom he called he also justified, and those whom he justified he also glorified."[37]

5. 2 Corinthians 13:14—"The grace of the Lord Jesus Christ and the love of God and the fellowship of the Holy Spirit be with you all."[38]

6. Galatians 2:15–21 (16–17)—"Nevertheless knowing that a man is not justified by the works of the Law but through faith in Christ Jesus, even we have believed in Christ Jesus, so that we may be justified by faith in Christ and not by the works of the Law; since by the works of the Law no flesh will be justified."[39]

7. Ephesians 2:1–10 (vs. 8–9)—"For by grace you have been saved through faith; and that not of yourselves, it is the gift of God, not as a result of works so that no one may boast."[40]

8. Titus 3:1–7 (vs. 5–7)—"He saved us, not on the basis of deeds which we have done in righteousness, but according to His mercy, by the washing of regeneration and renewing by the Holy Spirit, whom He poured out upon us richly through Jesus Christ our Savior, so that being justified by His grace we would be made heirs according to the hope of eternal life."[41]

9. 1 Peter 1:1–2—"Peter, an apostle of Jesus Christ, To those who are elect exiles of the dispersion in Pontus, Galatia, Cappadocia, Asia, and Bithynia, according to the foreknowledge of God the Father, in the sanctification of the Spirit, for obedience to Jesus Christ and for sprinkling with his blood: May grace and peace be multiplied to you."[42]

With all of the reasons and revelation God has given and provided, why is it that fallen man continues in his disobedience and rebellion against God? Why is man incapable of coming to God with all the evidence presented to him? The answer lies with the doctrine of regeneration. We explore this in the following chapter.

Why Reason and Revelation Alone Are Insufficient in Convincing an Atheist of God's Existence

Imagine this scene. An atheist you have known for some time approaches you. Perhaps because of your Christian testimony, he begins asking you questions regarding why you believe in the existence of God. Though initially taken by surprise, you do your best to answer each question thoughtfully, graciously, and accurately to the biblical text.

The atheist in question may be a coworker, a friend, or even a member of your immediate or extended family. Over the course of several meetings and conversations, your relationship with the individual continues to be cordial and friendly. You are encouraged and increasingly hopeful that this person will soon come to repent of their sins and trust Christ as their Savior and Lord.

However, after answering every question posed to you, your atheist friend or relative does not respond to your request for them to receive Jesus Christ as Savior and Lord. They become increasingly resistant to even the slightest suggestion that they need Jesus.

You are perplexed. You are confused. You have answered every one of their questions. You have addressed each of their objections. You were encouraged by their initial response to your sincere explanation of the basics of biblical Christianity and the evidence for God's existence. They even let you pray with them. Now, they want little or nothing to do with you or with your God. It is as if someone threw a switch to completely change the person you have come to know. What happened?

What all too often happens when we share the gospel, and a defense of the same, is that we mistakenly believe that reason and biblical revelation alone are sufficient to convince a person of their need for Christ. Not so! There is a necessary third component to a true biblical understanding of God and sin resulting in conversion to Christ. That indispensable component is monergistic regeneration.

Monergistic regeneration is the new birth or rebirth. This compound word contains the root word *generation* meaning creation, invention, initiation, and origination. The prefix *re* means once more, afresh, or anew. Therefore, regeneration refers to an afresh or new creation or origination. Pertaining to a sinner's relationship to the holy God of the Bible, it is a new birth resulting in justification and reconciliation with

God. Where once God was the sinner's enemy (Rom. 5:10), through regeneration the sinner becomes a child of God.

The noun *regeneration* occurs only twice in the Scriptures: in Matthew 19:28 regarding the renewal of the world immediately prior to the return of Christ and in Titus 3:5 where baptism is a sign and seal of regeneration. However, there are numerous texts that refer to regeneration by using various images and expressions. One such description is the new birth.

Is this new birth necessary? It is not only necessary but occurs only through the means and methods God has appointed resulting in a new pattern of living.

In Ezekiel 36:25–26 it reads, "I will sprinkle clean water on you, and you shall be clean from all your uncleanness's, and from all your idols I will cleanse you. And I will give you a new heart, and a new spirit I will put within you. And I will remove the heart of stone from your flesh and give you a heart of flesh."[1] As one commentator explains,

> This section is among the most glorious in all Scripture on the subject of Israel's restoration to the Lord and national salvation. This salvation is described in v. 25 as a cleansing that will wash away sin. Such washing was symbolized in the Mosaic rites of purification (cf. Num. 19:17–19; Ps. 119:9; Isa. 4:4; Zech. 13:1).For the concept of sprinkling in cleansing, see Ps. 51:7, 10; Heb. 9:13; 10:22. This is the washing Paul wrote of in Eph. 5:26 and Titus 3:5. Jesus had this very promise in mind in John 3:5. What was figuratively

described in Ezek. 36:25 is explained as literal in vv. 26–27. The gift of the "new heart" signifies the new birth, which is regeneration by the Holy Spirit (cf. 11:18–20). The "heart" stands for the whole nature. The "spirit" indicates the governing power of the mind, which directs thought and conduct. A "heart of stone" is stubborn and self-willed. A "heart of flesh" is pliable and responsive. The evil inclination is removed and a new nature replaces it. This is New Covenant character as in Jer. 31:31–34. The Lord will also give his "Spirit" to the faithful Jews (cf. Ezek. 39:29; Isa. 44:3; 59:21; Joel 2:28–29; Acts 2:16ff.). When Israel becomes the true people of God (Ezek. 36:28), the judgment promise of Hos. 1:9 is nullified. All nature will experience the blessings of Israel's salvation (Ezek. 36:29–30). When the Jews have experienced such grace, they will be even more repentant—a sign of true conversion (v. 31).[2]

In John 3:3, Jesus said, "Truly, truly, I say to you, unless one is born again he cannot see the kingdom of God."[3] Notice that Jesus said that if the new birth does not occur, the sinner in question cannot see or understand the rule of God over man. It is not that they will not, but it is that they cannot. Also, the order of the language surmises the new birth or regeneration occurs prior to one's placing faith in Christ. As Dr. R. C. Sproul recalls,

One of the most dramatic moments in my life for the shaping of my theology took place in a seminary classroom. One of my professors went to the blackboard and wrote these words in bold letters: "**Regeneration Precedes Faith**." These words were a shock to my system. I had entered seminary believing that the key work of man to effect rebirth was faith. I thought that we first had to believe in Christ in order to be born again. I use the words in order here for a reason. I was thinking in terms of steps that must be taken in a certain sequence. I had put faith at the beginning.[4]

Regeneration is called "renewal of the Holy Spirit" in Titus 3:5. It results in sinners becoming "new creations" in Christ (2 Cor. 5:17), being commanded to put on the "new self" because of Christ (Eph. 4:24) and to being referred to as "newborn babies" through Christ (1 Pet. 2:2).

Jesus also spoke extensively of the need for regeneration in John 6 where He describes Himself through the allegory of being the Bread of Life. In vs. 37 He says, "I am the bread of life; whoever comes to me shall not hunger, and whoever believes in me shall never thirst. But I said to you that you have seen me and yet do not believe. All that the Father gives me will come to me, and whoever comes to me I will never cast out."[5]

He continues this thought in vs. 44. He says, "No one can come to me unless the Father who sent me draws him. And I will raise him up on the last day."[6]

Jesus concludes His discourse on regeneration in vs. 60–65. He says,

> When many of his disciples heard it, they said, "This is a hard saying; who can listen to it?" But Jesus, knowing in himself that his disciples were grumbling about this, said to them, "Do you take offense at this? Then what if you were to see the Son of Man ascending to where he was before? It is the Spirit who gives life; the flesh is no help at all. The words that I have spoken to you are spirit and life. But there are some of you who do not believe." (For Jesus knew from the beginning who those were who did not believe, and who it was who would betray him.) And he said, "This is why I told you that no one can come to me unless it is granted him by the Father."[7]

Jesus also illustrated the importance of regeneration in raising Lazarus from the dead in John 11. The allegorical meaning of this familiar story is that as Lazarus was physically dead and in need of Jesus's power to effectively raise him from his physically deadened state, so too are fallen sinners spiritually dead or separated from God and need to be raised unto new life in Christ.

The Apostle Paul extensively addresses the subject of regeneration in Romans 8:1–10 and Ephesians 2:1–5. In Romans 8:1–10, he says,

> There is therefore now no condemnation for those who are in Christ Jesus. For the law of the Spirit of life has set you free in Christ Jesus from the law of sin and death. For God has done what the law, weakened by the flesh, could not do. By sending

his own Son in the likeness of sinful flesh and for sin, he condemned sin in the flesh, in order that the righteous requirement of the law might be fulfilled in us, who walk not according to the flesh but according to the Spirit. For those who live according to the flesh set their minds on the things of the flesh, but those who live according to the Spirit set their minds on the things of the Spirit. For to set the mind on the flesh is death, but to set the mind on the Spirit is life and peace. For the mind that is set on the flesh is hostile to God, for it does not submit to God's law; indeed, it cannot. Those who are in the flesh cannot please God.

You, however, are not in the flesh but in the Spirit, if in fact the Spirit of God dwells in you. Anyone who does not have the Spirit of Christ does not belong to him. But if Christ is in you, although the body is dead because of sin, the Spirit is life because of righteousness. If the Spirit of him who raised Jesus from the dead dwells in you, he who raised Christ Jesus from the dead will also give life to your mortal bodies through his Spirit who dwells in you.[8]

Paul indicates that the differences between the regenerated sinner and one who is unregenerated are significant. They live mutually exclusive lives indicated by the words *flesh* (referring to the sinful nature) and *mind* (referring to consciousness, understanding, and perception). The contrasts between the two categories of individuals are as follows:

1. Those who live according the flesh set their minds on the things of the flesh, while those who live according to the Spirit set their minds on the things of the Spirit.

2. For to set the mind on the flesh is death, but to set the mind on the Spirit is life and peace.

3. For the mind that is set on the flesh is hostile to God, for it does not submit to God's law; indeed it cannot. The logical contrasting inference is those whose mind is set on the Spirit is in harmony with God, for it does submit to God's law; indeed because it can.

4. Those who are in the flesh cannot please God, while those in the Spirit are able and do please God.

5. Those who are in the Spirit are indwelt by the Holy Spirit, while those who are in the flesh are not indwelt by the Spirit.

6. For those in the flesh, the body is dead because of sin, while those in the Spirit possess life and righteousness.

7. If the Spirit of him who raised Jesus from the dead dwells in you, He who raised Christ Jesus from the dead will also give life to your mortal bodies through his Spirit who dwells in you.

Paul further explains that there is a fundamental difference between the unregenerate and the regenerate. You can witness this by the fundamental differences in how the two groups think, feel, behave, and make decisions. The unregenerate are by nature hostile to God and His Word. By contrast, the regenerate individual not only loves God but also seeks to obey His Word as a sign of the change of heart and mind God has brought about by the Holy Spirit and through the preaching of the gospel.

Elsewhere in Ephesians 2:1–5, Paul continues this theme when he writes,

> And you were dead in the trespasses and sins in which you once walked, following the course of this world, following the prince of the power of the air, the spirit that is now at work in the sons of disobedience—among whom we all once lived in the passions of our flesh, carrying out the desires of the body and the mind, and were by nature children of wrath, like the rest of mankind. But God, being rich in mercy, because of the great love with which he loved us, even when we were dead in our trespasses, made us alive together with Christ—by grace you have been saved.[9]

In this familiar passage, Paul dictates what life is like for unregenerate sinners who are without Christ. They are (1) dead in trespasses and sins in which they walk or live; (2) they follow the course of this world's system of thought and philosophy, which is anti-God; (3) they follow the prince of the power of the air, which is Satan; (4) they are disobedient to God's Word due to the spirit that is at work in them; (5) they live in the passions of sin; (6) they carry out the desires of the body and the mind; and (7) they are by nature children of and the recipients of God's wrath.

By contrast, the regenerate is a recipient of God's grace, mercy, and love. God makes them alive in Christ and this is all because of God's amazing grace. Being made alive is a description of regeneration.

Not to be overlooked in this discussion of regeneration is the preceding word *monergistic*. The prefix being *mon* is short for *mono*. This refers to being alone or one. The root word *erg* comes from the Greek verb for "work." "Monergism is something that operates by itself or works alone as the sole active party."[10]

The reason behind this accompanying word to regeneration is the act of new birth is solely initiated by the Holy Spirit God. This act is not a cooperative effort between God and sinful man: that would be synergistic regeneration. Rather, monergistic regeneration is completely a work of God on behalf of sinful man. "Regeneration is always ascribed to the Holy Spirit as the efficient cause."[11]

Dr. Sproul continues by saying,

When the term *monergism* is linked with the word *regeneration*, the phrase describes an action by which God the Holy Spirit works on a human being without the person's assistance or cooperation. This grace of regeneration is called operative grace. Cooperative grace, on the other hand, is grace that God offers to sinners and that they may accept or reject, depending upon the sinner's disposition. Monergistic regeneration is exclusively a divine act.[12]

Unless the sinner receives the gracious regenerating work of God in their minds, emotions, and wills, they will not respond to the gospel and cannot respond to the gospel. "Unless we first receive the grace of regeneration, we will not and cannot respond to the gospel in a positive way. Regeneration must occur first before there can be any positive response of faith."[13]

What preceding cause activates the miracle of new birth within the deadened sinner's soul? The new birth occurs by nothing more, nothing less, and nothing else but the preaching of the gospel. It is through the heralding of the gospel of Jesus Christ that God brings to life the seed of truth that has been sown in the soul of sinful, fallen man thereby raising him unto new life.

Man is incapable of responding to the gospel on his own. He needs the Holy Spirit's divine work to occur in his life. Without it, he will not and cannot respond to the gospel no matter how much revelation or reasoning he has received.

Paul explains this inability to respond to the gospel and the resulting hostility to the same in 1 Corinthians 1:18–31.

> For the word of the cross is folly to those who are perishing, but to us who are being saved it is the power of God. For it is written, "I will destroy the wisdom

of the wise, and the discernment of the discerning I will thwart." Where is the one who is wise? Where is the scribe? Where is the debater of this age? Has not God made foolish the wisdom of the world? For since, in the wisdom of God, the world did not know God through wisdom, it pleased God through the folly of what we preach to save those who believe. For Jews demand signs and Greeks seek wisdom, but we preach Christ crucified, a stumbling block to Jews and folly to Gentiles, but to those who are called, both Jews and Greeks, Christ the power of God and the wisdom of God. For the foolishness of God is wiser than men, and the weakness of God is stronger than men. For consider your calling, brothers: not many of you were wise according to worldly standards, not many were powerful, not many were of noble birth. But God chose what is foolish in the world to shame the wise; God chose what is weak in the world to shame the strong; God chose what is low and despised in the world, even things that are not, to bring to nothing things that are, so that no human being might boast in the presence of God. And because of him you are in Christ Jesus, who became to us wisdom from God, righteousness and sanctification and redemption, so that, as it is written, "Let the one who boasts, boast in the Lord."[14]

There is much to glean from this passage of Scripture regarding the inability of man to come to Christ and his subsequent hostility toward the gospel. In this text, we make the following observations indicating man's hostility to the gospel in his fallen state.

1. For the word of the cross is folly to those who are perishing, but to us who are being saved it is the power of God (vs. 18).

2. God will destroy and thwart the wisdom of the wise (vs. 19).

3. God will make foolish the wisdom of the world (vs. 20).

4. The world does not come to know God through its wisdom. At the same time, God saves sinners through the folly of what is preached (vs. 21).

5. Jews demand signs, Greeks seek wisdom. But the preaching of Christ crucified will be a stumbling block to the Jews and folly to the Gentiles (vs. 22–23).

6. For those who are called by God, the gospel is the power and wisdom of God (vs. 24).

7. God is stronger than man's power and wiser than man's wisdom. (vs. 25).

8. God chose to save those who are unwise, weak and the ignoble. God chose what appears foolish to shame the wise. God chose what appears weak to shame the strong. God chose what is low and

despised in the world to bring the nobles to nothing (vs. 26–28).

9. God chose to save this way so that no one could boast in God's presence (vs. 29).

10. This resulting work of God makes the sinner wise, righteous, holy and redeemed (vs. 30–31).

Paul goes on to say in 1 Corinthians 2 that the fallen sinner's new birth does not occur because of some other person's ability to be a powerful motivational speaker.

> And I, when I came to you, brothers, did not come proclaiming to you the testimony of God with lofty speech or wisdom. For I decided to know nothing among you except Jesus Christ and him crucified. And I was with you in weakness and in fear and much trembling, and my speech and my message were not in plausible words of wisdom but in demonstration of the Spirit and of power so that your faith might not rest in the wisdom of men but in the power of God.[15]

The apostle did not want the Corinthians to think they came to Christ in and of themselves or that Paul was the operative force behind their conversion. Rather, he insisted they know that only through the sovereign work of the Holy Spirit does anyone come to Christ for conversion. Paul says that all that we know of God is solely because of the Spirit of God.

Yet among the mature we do impart wisdom, although it is not a wisdom of this age or of the rulers of this age, who are doomed to pass away. But we impart a secret and hidden wisdom of God, which God decreed before the ages for our glory. None of the rulers of this age understood this, for if they had, they would not have crucified the Lord of glory. But, as it is written, "What no eye has seen, nor ear heard, nor the heart of man imagined, what God has prepared for those who love him"—these things God has revealed to us through the Spirit. For the Spirit searches everything, even the depths of God. For who knows a person's thoughts except the spirit of that person, which is in him? So also no one comprehends the thoughts of God except the Spirit of God. Now we have received not the spirit of the world, but the Spirit who is from God, that we might understand the things freely given us by God. And we impart this in words not taught by human wisdom but taught by the Spirit, interpreting spiritual truths to those who are spiritual.[16]

Why is it absolutely necessary that man need the sovereign regeneration work by the Holy Spirit in order for man to understand the gospel and to come to know Christ as savior? Paul answers this question in vs. 14.

The natural person does not accept the things of the Spirit of God, for they are folly to him, and he is not able to understand them because they are spiritually discerned. The spiritual person judges all things but is himself to be judged by no one. "For who has understood the mind of the Lord so as to instruct him?" But we have the mind of Christ.[17]

The unregenerate sinner is unable to understand the nature of the gospel. He lacks the ability to comprehend the truth of the gospel. That is why he must first be regenerated by the Holy Spirit through the preaching of the gospel in order to understand the gospel that is preached.

I know as I answer each one of this atheist's questions, it will still require a sovereign work by the Holy Spirit for this individual to be converted to Christ. This should not deter me in my efforts to answer his objections to biblical truth, but rather give me a perspective in what I can do and what I cannot do. I cannot convert this man. That is God's job. But I can answer his objections to biblical Christianity as best as I can. Through reason, revelation, and sovereign regeneration, this man may be saved—but only by a sovereign work of God. It is with this perspective in mind that I now begin to answer an atheist who calls himself the godslayer.

Letter One

The bible (sic) is limited to the knowledge and ignorance of the primitive men who wrote it. The reason is clear: your god (sic) is imaginary and had nothing to do with your bible (sic). Your bible is as pathetic as is your god. The godslayer!

Dear deluded one;

I read with derision your spew about the bible (sic) and although I know the newspaper lacks the courage to print any but the religious "party line," I could not help but marvel at your naiveté... but then again you get your money from the gullible. But I must respond to your obsequious fawning over the Wholly Babble which of course was written by people who thought the earth was flat.

Have you ever wondered why one cannot get a copy of those writings that composed the bible (sic) after the King James toadies filtered out most of the absurdities and cruelties to make their (sic) "accepted" version?

Anyway, since you were brief, let me answer each your contentions about this vacuous tripe bible (sic) you put so much faith in.

1. *Claim of unity. Actually, there is no real unity. The bible (sic) is replete with contradictions and absurdities. One needs only to Google biblical contradictions to find thousands of them.*

2. *Claim of indestructibility. If this is true, then why does it need human interpretation? Why vagueness? What is your god (sic) afraid of? Our understanding of him as the monster he is? Remember also this indestructibility is directly responsible for programs, crusades for killing, witch burnings and inquisitions.*

3. *Claim of historical accuracy? And you say this with a straight face? There is no contemporary evidence of Jesus' existence and absolutely no recital of history that could not have been written long after the history had occurred.*

4. *Claim of scientific accuracy? Ha! According to your bible (sic), donkeys speak, iron axe handles float on water, and slugs melt as they crawl, bats are birds, and all thinking comes from the heart organ.*

5. *Claim of fulfilled prophecy? What of all unfulfilled prophecy? One example will suffice: the Christ will return before all then living shall die? How many 2,000 year old men do you know?*

6. *Claim of universal influence. How many murders, burnings, and tortures came from the pathetic attempt to Christianize the world? Note also that none of the Ten Commandments forbids rape or incest. Such a wonderful role model is your bible (sic).*

7. *Claim of consistency? This is an astonishing claim when you cannot get any other version.*

8. *Claim of circulation? Well if size is your criteria, the bible (sic) falls well behind the writings of Mao and if majority is an indication validity, then Hinduism is the only true religion.*

9. *Claim of honesty about the human condition? Your bible (sic) tells me to sell my daughter into slavery, kill all your enemies and their wives and their children and their animals, but of course keep all the unmarried virgins for yourself.*

10. *Claim of life transforming? Your god (sic) orders you to smash the heads of little babies of unbelievers against the rocks until their brains spill out as a sign of your piety. Have you done this, or have you picked and chose which of your god's (sic) order you will obey?*

This is your god (sic) given bible (sic). One that tells me to keep handicapped out of church, keep women silent, shun my wife during her menstrual period (which is as your god made her), and kill and maim ... this is your vaunted bible (sic).

Consider this, if your bible (sic) was written or inspired by a god (sic), one would expect a clear, non-contradictory and lovingly brilliant statement. Instead, we get replete contradictions, cruelty, injustice and stupidity. We should be awed by its brilliance and knowledge ... not knowledge limited to the knowledge and ignorance of the primitive men who wrote it. The reason is clear; your god (sic) is imaginary and had nothing to do with your bible (sic). Your bible (sic) is as pathetic as is your god (sic).

—The godslayer

We have several questions to answer and address from the godslayer. I begin by answering each issue point by point. First of all, did the writers of Scripture really believe the earth was flat and if not, where and when did this absurdity originate?

The Bible's affirmation of the Earth's spherical shape can be found in several Old Testament texts. To begin with, Isaiah 40:21–23 says,

> Do you not know? Do you not hear? Has it not been told you from the beginning? Have you not understood from the foundations of the earth? It is he who sits above the circle of the earth, and its inhabitants are like grasshoppers; who stretches out the heavens like a curtain, and spreads them like a tent to dwell in; who brings princes to nothing, and makes the rulers of the earth as emptiness.[1]

The word *circle,* which appears in vs. 22, means circuit or compass. The word *vault* is also used in some translations instead of circle. The word *vault* means a domed or circular throne room in the sky. The word *circle* and *vault* is therefore appropriate when describing the spherical shape of the earth.

This spherical concept of Earth is also supported by other biblical texts. These include Job 22:14, "Thick clouds veil him, so that he does not see, and he walks on the vault of heaven" (Job 22:14, esv)[2]; Job 26:10, "He has inscribed a circle on the face of the waters at the boundary between light and darkness."[3]; and Proverbs 8:27, "When he established the heavens, I was there; when he drew a circle on the face of the deep."[4]

Since the concept of a flat earth is not found in the Scriptures, it begs the question as to when and by whom did the theory of the earth being flat originate. The so-called Flat Earth Model originated from many ancient cultures and civilizations. These include Greece until the Classical Period (480 bc–323 bc), the Bronze Age (2900 bc), and Iron Age (1200 bc) civilizations of the Near East until the Hellenistic period (323 bc–146 bc), India until the Gupta period (early centuries ad) and China until the seventeenth century ad. It was also typically held in the native cultures of the Americas. A flat earth domed by the sky in the shape of an upturned bowl was widespread in pre-scientific cultures. The Jewish conception of a flat earth is even found in biblical and post biblical eras.

The common conception of the earth being flat was that it was a round flat wheel like an object resting in the surrounding waters known as oceans. Several classical Greek poets, such as Homer and Hesiod (eighth century BC) described the earth as this flat-like disc cosmos on the Shield of Achilles. This poetic custom of an earth-encircling (*Gaiaokhos*) sea (*Oceanus*) and a flat disc also appears in Stasinus of Cyprus, Mimnermus, Aristophanes, and Apollonius Rhodius. Homer's presentation of the flat earth theory extended well unto the fourth century AD.

The flat earth theory was also proposed by ancient Greek philosophers. Pre-Socratic philosophers who believed that the world was flat included Thales (c. 550 BC), Leucippus (c. 440 BC) and Democritus (c. 460–370 BC). The theory was also embraced in Ancient India, by the Norse and Germanic peoples, in ancient Japan and China.

The development of the spherical view of earth within various cultures and historical figures, aside from the testimony of Scripture, developed throughout the succeeding centuries and in many specific periods of history. These historical periods include

1. Classical World (8th–7th century BC–1000 AD).
2. Early Christian Church (33 AD–325 AD).

3. Early Middle Ages (5th–10th century AD).

4. High Middle Ages (11th–13th century AD).

5. Late Middle Ages (14th–16th century AD).

There are those today who still hold to a flat earth theory of the cosmos, but they are few and far between. However, the theory was not, and is not, proposed by Scripture.

Secondly, are there contradictions in the Bible? What about the seemingly endless evidence of contradictions and absurdities that atheists claim exist? Per the godslayer's suggestion, I Googled *Contradictions in the Scriptures* and found several Web sites that purport to reveal many so-called contradictions contained in the Scriptures. The sites would list comparative passages and the subsequent contradictions contained therein.

However, that is all that was done. There was no scholarly attempt to comment on the supposed contradictions or to in any way explain them. All I found were just lists of proposed disagreements. It was as if to say that the listing of apparent contradictions was sufficient in and of itself to prove the Bible is inaccurate.

This book's purpose does not provided enough space to address each and every apparent so-called contradiction submitted by atheists and agnostics. That is a subject for another book. However, I will address three examples of biblical contradictions I found online and attempt to explain their underlying unity.

The first example is about the identity of Joseph's father. The Joseph of whom I refer is the New Testament Joseph who was the husband of Mary, the mother of Jesus. Who is the father of Joseph? Matthew 1:16 states, "And Jacob begat Joseph the husband of Mary, of whom was born Jesus, who is called Christ."[5] However, Luke 3:23 says, "And Jesus himself began to be about thirty years of age, being [as was supposed] the son of Joseph, which was the son of Heli."[6]

The text from Luke seems to indicate that Heli was the father of Joseph. Who then was Joseph's father: Jacob or Heli?

The contradiction is solved when you understand that these are two distinct genealogies. Matthew's genealogy records the lineage of Jesus through his adopted father Joseph. Luke, on the other hand, traces Jesus's genealogy through his mother Mary. Therefore, Heli was not Joseph's father, but rather Mary's father, the father-in-law of Joseph and Jesus's maternal grandfather. No contradiction.

Let us examine a second apparent contradiction. Is Jesus equal to or lesser than God the Father? In John 10:30 we read, "I and my Father are one."[7] However, John 14:28 says, "You have heard how I said unto you, I go away, and come again unto you. If ye loved me, ye would rejoice, because I said, I go unto the Father: for my Father is greater than I."[8] Is Jesus equal to the Father or is He lesser than the Father?

In John 10:30, Jesus is acknowledging the unity of His nature and essence to that of God the Father. In effect, Jesus is calling Himself God. That is why the Jews, as recorded in John 10:31–33, took up stones to kill him. Why would they do such a thing? The text gives us the answer. "The Jews picked up stones again to stone him. Jesus answered them, 'I have shown you many good works from the Father; for which of them are you going to stone me?' The Jews answered him, 'It is not for a good work that we are going to stone you but for blasphemy, because you, being a man, make yourself God.'"[9]

However, Jesus was not speaking to His disciples in John 14:28 about His equality of nature and essence with God the Father. On the contrary, Jesus was speaking rather of His humiliation and subordination to the Father since the Incarnation. Jesus was going back to share equal glory with the Father that He had voluntarily relinquished while on this earth. These are two different statements from two different texts, which have two different contexts and two different meanings. One text speaks of Jesus's deity while the other addresses Jesus's humanity.

Our third example is found by comparing 1 Kings 4:26 with 2 Chronicles 9:25. 1 Kings 4:26 states, "And Solomon had forty thousand stalls of horses for his chariots, and twelve thousand horsemen."[10] Yet, 2 Chronicles 9:25 says, "And Solomon had four thousand stalls for horses and chariots, and twelve thousand horsemen; whom he bestowed in the chariot cities, and with the king at Jerusalem."[11]

The question is how many stalls and horsemen did King Solomon actually have?

What is evident here is what is known as a textual variant. This is an alternative reading between two texts based not upon the whims of the copyist but rather upon a human copyist's error in the recording from one text to another. As author, speaker, and pastor Dr. John MacArthur writes, "We are indebted to those select scholars who labor tediously in the field of textual criticism. Their studies recover the original text of Scripture from the large volume of extant manuscript copies that are flawed by textual variants."[12]

What is the definitive answer when one comes into an apparent discrepancy such as found in these two texts? The answer resides in the relying upon the oldest existing manuscripts available because of the perspective that the copy closest to the original is evaluated to be the most accurate. Therefore, biblical scholars have acknowledged that this discrepancy between these two texts are resolved by relying upon the oldest existing copy, 2 Chronicles 9:25, as being more accurate in listing Solomon's stalls of horses as 4,000 rather than 40,000 as listed in 1 Kings 4:25.

Throughout the Bible's existence, scholars who are involved in the science known as textual criticism continue to discover, preserve, catalogue, evaluate, and publish biblical manuscripts. The task at hand for the textual critic is to make sure that the original prophetic/apostolic inspired text remains unaltered.

Two important historical evidences reinforce confidence on the accuracy of our current Old Testament text. These include the striking similarity between the oldest existent Old Testament Hebrew text dated in the tenth century AD. and the Old Testament Greek translation known as the Septuagint, which is dated at 200–150 BC. The accuracy in the copying of the Old Testament text is striking.

The second evidence speaking of the Old Testament consistency would be the discovery of what is known as the Dead Sea Scrolls. From 1947–1956, an extensive collection of Old Testament manuscripts dated between 200–100 BC prove the continuity between the text then and today.

As previously noted in chapter two, the extensive New Testament manuscripts, numbering in excess of five thousand and dated to within twenty-five to fifty years of the originals, supports the claim of biblical accuracy. It is estimated by textual critics that 99.99 percent of the original writing have been reclaimed and of the remaining one hundredth of a percent does not impact the accuracy of Christian doctrine in any way.

With this wealth of biblical manuscripts in the original languages and with the disciplined activity of textual critics to establish with almost perfect accuracy the content of the autographs, any errors that have been introduced and/ or perpetuated by the thousands of translations over the centuries can be identified and corrected by comparing the translation or copy with the reassembled original. By this providential means, God has made good His promise to preserve the Scriptures.[13]

Regarding the godslayer's third point, what is the meaning of indestructibility? Is the Bible indestructible? How does this indestructibility have anything to do with biblical interpretation?

For anything to be identified as indestructible means that it is permanent, unyielding, durable, everlasting, imperishable, and eternal. It is therefore not fragile, breakable, or lacking durability. This is what is meant when believers articulate that the Bible is indestructible. It has stood, and continues to stand, the test of time.

As I previously mentioned in chapter two, one of the evidences of the Bible being God's Word is that it is indestructible. This is in spite of many philosophical, political, ecclesiastical, and even physical efforts to destroy it.

I am unsure as to what the Bible's continued indestructibility amidst mankind's attempts to destroy it has to do with interpretation. I acknowledge that the Bible has been used incorrectly to sanction all sorts of devastating programs and movements. Such is the sly work of the devil through those who claim to love God but in reality serve the adversary. However, this unfortunate misusage of God's Word does not negate the obvious: the Bible remains in existence in spite of efforts by the many and the few to eliminate it from the culture and also the church.

The godslayer states that the Scriptures contain vagueness and poses the question, "What is your god afraid of?" Is this because God is a monster?

Not in the least. The Bible, along with being God's Word, is literature. To approach the Bible without this basic understanding is to fail to grasp its fundamental structure. It is because of the Bible's varied genres or types of literature, which include such forms as law, history, poetry, wisdom, prophecy, biography, letters, and apocalyptic, that the student and interpreter of Scripture must follow particular tools and disciplines in order to rightly divide the Word of truth (2 Tim. 2:15). When careful exegesis, which is the explanation and interpretation of the text, is not followed, this lends itself to programs that hurt, crusades that kill, witch burnings that defame, and inquisitions that imprison.

Exegesis is defined as the competent and consistent application of sound interpretive principles to the biblical text. This is accomplished by addressing four basic questions in approaching the Bible for the purpose of knowing what a particular text says, what it means, and how it may be applied.

The four questions include the following: First, what did the text mean to the biblical audience? Two, what are the differences or similarities between the biblical audience and the Bible's audience today? Three, what is or are the theological and biblical doctrine(s) in the text under examination? Finally, how is the text to be applied in believer's lives today?

Fourth, what historical evidence do we have of Jesus's existence? How recent are the biblical documents to the original manuscripts that speak of this historical character, and are they trustworthy? The godslayer says that there is no contemporary evidence of Jesus's existence and absolutely no recital of history that could not have been written long after the history had occurred. Is this true?

The truth of Jesus Christ being an actual historical person is accepted by many religious scholars of all faiths. However, there are those who claim to this day that Jesus never existed. They are known as mythicists. Yet contemporary historians believe the evidence is especially strong in supporting the historicity of Jesus.

Bart Ehrman, professor of religious studies at the University of North Carolina at Chapel Hill and author of the book, *Did Jesus Exist? The Historical Argument for Jesus of Nazareth*, explains that he was surprised to discover how influential mythicists are. He says, "Historically, they've been significant and in the Soviet Union. In fact, the mythicist view was the dominant view. Even today, in some parts of the west—in parts of Scandinavia—it is the dominant view that Jesus never existed."[14]

Erhman continues in saying that the "Mythicists arguments are fairly plausible. According to them, Jesus was never mentioned in any Roman sources and there is no archeological evidence that Jesus ever existed. Even Christian sources, are problematic—the Gospels come long after Jesus' death written by people who never saw the man."[15] Erhman goes on to say "these mythicists point out that there are pagan gods who were said to die and rise again and so the idea is that Jesus was made up as a Jewish god who died and rose again."[16]

What evidence do believers have today that the authors of the Four New Testament Gospels are indeed Matthew, Mark, Luke, and John? Being able to intelligently respond to the assumption that the gospels were written long after Jesus lived will give credibility to the Bible's claim for being truth and having integrity. I refer the reader to any New Testament Introduction textbook for a fuller treatment of this subject, but I will at least address the basic arguments that the names of the four gospels represent their respective human authors.

There are several internal evidences that Matthew was the real author of the first gospel and that it was written around 50–70 AD. Both Mark and Luke use Matthew's surname, Levi, along with his first name (Mark 2:14; Luke 5:27) recalling Matthew's call into ministry. Matthew probably did not use this dual identification because his Jewish readers were already familiar with his full name.

Immediately following Matthew's calling, he hosted a dinner in his home (Mark 2:15). Luke verifies this (Luke 5:29). Matthew simply refers to the domicile as "the house"

(Matt. 9:10). Matthew's readers would undoubtedly know that it was his house.

There are also three different words used for money in Matthew's gospel. This would be consistent with Matthew's prior occupation as a tax collector. Also, the Gospel of Matthew is the only one to mention Jesus's payment of the temple tax (Matt. 17:24–27). These seemingly minute facts add up to considerable internal evidence regarding Matthew's authorship.

Although Mark was not an apostle as Matthew and John were, the early church recognized Mark as the author of the gospel that bears his name. Irenaeus said that "after the death of Peter and Paul, Mark delivered to us in writing things preached by Peter."[17] Other church fathers supporting Mark's authorship, with the Apostle Peter's influence and assistance in its composition, include Papias, Justin Martyr, Clement of Alexandria, Tertullian, Origen, and Eusebius.

"Internal evidence, though slight, confirms the conclusion. The account of the flight of the young man (Mark 14:51–52) found only in Mark, takes on special significance if that youth was really Mark. The detailed description of the upper room (14:12–16) is noteworthy if that room was indeed the house owned by Mark's mother (Acts 12:12; Col. 4:10)."[18]

Although the exact date of Mark's gospel is unknown, many scholars attribute a date of its writing as early as 45

AD and as late as 67–68 AD after Peter's martyrdom. There is no evidence to suggest that the gospel was written well into the latter third of the first century.

Luke's authorship of his gospel is supported by several early church fathers including Irenaeus, Tertullian, and Clement of Alexandria. Since both the Gospel of Luke and the Book of Acts were written by the same man to the same person, Theophilus (Luke 1:3; Acts 1:1), ascertaining who wrote Acts, will therefore identify the author of the corresponding gospel.

Significant passages in the Book of Acts include the "we" and "us" sections (Acts 16:10–17; 20:5–28:31) where Luke figures prominently. Additionally, the sections in which Luke is not directly a participant we find the pronouns "they" and "them."

Finally, the evidence for the Apostle John being the human author of the fourth gospel includes the support of such early church fathers as Irenaeus, Clement of Alexandria, Tertullian, Origen, and Hippolytus. Not only is there the previously mentioned external evidence, but there is also internal evidence for John's authorship contained within the biblical text itself.

To begin with, the author must have been a Jew because of the extensive references to the Old Testament (12:40; 13:18; 19:37). There is also the author's knowledge of the Jewish feasts (2:23; 5:1; 6:4; 7:2; 10:22; 13:1). The author was aware of minute details within Jewish customs, which includes weddings (2:1–10), purification (3:25; 11:55), along with the burial of the dead (11:38–44; 19:40).

Additionally, the author was familiar with the doctrine of the coming of the Messiah (1:19–28) and the differences between Jews and Samaritans (4:9–20). The author knew Jerusalem (5:2; 11:18; 11:54; 18:1; 19:13), Samaria (4:5–6; 4:11; 4:20–21), and Galilee (1:44–46; 2:1).

Furthermore, the author was an eyewitness of Jesus's glory (1:14). He was at the crucifixion (19:33–35), knew the size of the water pots used for the creation of wine (2:6), the approximate value of the anointing perfume (12:5) along with the number of fish that were caught (21:11).

The author identifies himself as the disciple "whom Jesus loved." This expression is used five times in the Gospel of John and only in the Gospel of John (13:23; 19:26; 20:2; 21:7; 21:20).[19] The author was also identified as the "other disciple" (18:15–16; 20:2; 21:1–2).[20]

The name for John the Apostle is conspicuously absent from the gospel. This makes it likely that humility would prevent John from identify himself by name as the fourth gospel's author. Finally, the language of the three Johannine Epistles is similar to the gospel bearing his name: especially as it pertains to the word *love*.

Even though Professor Ehrman supports the existence of Jesus Christ and compiles much supporting evidence, there are those who are still in denial. What historical evidence is there that Jesus Christ did indeed exist?

Josh McDowell's classic work, *Evidence that Demands a Verdict,* lists various ancient historians who validate Jesus Christ as a historical person. Many of these individuals were unbelievers with no religious agenda and who spoke supporting the historicity of Jesus Christ. Along with the twenty-seven New Testament books that affirm the historical Jesus, these ancient church fathers include Cornelius Tacitus (52–54 AD), Lucian of Samosata (second century AD), Flavius Josephus (born 37 AD), Suetonius (120 AD), Pliny the Younger (112 AD), Tertullian (197 AD), and Justin Martyr (150 AD). Additionally, there are the Jewish Talmuds (100–500 AD), Jewish civil and ceremonial law, which contains several references to Jesus Christ, including his crucifixion.

It is interesting to note that the dates of these ancient historians and their comments concerning the historicity of Jesus Christ are within one hundred years of His birth, life, death, burial, and resurrection. Rather than a long recital of history that could have been written long after the history had occurred, some of these recitals occurred within twenty years of Jesus's climatic ascension following His three-year ministry. Certainly, if Jesus did not exist, then these historians would have been refuted by their contemporaries.

The godslayer's next objection concerning the Bible's scientific accuracy does not negate God's miraculous intervention into the scientific laws that He Himself created. Nor does the Bible's scientific accuracy negate God's use of figurative language to communicate truth throughout the Bible's various genres. The Bible does record the occasion in which a donkey spoke (Num. 22), an iron axe handle floating on water (2 Kings 6:1–7), slugs melting as they crawled (Ps. 58:8), bats being birds (Lev. 11:13–19), and all thinking coming from the heart organ (Prov. 23:7). What is to be gleaned from these descriptive images?

Numbers 22 records the occasion when the prophet Balaam's donkey spoke to him. Balaam was a prophet of Israel who practiced divination and other magic arts. He consequently led Israel into apostasy and was identified as a false prophet by biblical writers Peter and Jude (2 Pet. 2:15–16; Jude 1:11). Fearing the encroaching Israelites, King Balak of Moab sent for Balaam recruiting his aid in resisting the Israelites by cursing them. The Lord spoke to Balaam and told him not to go to Balak, although the Lord changed His mind under the condition that Balaam would speak only His words. So Balaam saddled his donkey and went with the princes of Moab back to Balak.

But knowing Balaam's heart, the Lord became angry at Balaam because He knew Balaam's rebelliousness. Therefore, God sent an angel with a drawn sword to bar his way. Although Balaam couldn't see the angel, his donkey could, and she tried to discontinue the journey by going off the path, crushing Balaam's foot against the wall and lying down on the path.

Upset by her behavior, Balaam used his staff to beat the donkey three times. In Numbers 22:28, we learn that "the LORD opened the donkey's mouth, and she said to Balaam, 'What have I done to you to make you beat me these three times.'"[21] Then Balaam and the donkey proceeded to discuss the situation. Balaam angrily rebuked the donkey, after which the Lord opened Balaam's eyes to see the angel and understand why his journey was stopped.

The story evidences cause and effect from the perspective of the reader. If you believe in the existence of God, the occasion in which God gave a donkey the ability to speak is not inconsistent with the Bible's narrative that God created all living things. It is also accurate to say that if you do not believe in the existence of God, a talking donkey appears to be something of a fairy tale. What matters are one's presuppositions and the basis for those presuppositions in approaching the biblical text.

The same can be said concerning the story from 2 Kings 6:1–7 of a floating ax head. The text says,

> Now the sons of the prophets said to Elisha, "See, the place where we dwell under your charge is too small for us. Let us go to the Jordan and each of us get there a log, and let us make a place for us to dwell there." And he answered, "Go." Then one of them said, "Be pleased to go with your servants." And he answered, "I will go." So he went with them. And when they came to the Jordan, they cut down trees. But as one

Thomas Clothier

> was felling a log, his axe head fell into the water, and
> he cried out, "Alas, my master! It was borrowed." Then
> the man of God said, "Where did it fall?" When he
> showed him the place, he cut off atick and threw it in
> there and made the iron float. And he said, "Take it
> up." So he reached out his hand and took it.[22]

The narrative records a miracle in which God ultimately causes the greater weight of the ax head, presumably made of iron, to float to the surface while in the water. It stands to consistent reason that the God of the Bible, who created the universe and its natural laws, can circumvent those same natural laws while not compromising His holy character in doing so.

As the June, 2013 issue of *Tabletalk Magazine* indicates in an article entitled "Are Miracles for Today," "Theologians have a strict definition of miracles," as Dr. R. C. Sproul explains. "A miracle, properly speaking, is an 'extraordinary work performed by the immediate power of God in the external perceivable world, which is an act against nature that only God can do' (for example, resurrections and floating axe heads). Considered this way, it seems clear that miracles are not occurring in the present."[23]

Regarding the issue of the classification of bats as either a fowl/bird creature or a mammal, the biblical language clarifies any misunderstanding. Leviticus 11:13–19 states,

And these [are they which] ye shall have in abomination among the fowls; they shall not be eaten, they [are] an abomination: the eagle, and the ossifrage, and the ospray, And the vulture, and the kite after his kind; Every raven after his kind; And the owl, and the night hawk, and the cuckow, and the hawk after his kind, And the little owl, and the cormorant, and the great owl, And the swan, and the pelican, and the gier eagle, And the stork, the heron after her kind, and the lapwing, and the bat.[24]

It's pretty hard to read this passage and not understand that God identifies a bat as a kind of fowl. As we compare this text with Genesis 1:20–25, we see that there is no contradiction or confusion as to exactly what category bats belong. Genesis 1:20–25 states,

And God said, "Let the waters swarm with swarms of living creatures, and let birds fly above the earth across the expanse of the heavens." So God created the great sea creatures and every living creature that moves, with which the waters swarm, according to their kinds, and every winged bird according to its kind. And God saw that it was good. And God blessed them, saying, "Be fruitful and multiply and fill the waters in the seas, and let birds multiply on the earth." And there was evening and there was morning, the fifth day.[25]

Notice that in both the Hebrew and English, the two passages use the same word *fowl* (עוֹף). Therefore, the two passages are talking about the same thing; otherwise, they would have used different words.

With respect to all thinking coming from the heart organ, this question is answered by simply examining the meaning of the word *heart* not only from its original Hebrew word in the Old Testament, but also its meaning from the original Greek word in the New Testament.

The Hebrew word for *heart* is לֵבָב [*lebab* /lay·bawb/]. It occurs in the Old Testament as *heart* 231 times, *consider* five times, *mind* four times, *understanding* three times, and translated miscellaneously nine times. It refers to the inner man, mind, will, heart, soul, and understanding. This involves man's mind, knowledge, thinking, reflection, memory, inclination, resolution, and his determination (of will). Finally, the word also means conscience, moral character, along with the seat of emotions and passions.

Familiar passages where the word *heart* is predominant include Deuteronomy 6:6, "Hear, O Israel: The LORD our God, the LORD is one. You shall love the LORD your God with all your heart and with all your soul and with all your might. And these words that I command you today shall be on your heart."[26] A second passage is Proverbs 4:20–23, "My son, be attentive to my words; incline your ear to my sayings. Let them not escape from your sight; keep them within your heart. For they are life to those who find them, and healing to all their flesh. Keep your heart with all vigilance, for from it flow the springs of life."[27]

The Greek word for *heart* is parallel to the Hebrew. It is the word καρδία [*kardia* /kar·dee·ah/] in which there are 160 occurrences. The Authorized Version translates καρδία as "heart" 159 times, and "broken hearted" once. It can refer to the organ in the animal body, which is the center of the circulation of the blood, and hence was regarded as the seat of physical life. It also stands for the center of all physical and spiritual life. It is the vigor and sense of physical life, but also the center and seat of spiritual life, meaning the soul or mind, and as such it is the fountain and seat of the thoughts, passions, desires, appetites, affections, purposes, and endeavors. It is the source of understanding, the faculty and seat of the intelligence along with the will and character of the soul so far as it is affected and stirred in a bad way or good.

One of the most familiar passages in the New Testament using the word καρδία is Matthew 22:34–37, which says,

> But when the Pharisees heard that he had silenced the Sadducees, they gathered together. And one of them, a lawyer, asked him a question to test him. "Teacher, which is the great commandment in the Law?" And he said to him, "You shall love the Lord your God with all your heart and with all your soul and with all your mind. This is the great and first commandment. And a second is like it: You shall love your neighbor as yourself. On these two commandments depend all the Law and the Prophets."[28]

It is obvious with only a surface knowledge of the Bible's use of the word *heart* that it means more than just the physical organ with the body. Rather it points us to the very center and core of man's being. It stands to reason that man's thinking, feeling, and choosing would emanate from his heart.

The godslayer's objection to the Bible's fulfilled prophecy is interesting. He contends that there are many prophecies that remain unfulfilled. I would concur. There are many biblical prophecies that remained unfulfilled because Jesus has yet to fulfill them. It is not that they will never be fulfilled, but rather that they have yet to be, but soon will be.

The Apostle Peter addresses this common objection to the reliability of the Scriptures due to unfulfilled prophecies by commenting on those who critiqued the purported soon return of Christ. 2 Peter 3:1–9 states,

> This is now the second letter that I am writing to you, beloved. In both of them I am stirring up your sincere mind by way of reminder, that you should remember the predictions of the holy prophets and the commandment of the Lord and Savior through your apostles, knowing this first of all, that scoffers will come in the last days with scoffing, following their own sinful desires. They will say, "Where is the promise of his coming? For ever since the fathers fell asleep, all things are continuing as they were from the beginning of creation." For they deliberately overlook this fact, that the heavens existed long ago, and the

earth was formed out of water and through water by the word of God, and that by means of these the world that then existed was deluged with water and perished. But by the same word the heavens and earth that now exist are stored up for fire, being kept until the Day of Judgment and destruction of the ungodly. But do not overlook this one fact, beloved, that with the Lord one day is as a thousand years, and a thousand years as one day. The Lord is not slow to fulfill his promise as some count slowness, but is patient toward you, not wishing that any should perish, but that all should reach repentance.[29]

The godslayer offers one example to prove his point: the Christ will return before all then living shall die? How many two-thousand-year-old men do you know? I will guess that one of the texts to which he is referring must be Matthew 24:32–35, which states,

> From the fig tree learn its lesson: as soon as its branch becomes tender and puts out its leaves, you know that summer is near. So also, when you see all these things, you know that he is near, at the very gates. Truly, I say to you, this generation will not pass away until all these things take place. Heaven and earth will pass away, but my words will not pass away.[30]

What is the meaning of the phrase, "this generation will not pass away until all these things take place"? The context must dictate the meaning of the word *generation*. A closer examination of the context yields valuable results.

This cannot refer to the generation living at that time of Christ, for "all these things"—the abomination of desolation (v. 15), the persecutions and judgments (vv. 17–22), the false prophets (vv. 23–26), the signs in the heavens (vv. 27–29), Christ's final return (v. 30), and the gathering of the elect (v. 31)—did not "take place" in their lifetime. It seems best to interpret Christ's words as a reference to the generation alive at the time when those final hard labor pains begin. This would fit with the lesson of the fig tree, which stresses the short span of time in which these things will.[31]

What is the answer when the godslayer cites occasions of deplorable atrocities committed in the name of God and in so-called obedience to the Scriptures? What about rape and incest not specifically mentioned in the Ten Commandments?

I do not know what specific examples of deplorable atrocities committed by Christians to which the godslayer refers. Any student of history must acknowledge that there have been atrocities committed in God's name. However, those acts of violence are not condoned by the Scriptures, nor should be by true disciples and followers of Jesus.

1 John 4:7–12 explicitly declares,

> Beloved, let us love one another, for love is from God, and whoever loves has been born of God and knows God. Anyone who does not love does not know God,

because God is love. In this the love of God was made manifest among us, that God sent his only Son into the world, so that we might live through him. In this is love, not that we have loved God but that he loved us and sent his Son to be the propitiation for our sins. Beloved, if God so loved us, we also ought to love one another. No one has ever seen God; if we love one another, God abides in us and his love is perfected in us.[32]

With respect to rape and incest not being mentioned in the Ten Commandments, I would submit that they are implicitly mentioned in the explicit seventh commandment, which says, "You shall not commit adultery."[33] In this seventh commandment, God is declaring that any sexual activity outside of heterosexual marriage (Gen. 1:26–27; 2:18–25, ESV) is an abomination and must never be condoned. This would by implication include homosexuality, incest, rape, premarital sex, extramarital sex, adultery, bestiality, etc. God has set a fixed boundary on sexual activity, and any deviation from that unchanging standard is called sexual immorality. This deviant behavior is to be avoided. The Apostle Paul states in 1 Thessalonians 4:1–5,

> Finally, then, brothers, we ask and urge you in the Lord Jesus, that as you received from us how you ought to walk and to please God, just as you are doing, that you do so more and more. For you know what instructions we gave you through the Lord Jesus. For

> this is the will of God, your sanctification: that you
> abstain from sexual immorality; that each one of you
> know how to control his own body in holiness and
> honor, not in the passion of lust like the Gentiles who
> do not know God. [34]

As one commentator has written, "This commandment is directed toward protecting the sanctity of the home (Hebrews 13:4; Genesis 2:24; Matthew 19:1–12), the fundamental building block of society. The marital vow is a holy commitment that should not be violated by sexual unfaithfulness under any circumstances." [35]

Is the Bible the most sold book of all time? One of the evidences I previously submitted in chapter two regarding the Bible being the Word of God was that it was the all-time best-selling book. The godslayer took issue with this by stating "size is your criteria, the bible (sic) falls well behind the writings of Mao and if majority is an indication validity, then Hinduism is the only true religion." I set out then to discover if indeed the Bible is the all-time best-selling volume.

I made an interesting discovery in this investigation. Many publishers, bookstores, and Internet Web sites concerned with book sales statistics do not include the Bible in their calculations because of, in their words, various unreliable criteria in making such calculations. Others will group best-selling statistics into some three hundred separate categories rather than one definitive category of sales.

I also discovered that there is no central repository for total sales numbers for books. Publishers may not share sales numbers for individual books, or their reported numbers may be inaccurate because as one individual explains, "They seem prone to creative exaggeration, particularly when a movie version of the book is coming out soon." It also becomes complicated when you consider that many books are put out in multiple editions over the years, often by multiple publishers. Additionally, older works that are in the public domain might be published simultaneously by several different publishers. The fact is any worldwide sales figures for a book more than a few years old are educated guesses at best.

It is with this in mind that I submit the following figures, by Comcast.net, as the all-time Top Ten best-selling books. They are:

Rank Author	Book	First Publication Date	Approximate Sales
Various	*The Holy Bible*	1451–55	More than 6 billion
Mao Tse-tung	*Quotations from Chairman Mao*	1966	900 million
Noah Webster	*The American Spelling Book*	1783	Up to 100 million

Mark C. Young	*Guiness Book of World Records*	1955	More than 90 million
World Almanac. Editors.	*World Almanac*	1868	5 million
William Holmes McGuffey	*The McGuffey Readers*	1836	60 million
Benjamin Spock	*The Common Sense Book of Baby and Child Care*	1946	More than 50 million
Elbert Hubbard	*A Message to Garcia*	1899	More than 40 million
Charles Monroe Sheldon	*In His Steps*	1896	More than 30 million
Jacqueline Susann	*Valley of the Dolls*	1966	More than 30 million

Does the Bible condone and instruct anyone to sell a daughter into slavery, kill all one's enemies and their wives and their children and their animals, but of course keep all the unmarried virgins for yourself?

One of the most difficult things to do when responding to someone who is questioning the Christian faith, and who doubly keeps their identity anonymous, is to try to understand what they are asking when they pose a question or make a statement regarding biblical Christianity. Such is the case with the godslayer's previous question.

Since I am unsure of what specific biblical incident or text he refers, I am therefore at an inconvenience and furthermore susceptible of speaking in error. However, I will endeavor to address his question in general biblical principles even though I may refer to examples, which are not the specific ones he may have had in mind.

Exodus 21:7–11 says the following:

> When a man sells his daughter as a slave, she shall not go out as the male slaves do. If she does not please her master, who has designated her for himself, then he shall let her be redeemed. He shall have no right to sell her to a foreign people, since he has broken faith with her. If he designates her for his son, he shall deal with her as with a daughter. If he takes another wife to himself, he shall not diminish her food, her clothing, or her marital rights. And if he does not do these three things for her, she shall go out for nothing, without payment of money.[36]

Exodus 21 through Exodus 24 forms what is called the Book of the Covenant. The Book of the Covenant is separate from the Ten Commandments. The Book of the Covenant contains applications of the teaching contained in the commandments. It also addresses the specific needs of Israel as a society and culture at the time. It also contains general principles that are applicable to all areas of life by giving negative commands along with case laws or illustrations as to how the Ten Commandments may be applied to specific situations. Additionally, it contains exhortations and promises.

Exodus 21:1 begins with an introductory statement, "Now these are the rules that you shall set before them."[37] In verses two through six, there are laws concerning Hebrew slaves. In verses seven through eleven, we see instructions concerning the proper treatment of female slaves: those who would be considered the least in society.

There were basically two types of slaves in the Old Testament: a fellow Jew who sold himself in order to raise money to pay his debts (Lev. 25:39–55; Deut. 15:12–18) and a foreign prisoner of war. While Jewish slaves could receive their freedom after six years of servitude (Exod. 21:1–6), prisoners of war remained slaves for life (Exod. 21:20–26). However, if they were mistreated, they would become free.

The instruction regarding female slaves is treated separately. Female slaves were to be treated differently. Often, female slaves were concubines or secondary wives (Gen. 16:3; 22:24; 30:3, 9; 36:12; Judg. 8:31; 9:18). "Some Hebrew fathers thought it more advantageous for their daughters to become concubines of well-to-do neighbors than to become the wives of men in their own social class."[38] This did not necessarily make this practice right but rather cultural.

If a daughter who became a servant was not pleasing to her master, she was to be redeemed by a near kinsman

(Lev. 25:47–54) but never sold to foreigners (Exod. 21:8); she could also redeem herself. If she married her master's son, she was to be given family status (vs.9). If the master married someone else, he was required to provide his servant with three essentials: food, clothing, and shelter (marital rights probably means living quarters, not sexual privilege).[39]

As one other commentator writes, "A female slave who was married to her captor could not be sold again as a slave. If her master, now her husband, grew to hate her, she had to be liberated and was declared a free person."[40]

Why did God just not abolish slavery entirely? Why concede its existence when He could have abolished it outright? Why didn't God just abolish slavery in Israel? Here's the answer: I don't know. Neither does anyone else for that matter.

What about the claim that God could order us today to kill all our enemies and their wives and their children and their animals, but of course keep all the unmarried virgins for yourself? The text I believe the godslayer refers to is Numbers 31:31–41, which states,

> And Moses and Eleazar the priest did as the LORD commanded Moses. Now the plunder remaining of the spoil that the army took was 675,000 sheep, 72,000 cattle, 61,000 donkeys, and 32,000 persons in all, women who had not known man by lying with him. And the half, the portion of those who

> had gone out in the army, numbered 337,500 sheep, and the Lord's tribute of sheep was 675. The cattle were 36,000, of which the Lord's tribute was 72. The donkeys were 30,500, of which the Lord's tribute was 61. The persons were 16,000, of which the Lord's tribute was 32 persons. And Moses gave the tribute, which was the contribution for the Lord, to Eleazar the priest, as the Lord commanded Moses.[41]

The judgment that occurs was against the Midianites. The Midianites consisted of five families, linked to Abraham through Midian, son of the concubine Keturah. Abraham sent them away, with all his other sons by concubines, into the east (Gen. 25:1–6). The Midianites became nomads inhabiting the desert area south of the Dead Sea and immediately east of the Red Sea.

They were desert dwellers associated with the Ishmaelites and Medanites (Gen. 37:28, 36). Midianites traders sold Joseph to Potiphar, the Egyptian (Gen. 37:28–36). Moses had a Midianite wife and father-in-law, Zipporah and Jethro/ Reuel (Exod. 2:21; 3:1), and a brother-in-law, Hobab (Num. 10:29; Judg. 4:11). Hobab was asked by Moses to guide Israel in travelling through the wilderness due to his knowledge of the area (Num. 10:29–32).

It was some time later that the chiefs of Midian and Moab combined in hiring Balaam to curse Israel (Num. 22–24) and their people led Israel into idolatry and immorality (Num. 25). Therefore, they had to be vanquished (Num. 25:16–18; 31).

The five princes of Midian were colleagues of the Amorite king Sihon (Josh. 13:21). In the time of the judges, through Gideon and his small army (Judg. 6–8; 9:17), God delivered Israel from the scourge of camel-riding Midianites, Amalekites and other "children of the east" (Judg. 6:6–8; 9:17). This event is remembered by the psalmist Asaph and the prophet Isaiah (Ps. 83:9; Isa. 9:4; 10:26).

The theme of Numbers 31 is God's righteous and just judgment directed toward unrighteous sinners. We live in a current culture in which the love of God, whatever god it is that people worship, supersedes any biblical doctrine of the justice of God. This passage, and others similar to it, seem strangely antiquated. The truth is that God hates sin and will judge sin. See Psalm 5, 11 and Proverbs 6.

The Midianites were responsible for Israel's apostate behavior (Num. 25). The judgment from God was to be total annihilation of all the Midianites and the dedication of all material property to God (Deut. 2016–18l; Judg. 6:15–19).

The conflict against the Midianites proved successful with the death of all males (Num. 31:7–12). This would include the five Midianite kings along with the prophet Balaam. However, not all Midianites were executed. Moses became angry because of the survivors. Therefore, all remaining survivors were executed except 32,000 virgins (Num. 31:32–35). Ten percent (32) of these virgins were dedicated to the Lord. Unlike some liberal commentators who insinuate that these women were sacrificed, instead they would have functioned as servants to the priests or at the tabernacle (1 Sam. 2:22). The others would have served as slaves throughout the Israelite community as spoils of war.

The text reveals not only that God is just regarding the punishment of sin, but is also gracious towards sinners. Those who rightly deserved death would receive life and be spared from God's judgment. This parallels the salvation sinners receive from God through Jesus Christ: object of God's wrath receive His mercy (Eph. 2:4–10).

Finally, what about the claim that God orders believers to smash the heads of little babies of unbelievers against the rocks until their brains spill out as a sign of piety? Is this to be condoned?

I speculate as to what reference the godslayer is making, but I am assuming he is alluding to Psalm 137:9, which says, "Blessed shall he be who takes your little ones and dashes them against the rock."[42] This psalm is again an oracle of judgment upon heathen nations: specifically the nation of ancient Babylon. The psalm is explicitly about the Babylonian Captivity of Judah, which occurred between 605 BC until 535 BC.

The anonymous writer is prophesying against the Babylonians. The psalm is divided into three sections: (1) lamentation—vs. 1–4; (2) the conditions for lamentation—vs. 5–6; (3) the prayers against the wicked—vs. 7–9. It is within the midst of the psalmist's prayer against the wicked Babylonians that he states this impending judgment against their children.

The reason for this stark judgment must be as repayment for a similar act perpetrated by the Babylonians against Judah. The corresponding sorrow of Judah is recorded in Lamentations 1–2. The desire by the psalmist is that those who ravaged the land, and particularly Jerusalem, would find themselves ravaged by God. This would be fulfilled as recorded in Daniel 5. This would also illustrate the teaching from Galatians 6:7–8, which states, "Do not be deceived: God is not mocked, for whatever one sows, that will he also reap. For the one who sows to his own flesh will from the flesh reap corruption, but the one who sows to the Spirit will from the Spirit reap eternal life."[43]

Many questions! Biblical answers! Will they satisfy? One can only pray that they will. However, there are more questions to follow as evident in the next chapter.

Letter Two

Christianity: The belief that a cosmic Jewish zombie who was his own father can make you live forever if you symbolically eat his flesh and telepathically tell him you accept him as your master, so he can remove an evil force from your soul that is present in humanity because a rib woman was convinced by a talking snake to eat from a magical tree....

Yeah, makes perfect sense. The godslayer.

"The resurrection is important to the church because it claims ultimate and definitive proof of its beliefs and god's (sic) divinity. There was only one way to prove that Jesus rose from the dead...he had to appear to people. Supposedly, he (sic) appeared to hundreds and to Paul. The question then becomes, Why did Jesus stop these appearances? Why does he (sic) not appear today?"

"Obviously, Paul benefited from this alleged personal meeting so he could see for himself the resurrection and could ask questions. So why doesn't Jesus appear now to prove he (sic) is resurrected? There is nothing to stop Jesus from appearing in my living room, and if you think about

it, he(sic) really does need to appear now. If Paul needed a personal visit, so do we. The bible says he (sic) appeared to hundreds, so it's okay for him (sic) to appear; it wouldn't take away any of our free will."

"Since this god (sic) is supposedly all-powerful and tireless, it would be easy from him (sic) to appear. Moreover, if he (sic) did appear it would prove that he (sic) is real. Yet as we all know, he (sic) has not appeared for over 2000 years. There is nothing to stop him (sic) and several good reasons for him (sic) to actually appear."

"What if we all prayed to god (sic) to please appear and prove that his (sic) resurrection wasn't just another fairy tale? Matthew 7:7 and John 14:14 guarantees that we will get what we pray for. Yet, when we pray to him (sic), nothing ever happens. Isn't it odd that nothing ever happens given that fact that Jesus promised that it would?"

"Therefore, the resurrection story must be false, or Paul fabricated or hallucinated. Given that any rational and unprejudiced analysis it is clear that the resurrection story is a lie. There are plenty of other provable false stories in the bible. There is zero evidence to substantiate Paul's or the bible's story. There is zero reason to believe it: an obvious motive for the church to lie and plenty of alternative explanations."

"Every bit of provable evidence and logic mandates that the resurrection story is a myth. Jesus, if he (sic) existed at all, was clearly only a normal man and not a god (sic). Since the resurrection did not happen, we can see that god (sic) himself is imaginary. If god (sic) actually

*did exist and was playing any kind of a role whatsoever,
then he (sic) would never allow such a phony imposter like
Jesus."*

*"Now Tom, aren't you ashamed for spewing out such
garbage? Oh, I forgot, you get money from the blissfully
ignorant for your promoting this delusion. Well, if there
is a deity and if he (sic) is just, you will get what you
deserve. But there isn't, so I guess your con is safe."*

—*The godslayer*

Aside from the evidence submitted in chapter two, which
supports the viability of the bodily resurrection of Jesus
Christ beyond a reasonable doubt, I also submit to you a
fundamental flaw in the godslayer's reasoning regarding the
resurrection: seeing is not necessarily believing.

The godslayer contends that if Jesus were to appear today
it would be easy and logical to believe in Him as Savior and
Lord, let alone that He exists. Jesus supposedly appeared
to many as recorded in the Scriptures, so the godslayer's
contention is why doesn't Jesus appear in the same way to
people today? The godslayer's conclusion is because the
resurrection is a lie, Jesus Christ is a lie, and the concept of
God is the ultimate lie.

However, if Jesus Christ were to appear today, would
that necessarily mean that people would believe, follow, and
worship Him simply because they saw Him and what He
did? Does seeing necessarily result in believing? Will seeing
Jesus Christ in person result in a person's commitment,

trust, dependence, and worship of Him? Let us turn to the biblical text and examine people's reactions when they saw Jesus Christ in the past, and how they will react when they see Him in the future. I refer to the Gospel of John and the Book of Revelation.

Throughout John's gospel, we witness many people seeing Jesus in person while He performed many miracles. In fact, these miraculous events occur as early as John chapter two. However, do these miraculous occurrences and appearances result in people believing in Jesus Christ as Savior and Lord? John contends at the outset of his gospel account that they do not. He states in John 1:9–11, following his prologue on the deity of Jesus Christ, that, "The true light, which gives light to everyone, was coming into the world. He was in the world, and the world was made through him, yet the world did not know him. He came to his own, and his own people did not receive him."[1]

John says that Jesus came before two distinct groups: the world in general and the Jews in particular. Yet, in spite of His many appearances and miracles the world, even though created by Him, did not know Him. The word *know*, γινώσκω / *ginōskō*, means to understand, perceive, and to recognize. Additionally, in spite of Jesus's many appearances and miracles, the Jews in particular did not receive Him. The word receive, παραλαμβάνω / *paralambanō*, means to accept or acknowledge one to be what he professes to be. Even before John gives us ample evidence, he contends that seeing Jesus did not necessarily result in many people believing in Jesus.

John records seven specific miraculous signs to show that Jesus is the Messiah. They include changing water into wine (2:1–11), rising from the dead (2:13–22), healing the nobleman's son (4:46–54), healing the paralytic man (5:1–15), the feeding of the five thousand (6:1–15), the healing of the man born blind (9:1–41), and the raising of Lazarus from the dead (11:1–44). It is to these specific signs that we now look with the critical eye of understanding how people responded to these encounters with Jesus. Did everyone who beheld these appearances and acts of Jesus respond by believing in Jesus? Let's see!

> On the third day there was a wedding at Cana in Galilee, and the mother of Jesus was there. Jesus also was invited to the wedding with his disciples. When the wine ran out, the mother of Jesus said to him, "They have no wine." And Jesus said to her, "Woman, what does this have to do with me? My hour has not yet come." His mother said to the servants, "Do whatever he tells you."

> Now there were six stone water jars there for the Jewish rites of purification, each holding twenty or thirty gallons. Jesus said to the servants, "Fill the jars with water." And they filled them up to the brim. And he said to them, "Now draw some out and take it to the master of the feast." So they took it. When the

master of the feast tasted the water-now-become-wine, and did not know where it came from (though the servants who had drawn the water knew), the master of the feast called the bridegroom and said to him, "Everyone serves the good wine first, and when people have drunk freely, then the poor wine. But you have kept the good wine until now." This, the first of his signs, Jesus did at Cana in Galilee, and manifested his glory. And his disciples believed in him. After this he went down to Capernaum, with his mother and his brothers and his disciples, and they stayed there for a few days.[2]

As the narrative begins, the comment to the third day refers the reader to the immediate preceding context of John 1:35–51. Jesus has begun calling men to follow Him. These included Andrew, Simon Peter, Nathaniel, and Phillip.

Weddings in Israel could last a week. The groom assumed the financial responsibility to ensure that all the guests were amply supplied with food and drink for the celebration. To run out of wine on such an occasion would have been a major embarrassment. In fact, some historians indicate that such a faux pas might result in a potential lawsuit by the bride's relatives against the groom. Therefore, to run out of wine was no small matter.

While the exact location of the wedding feast in Cana is not known, the text does say that Jesus and His disciples had been invited. The possibility exists that the bride and groom may have known Jesus and His family. Also invited were Andrew, Simon Peter, Nathaniel, Phillip, and an unnamed disciple (1:35).

Wine at this time in history was a fermented drink. In order to quench one's thirst, and not become drunk (Ps. 104:15; Prov. 20:1; 23:20–21, 29–35; 31:4–5; Eph. 5:18), it would be diluted with water from one-third to one-tenth its original potency. Because of the climate in Israel, new or sweet wine would quickly ferment. Additionally, the lack of proper water purification made the drinking of wine, even to this day, a much safer drink than water. It should be noted that while the Bible condemns drunkenness, it does not teach total or complete abstinence.

Somehow there was not sufficient wine. It ran out. For the reasons previously stated, this would be a most difficult and potentially awkward situation. Somehow, as moms are prone to discover such things, Mary found out that there was no more wine to serve the wedding guests. This was probably because the women's quarters were near the place where the wine was stored. It is reasonable to assume that is how Mary discovered the shortage.

She came to Jesus to inform Him of the situation. Perhaps she felt that He would have an answer or a solution to this problem. His immediate response to her is interesting and may be misunderstood. Jesus used the title "woman" in addressing His mother. He was not being derogatory or impolite to Mary. He was in effect calling her "ma'am." A term many use even today indicating respect for a woman. He may also have been distancing Himself from her parental control due to the significant fact that He was and is God.

When Jesus responded with the statement "what does this have to do with us,"[3] He was making it clear that His mission on earth as the promised Messiah involved far more important things than a wedding feast running out of a beverage for its guests. He was not reproaching her but clearly indicating that He would not be distracted from His overall mission.

Jesus also said, "My hour has not yet come."[4] Jesus was referring to His substitutionary death on the cross and His subsequent resurrection from the dead (7:30; 8:20; 12:23–27; 13:1; 17:1). From this divine mission, He would not be deterred or distracted.

Mary then instructed the servants to do whatever Jesus told them to do. Why and how Mary could exude such seeming authority to order servants to do her bidding remains a mystery. However, like many Old Testament saints of God, she would not take no for an answer (Gen. 32:26–30; Exod. 33:12; 34:9; 1 Kings 18:36–37; 2 Kings 2:1–9; 4:14–28). "Mary acts in confidence that Jesus will hear her entreaty."[5]

The servants did as instructed and per Jesus's direction filled six stone water pots that were normally used for Jewish purification rites. The text indicates that they contained twenty to thirty gallons each. The servants did as they were told and filled each one with water.

After doing so, Jesus told them to draw some of the liquid out and give it to the headwaiter, or the master of the banquet. The headwaiter tasted the water, which had become wine, and was ignorant of where it had come from, although the text indicates that the servants knew. The headwaiter was curious and spoke with the bridegroom as to why he did not serve the best wine first to be then followed by the lesser in quality wine being served last? The practice was normally followed due to the fact that the guest's taste buds would be diluted after a period of time and would not notice the decline in the wine's quality. The indication is that the wine Jesus miraculously created was better than any previously served wine at the wedding.

The result of this first recorded miracle by Jesus is that by manifesting His glory, Jesus's disciples (those five mentioned within this context) believed in Him. However, we must also take notice of those who also saw Jesus manifest His glory and who did not believe in Him: the servants. The text indicates that they knew about the miraculous event of the water they placed in the six stone jars becoming wine. Yet there is no mention of them trusting in Jesus and following Him, while this is said of His disciples. The point of the lesson: seeing does not necessarily result in believing.

In the immediate aftermath of the water turned into wine, Jesus traveled to Jerusalem for the Passover and subsequently cleansed the temple.

> The Passover of the Jews was at hand, and Jesus went up to Jerusalem. In the temple he found those who were selling oxen and sheep and pigeons, and the money-changers sitting there. And making a whip of cords, he drove them all out of the temple, with the sheep and oxen. And he poured out the coins of the money-changers and overturned their tables. And he told those who sold the pigeons, "Take these things away; do not make my Father's house a house of trade." His disciples remembered that it was written, "Zeal for your house will consume me."

> So the Jews said to him, "What sign do you show us for doing these things?" Jesus answered them, "Destroy this temple, and in three days I will raise it up." The Jews then said, "It has taken forty-six years to build this temple, and will you raise it up in three days?" But he was speaking about the temple of his body. When therefore he was raised from the dead, his disciples remembered that he had said this, and they believed the Scripture and the word that Jesus had spoken.[6]

The account of Jesus's cleansing is one of the more visual and familiar stories and scenes from the Scriptures. There have been many films and television programs devoted to the life of Christ, and most, if not everyone, of them depicts this scene. However, it is what occurs after this dramatic turn of events that should intrigue us.

When Jesus had cleansed the temple by driving out the money-changers, the Jewish religious leaders of His day asked by what authority Jesus would do such a thing. Jesus's response was cryptic. He said, "Destroy this temple and in three days I will raise it up."[7] The religious leaders were unaware of Jesus's true meaning and thought that He was referring to the actual physical temple building or structure. However, the text indicates that Jesus was referring to His bodily resurrection.

The text also states that following His resurrection, "his disciples remembered that he had said this, and they believed the Scripture and the word that Jesus had spoken."[8] However, John does not record that the religious leaders remembered and believed in Jesus after His resurrection. Even though they saw Him and the ample evidence as to His identity by His many miracles and teachings, they did not come to saving faith.

Rather, the religious leaders did everything they could to hinder the message of the empty tomb and the proclamation of the gospel. Instead of believing, they sought to hinder the spread of the gospel.

One of the most definitive statements about the trusting in the truth of the resurrection, instead of relying upon one's personal experience of actually seeing the risen Christ as the godslayer contends should occur, is the account of doubting Thomas. As you may recall, John 20:24–25 records that, "Thomas, one of the Twelve, called the Twin, was not with them when Jesus came. So the other disciples told him, 'We have seen the Lord.' But he said to them, 'Unless I see in his hands the mark of the nails, and place my finger into the mark of the nails, and place my hand into his side, I will never believe.'"[9]

It was eight days later that Jesus appeared again to His followers, and this time Thomas was with them. John 20:26–29 records what happened during that encounter.

> Eight days later, his disciples were inside again, and Thomas was with them. Although the doors were locked, Jesus came and stood among them and said, "Peace be with you." Then he said to Thomas, "Put your finger here, and see my hands; and put out your hand, and place it in my side. Do not disbelieve, but believe." Thomas answered him, "My Lord and my God!" Jesus said to him, "Have you believed because you have seen me? Blessed are those who have not seen and yet have believed.[10]

Therein is the definitive statement from Jesus. He pronounced a blessing, much like an Old Testament prophet declaring an oracle of blessing from God, that those who would believe in the resurrection, yet had not seen Jesus in person following this event, would be blessed by God. While the godslayer argues that seeing is believing, Jesus contends that believing is truly seeing.

Let us now direct our attention to the third miraculous sign John records Jesus performing to demonstrate and display that He is God. The story is found in John 5:1–17. It is the account of Jesus healing the paralytic man by the pool of Bethesda. It was a public miracle and one that stirred much commotion and conversation, but would it result in conversions because of what people witnessed? Let us examine the text.

> After this there was a feast of the Jews, and Jesus went up to Jerusalem. Now there is in Jerusalem by the Sheep Gate a pool, in Aramaic called Bethesda, which has five roofed colonnades. In these lay a multitude of invalids—blind, lame, and paralyzed. One man was there who had been an invalid for thirty-eight years. When Jesus saw him lying there and knew that he had already been there a long time, he said to him, "Do you want to be healed?" The sick man answered him, "Sir, I have no one to put me into the pool when the water is stirred up, and while I am going another steps down before me." Jesus said to him, "Get up, take up your bed, and walk." And at once the man was healed, and he took up his bed and walked.
>
> Now that day was the Sabbath. So the Jews said to the man who had been healed, "It is the Sabbath, and it is not lawful for you to take up your bed." But he answered them, "The man who healed me, that man

said to me, 'Take up your bed, and walk.'" They asked him, "Who is the man who said to you, 'Take up your bed and walk'?" Now the man who had been healed did not know who it was, for Jesus had withdrawn, as there was a crowd in the place. Afterward Jesus found him in the temple and said to him, "See, you are well! Sin no more, that nothing worse may happen to you." The man went away and told the Jews that it was Jesus who had healed him. And this was why the Jews were persecuting Jesus, because he was doing these things on the Sabbath. But Jesus answered them, "My Father is working until now, and I am working."[11]

The healing of the paralytic man is another example that seeing what Jesus did does not necessarily result in believing in who Jesus is. In the story John presents in John 5, Jesus heals a man who had been an invalid for thirty-eight years. Jesus tells the man to take up his mat and walk, and when Jesus heals the man, he obeys by taking up his mat and to begin walking.

However, all the Jewish religious leaders focus on is not the miraculous healing of the paralytic man by Jesus, but rather the fact that Jesus had the audacity, in their eyes, of healing the man on the Sabbath. The Jews inquire of the man why he is breaking the law, which he was not doing, by taking up his bed. The man replied that he was healed by someone who told him to take up his bed and walk.

When Jesus found the man in the temple, probably because the man was being inspected by the priests per the instruction from the Old Testament Law, He told him to go and sin no more. It was then that the man told the Jewish leaders that Jesus had healed him.

As a result, the Jewish leaders began persecuting Jesus because He healed on the Sabbath. Notice that the Jews did not deny Jesus had healed the man, they just were not pleased that the healing took place on the Sabbath. Talk about not seeing the forest for the trees. The Jewish religious leaders were so incensed that Jesus broke one of their traditions that they could not recognize His miracle even when it stood before them in the flesh. Seeing did not result in believing.

The fourth miraculous sign Jesus performed is recorded in John 6:1–15. It is one of the most dramatic and visual. It is the feeding of the five thousand.

> After this Jesus went away to the other side of the Sea of Galilee, which is the Sea of Tiberias. And a large crowd was following him, because they saw the signs that he was doing on the sick. Jesus went up on the mountain, and there he sat down with his disciples. Now the Passover, the feast of the Jews, was at hand. Lifting up his eyes, then, and seeing that a large crowd was coming toward him, Jesus said to Philip, "Where are we to buy bread, so that these people may eat?" He said this to test him, for he himself knew what he would do. Philip answered him, "Two hundred denarius worth of bread would not be enough for each of them to get a little." One of his disciples,

Andrew, Simon Peter's brother, said to him, "There is a boy here who has five barley loaves and two fish, but what are they for so many?" Jesus said, "Have the people sit down." Now there was much grass in the place. So the men sat down, about five thousand in number. Jesus then took the loaves, and when he had given thanks, he distributed them to those who were seated. So also the fish, as much as they wanted. And when they had eaten their fill, he told his disciples, "Gather up the leftover fragments, that nothing may be lost." So they gathered them up and filled twelve baskets with fragments from the five barley loaves left by those who had eaten. When the people saw the sign that he had done, they said, "This is indeed the Prophet who is to come into the world!" Perceiving then that they were about to come and take him by force to make him king, Jesus withdrew again to the mountain by himself.[12]

This story is an all-time favorite for Sunday school teachers and for their students, especially children. It is also frequently depicted in films on the life of Christ. What a visual image! Five thousand men, not including women and children, which makes the sum total come to approximately twenty thousand, are fed by Jesus and His disciples beginning with two fish and five loaves of bread. What a striking event resulting in everyone being filled in their stomachs, and twelve baskets full remain with leftovers. What more can be said and gleaned from this all-too-familiar account? Much!

Rather than focus our attention on all that transpired on that significant day and event, let us instead focus our attention on what happened the following day. What happened between the same people and Jesus? In light of everything they experienced and witnessed, did they come to saving faith in Christ? Let us examine the text.

> On the next day the crowd that remained on the other side of the sea saw that there had been only one boat there, and that Jesus had not entered the boat with his disciples, but that his disciples had gone away alone. Other boats from Tiberias came near the place where they had eaten the bread after the Lord had given thanks. So when the crowd saw that Jesus was not there, nor his disciples, they themselves got into the boats and went to Capernaum, seeking Jesus.
>
> When they found him on the other side of the sea, they said to him, "Rabbi, when did you come here?" Jesus answered them, "Truly, truly, I say to you, you are seeking me, not because you saw signs, but because you ate your fill of the loaves. Do not work for the food that perishes, but for the food that endures to eternal life, which the Son of Man will give to you. For on him God the Father has set his seal." Then they said to him, "What must we do, to be doing the works of God?" Jesus answered them, "This is the work of God, and that you believe in him whom he

has sent." So they said to him, "Then what sign do you do, that we may see and believe you? What work do you perform? Our fathers ate the manna in the wilderness; as it is written, 'He gave them bread from heaven to eat.'" Jesus then said to them, "Truly, truly, I say to you, it was not Moses who gave you the bread from heaven, but my Father gives you the true bread from heaven. For the bread of God is he who comes down from heaven and gives life to the world." They said to him, "Sir, give us this bread always." Jesus said to them, "I am the bread of life; whoever comes to me shall not hunger, and whoever believes in me shall never thirst.[13]

It was the following day that the crowd sought Jesus. They were persistent and relentless. They were determined to find where He had gone. Why? Was it because they wanted to confess Him as Savior because of what they had seen and experienced with the miracle Jesus had performed? Or was there another reason?

Jesus clearly understands the crowd's intentions. He knew what they were looking for and why they were looking for Him. The multitude was no more interested in Jesus as Savior and Lord any more than people would be today if they witness the Lord in person. The crowd was more interested in a full stomach then they were in a redeemed soul.

Jesus clearly states this. He told them, "Truly, truly, I say to you, you are seeking me, not because you saw signs, but because you ate your fill of the loaves."[14] The people were looking for someone, anyone, who provided a convenient and inexpensive welfare state where their every want and need would be provided. However, for most people, these wants and needs extended merely to the physical and not to the spiritual. They were interested in the physical nourishment of the body but not necessarily in the nourishment of the soul provided by the God of truth.

Do not misunderstand me. They enjoyed the miracle from the previous day. They wanted more of the same. "So they said to him, "Then what sign do you do, that we may see and believe you? What work do you perform? Our fathers ate the manna in the wilderness; as it is written, 'He gave them bread from heaven to eat.'"[15] Did not Jesus just do this very thing the day before? How quick people forget and how insistent they are in what they want in the present.

Jesus's intention, as the rest of John 6 attests, was to use this miracle to illustrate that He and He alone is the bread of life: the true source of spiritual nourishment that never leaves a soul unsatisfied. However, the point being made here is that in spite of Jesus's appearance and miracle, people did not comprehend who He was. The same can be said today. Jesus could appear on earth, and will appear, but His appearing will not solicit faith. Faith is in itself a miraculous event wrought by the Holy Spirit through the preaching of the gospel. Belief in Jesus does not come by physical sight but rather by God sovereignly choosing the sinner to believe (Acts13:48) and in effect, to receive spiritual sight. It is that illustrated truth we now focus our attention.

> As he passed by, he saw a man blind from birth. And his disciples asked him, "Rabbi, who sinned, this man or his parents, that he was born blind?" Jesus answered, "It was not that this man sinned, or his parents, but that the works of God might be displayed in him. We must work the works of him who sent me while it is day; night is coming, when no one can work. As long as I am in the world, I am the light of the world." Having said these things, he spit on the ground and made mud with the saliva. Then he anointed the man's eyes with the mud and said to him, "Go, wash in the pool of Siloam" (which means Sent). So he went and washed and came back seeing.
>
> The neighbors and those who had seen him before as a beggar were saying, "Is this not the man who used to sit and beg?" Some said, "It is he." Others said, "No, but he is like him." He kept saying, "I am the man." So they said to him, "Then how were your eyes opened?" He answered, "The man called Jesus made mud and anointed my eyes and said to me, 'Go to Siloam and wash.' So I went and washed and received my sight." They said to him, "Where is he?" He said, "I do not know."
>
> They brought to the Pharisees the man who had formerly been blind. Now it was a Sabbath day when Jesus made the mud and opened his eyes. So the

Pharisees again asked him how he had received his sight. And he said to them, "He put mud on my eyes, and I washed, and I see." Some of the Pharisees said, "This man is not from God, for he does not keep the Sabbath." But others said, "How can a man who is a sinner do such signs?" And there was a division among them. So they said again to the blind man, "What do you say about him, since he has opened your eyes?" He said, "He is a prophet."

The Jews did not believe that he had been blind and had received his sight, until they called the parents of the man who had received his sight and asked them, "Is this your son, who you say was born blind? How then does he now see?" His parents answered, "We know that this is our son and that he was born blind. But how he now sees we do not know, nor do we know who opened his eyes. Ask him; he is of age. He will speak for himself." (His parents said these things because they feared the Jews, for the Jews had already agreed that if anyone should confess Jesus to be Christ, he was to be put out of the synagogue.) Therefore his parents said, "He is of age; ask him."

So for the second time they called the man who had been blind and said to him, "Give glory to God. We know that this man is a sinner." He answered, "Whether he is a sinner I do not know. One thing I do know, that though I was blind, now I see." They said to him, "What did he do to you? How did he open your eyes?" He answered them, "I have told you already, and you would not listen. Why do you want to hear it again? Do you also want to become his disciples?" And they reviled him, saying, "You are his disciple, but we are disciples of Moses. We know that God has spoken to Moses, but as for this man, we do not know where he comes from." The man answered, "Why, this is an amazing thing! You do not know where he comes from, and yet he opened my eyes. We know that God does not listen to sinners, but if anyone is a worshiper of God and does his will, God listens to him. Never since the world began has it been heard that anyone opened the eyes of a man born blind. If this man were not from God, he could do nothing." They answered him, "You were born in utter sin, and would you teach us?" And they cast him out.

Jesus heard that they had cast him out, and having found him he said, "Do you believe in the Son of Man?" He answered, "And who is he, sir, that I may believe in him?" Jesus said to him, "You have seen him, and it is he who is speaking to you." He said, "Lord, I believe," and he worshiped him. Jesus said, "For judgment I came into this world, that those who do not see may see, and those who see may become blind." Some of the Pharisees near him heard these things, and said to him, "Are we also blind?" Jesus said to them, "If you were blind, you would have no guilt; but now that you say, 'We see,' your guilt remains."[16]

The story of the healing of the man born blind is not only notable for the miracle, but also for people's reaction to the miracle. There was astonishment by his neighbors.

There were those who doubted the man who now could see was indeed ever blind, but merely resembled the man in question. The Jewish leaders did not believe the man truly received sight and were incredulous that Jesus healed on the Sabbath. Even the man's parents were cautious because if they attributed their son's miraculous sight to Jesus, they would be excommunicated from the synagogue. Even as the man confessed again and again what Jesus did for him, the response was skepticism and rebuke.

The tragedy is that other than the man Jesus healed, no one believed in Jesus. In spite of the conspicuous evidence of a former blind man acknowledging what Jesus did for him, no one responded in faith.

However, what if Jesus could raise the dead? Certainly that would result in people believing in Him as Savior and Lord if they witnessed such an event. Would it? Let us see as we turn our attention of John 11.

> Now a certain man was ill, Lazarus of Bethany, the village of Mary and her sister Martha. It was Mary who anointed the Lord with ointment and wiped his feet with her hair, whose brother Lazarus was ill. So the sisters sent to him, saying, "Lord, he whom you love is ill." But when Jesus heard it he said, "This illness does not lead to death. It is for the glory of God, so that the Son of God may be glorified through it."
>
> Now Jesus loved Martha and her sister and Lazarus. So, when he heard that Lazarus was ill, he

stayed two days longer in the place where he was. Then after this he said to the disciples, "Let us go to Judea again." The disciples said to him, "Rabbi, the Jews were just now seeking to stone you, and are you going there again?" Jesus answered, "Are there not twelve hours in the day? If anyone walks in the day, he does not stumble, because he sees the light of this world. But if anyone walks in the night, he stumbles, because the light is not in him." After saying these things, he said to them, "Our friend Lazarus has fallen asleep, but I go to awaken him." The disciples said to him, "Lord, if he has fallen asleep, he will recover." Now Jesus had spoken of his death, but they thought that he meant taking rest in sleep. Then Jesus told them plainly, "Lazarus has died, and for your sake I am glad that I was not there, so that you may believe. But let us go to him." So Thomas, called the Twin, said to his fellow disciples, "Let us also go, that we may die with him."

Now when Jesus came, he found that Lazarus had already been in the tomb four days. Bethany was near Jerusalem, about two miles off, and many of the Jews had come to Martha and Mary to console them concerning their brother. So when Martha heard that Jesus was coming, she went and met him, but Mary remained seated in the house. Martha said to Jesus, "Lord, if you had been here, my brother would not have died. But even now I know that whatever you ask from God, God will give you." Jesus said to her, "Your brother will rise again." Martha said to him, "I know that he will rise again in the resurrection on the last day." Jesus said to her, "I am the resurrection and the life. Whoever believes in me, though he die, yet shall he live, and everyone who lives and believes in me shall never die. Do you believe this?" She said to him, "Yes, Lord; I believe that you are the Christ, the Son of God, who is coming into the world."

When she had said this, she went and called her sister Mary, saying in private, "The Teacher is here and is calling for you." And when she heard it, she rose quickly and went to him. Now Jesus had not yet come into the village, but was still in the place where Martha had met him. When the Jews who were with her in the house, consoling her, saw Mary rise quickly and go out, they followed her, supposing that she was going to the tomb to weep there. Now when Mary came to where Jesus was and saw him, she fell at his feet, saying to him, "Lord, if you had been here, my brother would not have died." When Jesus saw her weeping, and the Jews who had come with her also weeping, he was deeply moved in his spirit and greatly troubled. And he said, "Where have you laid him?" They said to him, "Lord, come and see." Jesus wept. So the Jews said, "See how he loved him!" But some of them said, "Could not he who opened the eyes of the blind man also have kept this man from dying?"

Then Jesus, deeply moved again, came to the tomb. It was a cave, and a stone lay against it. Jesus said, "Take away the stone." Martha, the sister of the dead man, said to him, "Lord, by this time there will be an odor, for he has been dead four days." Jesus said to her, "Did I not tell you that if you believed you would see the glory of God?" So they took away the stone. And Jesus lifted up his eyes and said, "Father, I thank you that you have heard me. I knew that you always hear me, but I said this on account of the people standing around, that they may believe that you sent me." When he had said these things, he cried out with a loud voice, "Lazarus, come out." The man who had died came out, his hands and feet bound with linen strips, and his face wrapped with a cloth. Jesus said to them, "Unbind him, and let him go."

Many of the Jews therefore, who had come with Mary and had seen what he did, believed in him, but some of them went to the Pharisees and told them what Jesus had done. So the chief priests and the Pharisees gathered the council and said, "What are we to do? For this man performs many signs. If we let him go on like this, everyone will believe in him, and the Romans will come and take away both our place and our nation." But one of them, Caiaphas, who was high priest that year, said to them, "You know nothing at all. Nor do you understand that it is better for you that one man should die for the people, not that the whole nation should perish." He did not say this of his own accord, but being high priest that year he prophesied that Jesus would die for the nation, and not for the nation only, but also to gather into one the children of God who are scattered abroad. So from that day on they made plans to put him to death.

Jesus therefore no longer walked openly among the Jews, but went from there to the region near the wilderness, to a town called Ephraim, and there he stayed with the disciples.

Now the Passover of the Jews was at hand, and many went up from the country to Jerusalem before the Passover to purify themselves. They were looking for Jesus and saying to one another as they stood in the temple, "What do you think? That he will not come to the feast at all?" Now the chief priests and the Pharisees had given orders that if anyone knew where he was, he should let them know, so that they might arrest him.[17]

The raising of Lazarus from the dead is second only to Jesus's own resurrection with respect to the claim and evidence that Jesus is God in the flesh. It was a public miracle and a witnessed miracle. Many people were in attendance to mourn the death of Lazarus, and those same people were there to witness his resurrection.

When Jesus raised Lazarus, the text says that "Many of the Jews therefore, who had come with Mary and had seen what he did, believed in him, but some of them went to the Pharisees and told them what Jesus had done."[18] This is John's first mention that anyone actually believed after witnessing Jesus perform a miracle. However, those who believed were counterbalanced by those who refused to do so. They both witnessed the same miracle but came to equally different conclusions.

In fact, the religious leaders, upon hearing what Jesus had done, did not dispute His miracle but rather sought how to keep the people from believing in Him. Rather than evaluate the evidence before them, they rejected it outright and began to make plans regarding how they would kill Jesus.

A similar response is found not only in John's gospel but also in the Book of Revelation. When the world-shattering disturbances occur on the earth prior to Christ's coming, those without Christ will seek many different sources of protection and comfort but will still refuse to repent and trust Christ as their Savior. John states,

> When he [Christ] opened the sixth seal, I looked, and behold, there was a great earthquake, and the sun became black as sackcloth, the full moon became like blood, and the stars of the sky fell to the earth as the fig tree sheds its winter fruit when shaken by a gale. The sky vanished like a scroll that is being rolled up, and every mountain and island was removed from its place. Then the kings of the earth and the great ones and the generals and the rich and the powerful, and everyone, slave and free, hid themselves in the caves and among the rocks of the mountains, calling to the mountains and rocks, "Fall on us and hide us from the face of him who is seated on the throne, and from the wrath of the Lamb, for the great day of their wrath has come, and who can stand?"[19]

The unsaved will hide, they will recognize the source of their impending judgment, but what they will not do is repent and believe—in spite of what they see. Seeing does not necessarily result in believing. It never has. True biblical faith in Christ does not come by seeing what Jesus has done, or conceivably would do if He were to appear today, but rather through the monergistic regenerating work of the Holy Spirit within the deadened soul of sinful man.

8

Letter Three

"*The popular faith in words is a veritable disease of the mind.*" Carl Justav Jung You claim the resurrection is important to the Christian faith and I must concede you are right, but only so far as fantasy and mythology is important to the gullible. As Mark Twain put it, "*Faith is believing in what you know ain't so.*"

It seems to me however that you are begging the question. The real question is not why the resurrection of the fabled Jesus is important but rather why was there a need for a resurrection at all? Everyone celebrates Easter as a triumph for a god, but I submit that it only shows the evil of your god.

Allegedly, Jesus was born to be tortured and killed so mankind could be reconciled to god. Putting aside for a minute the absurdity of this, it does make one wonder about a "loving" deity who could only be pacified by torturing and murdering his only son. A "forgiving" god who just couldn't forgive?

Anyway, the party line is that Easter was to save us from sin...but what is sin? Sin is the willful violation, *either by commission or omission, of a purported rule of this god or one promulgated by his "special" clerical representatives. Of course these rules change according to culture, science, education, who is in power at the time, and ages. Remember when it was a sin to let a witch suffer to live, or not to kill a Jew, or to eat meat on Friday or any of several other idiocies?*

Also, when the Christian church couldn't reconcile the evil of god through non-man attributable acts such as earthquakes, floods, cancer, etc., it fabricated the idea of original sin which declares that man is evil just because he was born. It is amazing that all ministers don't have Pinocchio noses when they preach this drivel.

Anyway, the only reason for this reconciliation is so god wouldn't get pissed off at man for violating rules he made, or that he let others claim he made. I could speak volumes about the Adam/Eve myth and hypocrisy of this monster god but a single example will serve here: this "just" god damned an entire race forever because someone ate a bite of fruit of the tree of good and evil before they knew what good and evil was and therefore couldn't have known it was wrong to disobey god. So much for justice!

Does the only way this god allows himself to be pacified is to kill his own son? And even that is not enough for he still keeps his hell filled. I say that this religious claptrap is all patent (expletive) and that the only true line in the Bible is Isaiah 45:7, "I form light and create darkness, I make well-being and create calamity, I am the Lord, *who does all these things" (Isaiah 45:7* esv).

Will you now tell the truth about this monster god of yours …or will you keep your smug naiveté and keep living off the labor of your gullible flock? Surely, it is clear that your religion is as empty and transparent as your monster god.

—The godslayer

There are several questions the godslayer raises in this letter. First, what is sin? Second, why did Adam and Eve's sin affect the rest of mankind? Third, how could God hold Adam and Eve responsible for their sin when they did not know what good and evil was and therefore could not have known it was wrong to disobey God? Fourth, why did Jesus Christ die on the cross on behalf of sinners if God, who is supposedly forgiving, could have just forgiven man his sin and left it at that?

Before we address these questions, let me first respond to the godslayer's contention that the only true line in the Bible is Isaiah 45:7, "I form light and create darkness, I make well-being and create calamity, I am the LORD, who does all these things."[1] If it is reasonable to conclude that if one verse of the Bible is false the possibility of the entire Bible being false is a true statement, therefore then does it not seem logical that the opposite proposition is also true? If one verse of the Bible is true, then the possibility remains that the rest of the Bible is also true. The godslayer acknowledges Isaiah 45:7 as truth. In his own words, "the only true line in the Bible."

If this is accurate, then it stands to reason that if one line in the Bible is true, then could not other lines in the Bible also be true? How do you determine what lines are true in the Scriptures and which ones are not? Any "free thinking" individual who is intelligent can see the mammoth implication in this admission by the godslayer. By acknowledging one line of Scripture to be true, he opens up the possibility for the entire Bible to be regarded as true.

Dr. Harold Lindsell, in his book *The Battle for the Bible*, sets forth three possibilities regarding the Bible being a reliable guide to religious knowledge: that what it says corresponds to reality or truth. What he wrote over forty years ago remains significant for evangelicals today in their defense of biblical truth. The three possibilities Dr. Lindsell set forth are as follows.

The first possibility is that the Bible is not at all trustworthy. It is not truth. Dr. Lindsell contends, "If this answer is correct, then Christianity stands upon a false foundation. Anyone who professes a faith founded on a source that cannot be trusted is a fool, is naïve or is deluded."[2]

The second possibility is that the Bible can be trusted because it is truthful in all of its parts. The Bible does not contain error of any kind. It is inerrant and infallible. This is what Dr. Lindsell, and evangelical Protestants throughout the centuries and today, contend as the biblical perspective.

The third possibility is that the Bible contains some truth and some error. The Bible is neither completely truth nor is it completely false. However, how does anyone make the determination as to what is true in the Scriptures and what is not? What standard does anyone use to determine the Bible's truthfulness? Feelings? Church creeds? Governmental laws? A pastor's perspective? What?

Furthermore, to say that the Bible contains some error is to open the possibility that the entire biblical canon is completely false. The same can also be said for the Bible being true. If anyone acknowledges any part of the Scriptures as truth, it stands to reason the possibility exists that all of the Bible can be so categorized.

The godslayer makes a significant concession with his comment concerning the truth of Isaiah 45:7, the implication of which he, along with others, may not fully grasp. With this consideration in mind, let us look again at the biblical reasons for the resurrection with the understanding that there is not only one line in the Bible that is true, but that every one line is true. Every word, sentence, paragraph, chapter, discourse, book, and testament is the biblical truth God has chosen to reveal.

Regarding the reasons for the resurrection of Jesus from the dead, I refer the reader to Chapter Two. However, let us specifically review why was it so imperative for Jesus to conquer death, hell, and the grave? Let us examine the biblical reasons given in 1 Corinthians 15:12–19.

> Now if Christ is proclaimed as raised from the dead, how can some of you say that there is no resurrection of the dead? But if there is no resurrection of the dead, then not even Christ has been raised. And if Christ has not been raised, then our preaching is in vain and your faith is in vain. We are even found to be misrepresenting God, because we testified about God that he raised Christ, whom he did not raise if it is true that the dead are not raised. For if the dead are not raised, not even Christ has been raised. And if Christ has not been raised, your faith is futile and you are still in your sins. Then those also who have fallen asleep in Christ have perished. If in Christ we have hope in this life only, we are of all people most to be pitied.[3]

The Apostle Paul gives the Corinthian believers, as well as you and me, some clear and concise reasons why the resurrection of Jesus Christ from the grave is so essential to the gospel. He addresses the reasons in ascending order.

First, if there is no resurrection of the dead, then not even Christ rose. If that is the case, then secondly it stands to reason that preaching the gospel is futile and makes no sense at all. Thirdly, the Christian's faith therefore is also futile. Fourth, those of us who proclaim the gospel are misrepresenting God because we preach God raised Christ. Fifth, if the dead are not raised, not even Christ has been raised, and not only is our faith futile, but everyone remains in their sins. There is no just and substitutionary payment for the punishment of our sin. We ourselves bear the punishment individually and eternally. Paul's conclusion is that we are to be pitied.

Pity toward Christians may seem fine to the many so-called godslayers in the world, but we are not concerned with what to them seems fine but rather with what is true. The truth is that there is ample evidence that Christ indeed rose from the dead as previously noted in an earlier chapter.

The godslayer says that the real question is not why the resurrection of the fabled Jesus is important but rather why was there a need for a resurrection at all? He submits that everyone celebrates Easter as a triumph for a God, but that it only shows the evil of God. The evil to which the godslayer specifically refers to is the crucifixion of Jesus Christ on the cross. Allegedly, Jesus was born to be tortured and killed so mankind could be reconciled to God. He contends that God's behavior was evil by torturing and murdering his only son. He wonders why a "forgiving" God could not just forgive.

The Bible says the word of the cross is foolishness to those who are perishing (1 Cor. 1:18–25). The godslayer certainly displays this attitude. His hostility toward the cross is conspicuous. However, let us continue by biblically answering the question as to what is sin. The Bible leaves no doubt as to the meaning and severity of sin.

Sin is defined as transgressing God's law (1 John 3:4). Sin is not what man or a culture defines as sin, because as the godslayer rightly contends, man's definition of sin is constantly changing. Rather, sin is what God has set forth as violating His standards.

The Scriptures contend that sin is of the devil (1 John 3:8; John 8:44), is unrighteousness (1 John 5:17), is the failure to do what we know to be good (James 4:17), and whatever is not of faith in God (Rom. 14:23). Sin is also defined as any thought of foolishness (Prov. 24:9) and the imaginations of the unregenerate heart (Gen. 6:5; 8:21).

Sin is described as coming from man's thinking, feeling, and choosing (Matt. 15:19), the fruit of lust (James 1:15), the sting of death (1 Cor. 15:56), rebellion against God (Deut. 9:7; Josh. 1:18) the works of darkness (Eph. 5:11), and the product of man's dead works (Heb. 6:1; 9:14). It is also the abominable thing that God hates (Prov. 15:9; Jer. 44:4, 11), and what is reproaching to the Lord (Num. 15:30; Ps. 74:18).

The Bible states that sin entered into the world by Adam's disobedience to God (Gen. 3:6, 7; Rom. 5:12–21), that as a consequence of Adam's sin all men are conceived and born in sin (Gen. 5:3; Job 15:14; 25:4; Ps. 51:5), no man is without sin (1 Kings 8:46; Eccles. 7:20), and Scripture concludes all are under God's condemnation because of sin (Gal. 3:22). This is why Adam and Eve's sin affected mankind.

Man is by nature a sinner (Eph. 2:1–3) because the Bible says so. This is not a doctrine the church came up with on the fly. It always amazes me when the culture, specifically the news media, attempts to explain why sinful man does the evil that he does. Numerous explanations are given but seldom, if ever, are the reasons for man's behavior due to the fact that he is a sinner by nature and the evil he does verifies this fact.

Sin is defiling (Prov. 30:12; Isa. 59:3), deceitful (Heb. 3:13), disgraceful (Prov. 14:34), often very great (Exod. 32:20; 1 Sam. 2:17), often mighty (Amos 5:12), often manifold (Amos 5:12), often presumptuous (Ps. 19:13). Sin is sometimes open and manifest (1 Tim. 5:24), sometimes done in secret (Ps. 90:8; 1 Tim. 5:24), besetting (Heb. 12:1), like scarlet and crimson (Isa. 1:18), and reaching to heaven (Rev. 18:5).

God hates sin (Deut. 25:16; Prov. 6:16–19), identifies sin (Job 10:14), remembers sin (Rev. 18:5), is provoked to jealousy by sin (1 Kings 14:22), is provoked to anger by sin (1 Kings 16:2), can alone forgive sin (Exod. 34:7; Dan. 9:9; Micah 7:18; Mark 2:7), repays the sinner for his sin (Jer. 16:18; Rev. 18:6), and punishes man for his sin (Isa. 13:11; Amos 3:2).

The law of God is transgressed by every sin (James 2:10, 11; 1 John 3:4), gives knowledge of sin (Rom. 3:20; 7:7), shows the exceeding sinfulness of sin (Rom. 7:13) and was made by God to restrain sin (1 Tim. 1:9, 10). The law's strictness stirs up sin (Rom. 7:5, 8, 11), is the strength of sin (1 Cor. 15:56), curses those guilty of sin (Gal. 3:10). Sin leads to shame (Rom. 6:21), unrest (Ps. 38:3), and disease (Job 20:11). Sin also resulted in the ground being cursed on account of it (Gen. 3:17, 18), toil and sorrow originate from it (Gen. 3:16, 17, 19; Job 14:1), and it excludes all from heaven because of it (1 Cor. 6:9, 10; Gal. 5:19–21; Eph. 5:5; Rev. 21:27). Sin brings forth death (James 1:15), the wages of sin is death (Rom. 6:23), the punishment of sin results in death (Gen. 2:17; Ezek. 18:4).

The wicked are servants to sin (John 8:34; Rom. 6:16), are separated from God (dead) in their sin (Eph. 2:1), are guilty in everything they do because of their sin (Prov. 21:4; Ezek. 21:24), seek to excuse their sin (Gen. 3:12–13; 1 Sam. 13:11–12; 15:13–15), encourage themselves in their sin (Ps. 64:5), defy God in committing sin (Isa. 5:18,19), boast of their sin (Isa. 3:9), and make fun of their sin (Prov. 14:9). The wicked also expect God will forget their sin (Ps. 10:11; 50:21; 94:7), while all the while they cannot cease from sinning (2 Pet. 2:14).

The wicked heap up sin (Ps. 78:17; Isa. 30:1), are encouraged in, and by the temporary prosperity from sin (Job 21:7–15; Prov. 10:16). They are led by despair to continue in sin (Jer. 2:25; 18:12), they try to conceal their sin from God (Gen. 3:8, 10; Job 31:33), blame God for their sin (Gen. 3:12; Jer. 7:10), or seek to blame others (Gen. 3:12, 13; Exod. 32:22–24). The wicked also tempt others to sin (Gen. 3:6; 1 Kings 16:2; 21:25; Prov. 1:10–14), delight in those who commit sin (Ps. 10:3; Hos. 7:3; Rom.

1:32), and will bear the shame of their sin (Ezek. 16:52). Their sin will be revealed (Num. 32:23).

It should be conspicuous to anyone that the Bible has much to say concerning the severity of sin. Due to man's sinful condition, he cannot cleanse himself from sin (Job 9:30–31; Prov. 20:9; Jer. 2:22) or atone for his sin (Micah 6:7). Is there any hope for sinners?

The only hope for sinners is Jesus Christ. Jesus Christ alone was without sin (2 Cor. 5:21; Heb. 4:15; 7:26; 1 John 3:5), provides cleansing from sin (Zech. 13:1), was manifested to take away sin (John 1:29; 1 John 3:5), and whose blood redeems (Eph. 1:7) and cleanses (1 John 1:7) sinners of their sin. Those who receive God's forgiveness and righteousness through faith in Jesus Christ (John 1:12–13) are made free from the guilt and punishment of their sin (Rom. 6:18), and are now dead to their sin (Rom. 6:2, 11; 1 Pet. 2:24).

If you were to ask children in church why Jesus came to earth, most of them would probably say "to die on the cross to save us from our sin." While that is not an incorrect answer, it is not a complete answer. True, Jesus had to die on the cross, but He also had to live a righteous life prior to His substitutionary death on the cross.

John the Baptist refers to Jesus as the sinless and spotless Lamb of God (John 1:29).Jesus challenged the Pharisees to tell Him what sins He had committed (John 8:46). The answer to Jesus's rhetorical question was "none."The writer of the Book of Hebrews states that Jesus was tempted as we are but was without sin (Heb. 4:15). The Apostle Paul declares Jesus was without sin (2 Cor. 5:21).

The reason Jesus's righteous life prior to the cross is such a significant aspect of the gospel is that while our sins were imputed (credited) to Christ while on the cross, His righteousness is imputed (credited) to sinners by grace alone, through faith alone, in Christ alone. This is what the Bible calls justification. The only way any sinner can stand before God is by the imputed righteousness of Christ credited to their eternal soul's account. See Romans 3:21–26; 4:1–25; Philippians 3:1–9.

Due to their new relationship with God through Jesus Christ, sinners profess to have ceased from sin (1 Pet. 4:1), cannot live in sin (1 John 3:9; 5:18), resolve against sin (Job 34:32), are ashamed of having committed sin (Rom. 6:21), and abhor themselves on account of sin (Job 42:6; Ezek. 20:43). Even though Christ accomplishes all this for sinners, they yet still have the remains of sin within them (Rom. 7:17, 23; Gal. 5:17). However, the reverential fear of God restrains the believer from sinning (Exod. 20:20; Ps. 4:4; Prov. 16:6), as does the Word of God (Ps. 17:4; 119:11). Additionally, the Holy Spirit convicts believers of their sin (John 16:8–9).

Within the believer in Christ, sin should be confessed (1 John 1:8–10; Job 32:27; Prov. 28:13), mourned over (Ps. 38:18; Jer. 3:21), hated (Ps. 97:10; Prov. 8:13; Amos 5:15), abhorred (Rom. 12:9), put away (Job 11:14), departed from (Ps. 34:14; 2 Tim. 2:19), avoided even in appearance (1 Thess. 5:22), guarded against (Ps. 4:4; 39:1), struggled against (Heb. 12:4), mortified (Rom. 8:13; Col. 3:5), and completely destroyed (Rom. 6:6).

Believers should realize that sin hinders our prayers (Ps. 66:18; Isa. 59:1–2), and that God's blessings are withheld on account of sin (Jer. 5:25). Therefore, they should also pray to God that He would search for sin in their hearts (Ps. 139:23–24), make them know their sin (Job 13:23), forgive them their sin (Exod. 34:9; Luke 11:4), keep them from sin (Ps. 19:13), deliver them from sin (Matt. 6:13), and continually cleanse them from sin (Ps. 51:2). Finally, ministers of the gospel should warn the wicked to forsake their sin (Ezek. 33:9; Dan. 4:27).

With this wealth of revelation from God concerning sin, we must not fail to answer the godslayer's question concerning the offensiveness of the cross. It makes him, and I am sure others as well, wonder about a "loving" deity who could only be pacified by torturing and murdering his only son. A "forgiving" god who just couldn't forgive? Why was the cross so absolutely necessary? Could there have been another way to redeem man from consequences of sin? In the message entitled "Necessary Blood," Dr. R. C. Sproul recalls the following incident:

It's been a little over 50 years that I have been studying the mystery of the cross of Christ, and I've come to the conclusion that the day that I die and enter into Paradise, in the first 30 seconds that I'm there that I will have a quantum leap in my understanding of what took place on the cross. Now I must be satisfied with the feeble efforts of my own study during my lifetime, and trying to penetrate all that was involved in that action on the cross outside of Jerusalem. We look at its exposition in the New Testament and we see it is multi-faceted. Many nuances of the cross are set forth. It's like a magnificent tapestry that is woven by several brightly hued strands. Here is the idea of satisfaction. Over here is the idea of substitution. Over there is the concept of ransom. Here the paying of the bridal price. Still back there the idea of the kinsman redeemer. Even in Galatians we find the motif of horror, the motif of the cross of curse that Christ endured at Calvary.

But in all of these nuances and facets runs that flow of blood from Emmanuel's veins, and the question we ask is why? Why all of this blood? Was it really necessary that this blood be spilled for our redemption? It was 40 years ago before the founding of the Philadelphia Conference on Reformed Theology that I was asked to speak here in Philadelphia to a Quaker meeting. At that time I was the professor of philosophical theology at the Conwell School of Theology on Broad Street in Temple University. I was asked by the Friends to come and explain to them the relationship between the Old Testament and the New Testament. So I looked at the Passover. I looked at the Day of Atonement, and then I brought it forward to the crucifixion of Jesus.

In the middle of that address, there was a man who was quite hostile in the back of the meeting, who was anything but friendly for a Quaker, and he interrupted my message by shouting out "That's primitive and obscene." What do you do when someone interrupts your message with a statement like that? Well, just to give myself a moment to gather my thoughts, I said, "What was it you said?" as if I hadn't heard him. He said, "I said that's primitive and obscene." I looked at him and said, "You know, you're right. It is primitive." I like that term because the naked simplicity of this body right of sacrifice is so graphic, so crass, that even an uneducated person can grasp its meaning.

Isn't it wonderful that our God does not require a PhD in theology to understand His method of redemption? The salvation is not restricted to some agnostic elite group who can penetrate this event of redemption. "I like that word primitive," I said, "but the one I really like is the other word you used— obscene—because in the sight of a holy God, there is nothing more obscene than sin. When God takes the cumulative sin of the people that he places upon his beloved Son after our sin has been imputed to Jesus, that cumulative concentration that hung on the cross was the most obscene thing the world had ever seen. In fact it was so obscene that God refused to look at

> it. That God turned His back upon it. He turned off
> the lights. It is primitive and it is obscene, and maybe
> these dimensions may cause us to choke a little bit.[4]

The cross is primitive and offensive. It is brutal and bloody. Even to this day it evokes strong emotion: both negative and positive (1 Cor. 1:18–25). However, there was no other way for God to forgive and reconcile sinners to Himself without the cross. This is due to the fact that the cross does not represent a petulant God who delights in torture and murder simply for the sake of torture and murder. Rather, the cross displays the holy righteousness of God who must punish sin in order to be consistent to His holiness and justice. The cross displays God's penal, substitutionary atonement exclusively through His Son, our Savior and Lord Jesus Christ.

Primarily there are just three theological schools of thought regarding the cross. Where an individual stands in any of these paradigms determines their perspective on the necessity of the cross.

The first is theological modern day liberalism. It is either regarded as sub-Christian or anti-Christian. At its heart it denies man's inherent sinfulness and fallen nature thereby denying the need for the substitutionary atonement by Jesus Christ on the cross in the first place. Salvation and subtitutionary atonement is unnecessary. The cross, at best, is a moral example for people to follow.

The second perspective is that the cross is only necessary hypothetically. God could have redeemed sinners in any one of a number of ways, but He chose to use the cross. The cross was not absolutely necessary but was the methodology God selected. In short, the cross was one option of many.

The third perspective I am convinced is the biblical view: the cross was absolutely necessary for God to accomplish our redemption and justification through Jesus Christ. Why? It is because the cross, in all its brutality, displays the justice and righteousness of God in the necessity of punishing sin while at the same time displaying God's love and grace for sinners.

Let us examine a phrase I mentioned earlier: penal substitutionary atonement. What does this mean? Unless this statement is unpacked and examined, we may fail to grasp the significance of the cross and our salvation in Jesus Christ. Therefore, let us look at these three words separately in order to understand what they collectively mean.

Penal is short for penalty. Synonyms include punitive, punishing, severe, and strict. One of my favorite movies is *Papillion* starring Steve McQueen. The film tells the story of men imprisoned in a French "penal" colony in French Guiana, South America. These prisoners were incarcerated because they had broken the law. Therefore, they were being punished for their crimes. The film depicts these prisoners' struggle against their incarceration, their captors, and their environment.

McQueen plays the character Henri "Papillion" Charriere. A petty criminal, Papillion is wrongly convicted of murder and sentenced to life in prison. The film depicts not only his efforts to escape from his penal colony prison, but also his struggle in solitary confinement when he is recaptured following several attempted escapes.

As sinners, all of us have broken God's law: by our thoughts, our words, and our behavior. God's word states that all transgressors of the Law must be punished with death (Ezek. 18:3–4; 20; Rom. 6:23). God told Adam and Eve that death would be the ultimate consequence in disobeying Him (Gen. 2:15–17). They may not have known what good and evil was, but they knew God and they understood what He said (Gen. 3:1–3). That should have been sufficient. It was this commandment the devil denied (Gen. 3:4–5) and that our first parents rejected (Gen. 3:6).

God was under no obligation to save Adam and Eve, or for that matter any sinner. Each of us are deserving of receiving from God the due penalty for our sins: death. However, what if there was one way for God to satisfy His justice in punishing the sinner's sin while at the same time rescuing the sinner from a just and eternal condemnation? God provides such a way. It is with a substitute.

The second word we now examine is the word *subsitutionary*. It means substitution or to the take the place of. All of us probably remember when we were in school a time when our teacher was absent from class. Rather than cancel class, the school system hired a substitute to take our teacher's place until such time he/she could return to class. This is the central idea of substitutionary.

God provided a substitute for those He chose to redeem. Instead of the sinner paying the price for their sin, and rightly so in the eyes of God, He provided a substitute to take the place of the guilty. God did not have to do this. God was under no obligation to do this. He chose to do this on the basis of His grace and mercy toward sinners. Amazingly, God chose to do this before the foundation of the world (Eph. 1:3–14).

It is this doctrine of substitution that God displays in Genesis 3 when He graciously clothes Adam and Eve with garments of skin (Gen. 3:21). An innocent animal died in order for God to clothe sinners and cover their shame because of their sin. This concept is found throughout the Bible. Examples include Abraham's sacrifice of his son Isaac (Gen. 22), the Passover (Exod. 12), the sacrifices at the Tabernacle/Temple (Lev. 1–6) along with the words of John the Baptist (John 1:29) and Jesus (John 10:11–18). It is beautifully illustrated in Zechariah 3:1–7.

The most common and striking biblical image of what was used in place of man for God to punish sin was a lamb. The most striking and significant prophecy depicting this act of substitution is found in Isaiah 52:13–53:12. It is often referred as the gospel according to Isaiah.

Behold, my servant shall act wisely; he shall be high and lifted up, and shall be exalted. As many were astonished at you—his appearance was so marred, beyond human semblance, and his form beyond that of the children of mankind— so shall he sprinkle many nations; kings shall shut their mouths because of him; for that which has not been told them they see, and that which they have not heard they understand. Who has believed what he has heard from us? And to whom has the arm of the LORD been revealed? For he grew up before him like a young plant, and like a root out of dry ground; he had no form or majesty that we should look at him, and no beauty that we should desire him. He was despised and rejected by men; a man of sorrows, and acquainted with grief; and as one from whom men hide their faces he was despised, and we esteemed him not. Surely he has borne our griefs and carried our sorrows; yet we esteemed him stricken, smitten by God, and afflicted. But he was wounded for our transgressions; he was crushed for our iniquities; upon him was the chastisement that brought us peace, and with his stripes we are healed. All we like sheep have gone astray; we have turned—every one—to his own way; and the LORD has laid on him the iniquity of us all. He was oppressed, and he was afflicted, yet he opened not his mouth; like a lamb that is led to the slaughter, and like a sheep that before its shearers is silent, so he opened not his mouth. By oppression and judgment he was taken away; and as for his generation, who considered that he was cut off out of the land of the living, stricken for the transgression of my people? And they made his grave with the wicked and with a rich man in his death, although he had done no violence, and there was no deceit in his mouth. Yet it was the will of the LORD to crush him; he has put him to grief; when his soul makes an offering for guilt, he shall see his offspring; he shall prolong his days; the will of the LORD shall prosper in his hand. Out of the anguish of his soul he shall see and be satisfied; by his knowledge shall the righteous one, my servant, make many to be accounted righteous, and he shall bear their iniquities. Therefore I will divide him a portion with the many, and he shall divide the spoil with the strong, because he poured out his soul to death and was numbered with the transgressors; yet he bore the sin of many, and makes intercession for the transgressors.[5]

What did God accomplish by this punitive act of substitution? Atonement! What is meant by atonement? The word *atonement* is one of the few theological terms from an Anglo-Saxon heritage. It means "a making at one," and displays the act of reconciling God and man who are alienated and separated because of God's holiness and man's sinfulness. "Its use in theology is to denote the work of Christ in dealing with the problem posed by the sin of man and in bringing sinners into right relation with God."[6]

Jesus Christ's atoning work on the cross accomplished this reconciliation between God and sinners (2 Cor. 5:17–

21). This is why the cross was absolutely necessary. The cross was brutal and bloody because God treats sin that seriously. Sinners do not, but God does.

The godslayer poses the question as to why God could not just forgive. Why is the punishment of sin necessary? The answer is to satisfy God's justice. This is illustrated time and again in our own justice system.

Ariel Castro held three Cleveland, Ohio, women hostage in his home for a decade. Following the women's rescue and release in May 2013, Judge Michael J. Russo of Cuyahoga County Common Pleas Court sentenced Castro to life in prison without possibility of parole, and one thousand years. The punishment, rendered in August 2013, was the result of a plea deal between Mr. Castro and prosecutors that allowed him to avoid a possible death sentence.

Now to use the godslayer's own words, why couldn't these three women and the judicial system of the State of Ohio just forgive this man of his crimes? He testified in court he was a victim of sexual addiction. He said the reason he abducted and abused the three women was because he was sick. Why not just forgive and forget?

Even in man's fallen, sinful condition, we still retain some portion of God's image within us. It is this intelligence, emotion, and will corresponding to God's righteous character that causes us to recoil at crimes committed by such individuals as Ariel Castro. There remains within us a sense and desire for justice and for punishment to fit the crime. We cry for justice to be served and are troubled when it is not. What holds true for man also holds true for God.

The cross was not just a display of primitive and obscene violence. It displayed God's righteous justice. While we humans clearly see justice for others, and ignore it when we deserve it, God does no such thing. He remains faithful to merit His justice where and when it is deserved, and every sinner deserves God's justice.

Why did God choose to do this atoning work through His Son, Jesus Christ, on behalf of sinners? The cross displays an attribute of God that is not immediately seen in the bloody scene at Calvary: God's love. Not only God's love for sinners in need of salvation from God's justice, but the cross also displays Jesus Christ's love for God the Father in submitting to the cross to carry out the Father's will in saving sinners from God's righteous wrath.

This is what the Apostle John means when he writes "For God so loved the world that He gave His only begotten Son that whoever believes in Him shall not perish by have eternal life."[7] This is also what John addresses in 1 John 4:7–11:

> Beloved, let us love one another, for love is from God, and whoever loves has been born of God and knows God. Anyone who does not love does not know God, because God is love. In this the love of God was made manifest among us, that God sent his only Son into the world, so that we might live through him. In this

> is love, not that we have loved God but that he loved
> us and sent his Son to be the propitiation for our sins.
> Beloved, if God so loved us, we also ought to love one
> another.[8]

The concept of propitiation is illustrated in the cover of the Ark of the Covenant in the Holy of Holies, which was sprinkled with the blood of the expiatory victim on the annual Day of Atonement (Lev. 16). "This rite signifying that the life of the people, the loss of which they had merited by their sins, was offered to God in the blood as the life of the victim, and that God by this ceremony was appeased and their sins expiated; hence the lid of expiation, the propitiatory sacrifice"[9] (Strong's). Jesus Christ became the sinner's mercy seat or substitute.

The word *propitiation* is often used synonymously with the word *expiation*. In fact, the same Greek word (ἰλαστήριον/*hilasterion*) is often used for both words. However, there is a distinction between the two terms that must be noted. Whereas expiation addresses the act of the Christ's substitutionary atonement on the cross, propitiation is the result of that act: God has turned His wrath from the believing sinner for His wrath has been placated by the Son. However, as one author has written,

> The objection to propitiation arises largely from an
> objection to the whole idea of the wrath of God,
> which many exponents of this view relegate to the
> status of an archaism. They feel that modern men

cannot hold such an idea. But the men of the OT had no such inhibitions. For them 'God is angry with the wicked every day' (Psalm 7:11). They had no doubt that sin inevitably arouses the strongest reaction from God. God is not to be accused of moral flabbiness. He is vigorously opposed to evil in every shape and form while he may be 'slow to anger' (Nehemiah 9:17), his anger is yet certain in the face of sin. We may even read 'The Lord is slow to anger, and abounding in steadfast love, forgiving iniquity and transgression, but he will by no means clear the guilty' (Numbers 14:18). Even in a passage dealing with the longsuffering of God his refusal to condone guilt finds mention. The thought that God is slow to anger is to men of the OT far from being a truism. It is something wonderful and surpassing. It is awe-inspiring and totally unexpected. God who has provided the only means by which sinful man may be, and can be, saved from his sinful state.[10]

If this is so, then why is there still a hell filled with sinners? It is because man has refused to repent of his sin and believe in the sinless Son of God's work on the cross as the only hope for salvation from the condemnation of sin, which is hell. Faith, rather than believing in something you know is not so, is rather a trust in, a commitment to, a dependence upon and a worship of the One True God who alone can deliver sinful man from the condemnation of sin: hell.

The cross also displays God's grace and mercy. God's unmerited favor toward guilty sinners is expressed in Ephesians 2:1–9.

> And you were dead in the trespasses and sins in which you once walked, following the course of this world, following the prince of the power of the air, the spirit that is now at work in the sons of disobedience—among whom we all once lived in the passions of our flesh, carrying out the desires of the body and the mind, and were by nature children of wrath, like the rest of mankind. But God, being rich in mercy, because of the great love with which he loved us, even when we were dead in our trespasses, made us alive together with Christ—by grace you have been saved—and raised us up with him and seated us with him in the heavenly places in Christ Jesus, so that in the coming ages he might show the immeasurable riches of his grace in kindness toward us in Christ Jesus. For by grace you have been saved through faith. And this is not your own doing; it is the gift of God, not a result of works, so that no one may boast. For we are his workmanship, created in Christ Jesus for good works, which God prepared beforehand, that we should walk in them.[11]

The godslayer referred to a statement by nineteenth-century Swiss psychologist Carl Gustav Jung that "the popular faith in words is a veritable disease of the mind." However, I find it ironic that Jung, and the godslayer, use words to articulate and express their faith in their own personal perspectives in the belief of a non-god.

The word of the cross provides the only message of deliverance from the wrath of God. Without the cross there can be no forgiveness of sins. The cross, the righteousness of Christ, and the grace of God alone provides the basis for God forgiving the sinner of his sin. This is the gospel. This is what the godslayer does not understand. Do you?

9

Letter Four

The god of Christians is a father who is a great deal more concerned about his apples than he is about his children.

—Diderot

Again, you amaze me for a defender of god; I can only wonder why you only preach to the choir with faulty logic that assumes its conclusions. Also, you think only from the Bible. Putting aside for a minute the question of why a "perfect" god would give us a bible replete with contradictions, facts contrary to popular science, and obscurity in explanations, one can only marvel at the logic that says, "The Bible is true because it says it is true and therefore it must be true."

It is no wonder that apostasy is growing by leaps and bounds as you ignore the hard questions and wrote only of trivial issues of doctrine. I know why you ignore the hard issues of life. It is because you know you have no answer and the purported religious dogma has only unsubstantial responses, erroneous syllogisms, and must retreat to blind faith for justification of its empty philosophy.

In a minute I will challenge you to answer a real question, but first I submit the following examples showing how faulty is your Bible as to its god.

First, Acts 20:35 claims Jesus said it was "more blessed to give than receive" in the Scriptures. Sounds good doesn't it. The only problem is that nowhere in the Scriptures does he say that. Or again in John 7:38 is says that according to Scripture "out of belly shall flow rivers of flowing water." Again, nowhere in Scriptures does this phrase occur.

Since these quoted words appear nowhere else in the bible, one can only ponder why a "perfect" god would allow such an imperfect book. One might object to these examples as trivial, and in and of themselves they are, but I could fill volumes citing all the inconsistencies, contradictions, and absurdities replete in the bible that you use for your references.

Why are these referred to cite not in the bible? Who left them out, if they ever existed in the first place? And consider Revelation 22:19 that those will be damned who take away from the Scriptures. So who should be damned? The writer of the gospel? The scribes? John? Jesus? God himself? (What an inspirational thought that is).

Second, Jesus was not the messiah prophesized. Isaiah 9:6–7 states very clearly that the prince of peace messiah would bring with him endless peace (which coincidently contradicts Revelation that the messiah's return to wage terrible war). As we all know, after Jesus' reported appearance there has never been an age of peace.

From these examples, we can see how faulty is the bible as a reference and I haven't even mentioned it saying the earth is the center of the universe, or being flat, or talking donkeys, or slugs melting or any of the other absurdities.

Don't you see the fallacy of your logic? Just because something is written and says that it is true, doesn't make it true. This is especially valid when there is no empirical verification of its claims. But still you persist in claiming the bible is true. Don't you see the total emptiness of your assertion?

Now for a challenge. I dare you do give an honest and credible answer to the following. It is a simple question but no one religion, or priest, or rabbi has been able to answer: why do people have to die?

This should be simple if your god was honest and didn't always hide behind obscure parables and his eternal silence as if he feared man thinking for himself.

Do not give me that Adam/Eve myth which is so totally illogical as to be incomprehensible and unbelievable. Nor will I accept the fiction of original sin that man is evil just because he was born (the way god wanted him)?

Also, I will consider either of the following two responses to be proof of your intellectual failure and cowardice. First, that god is infinite and man is finite so we cannot possibly comprehend his thinking. Second, the argument that although it makes no sense, we must have blind faith and assume god is good and rational.

There is your challenge. Answer for once a real question. I await to see if you have the courage.

—The godslayer

Amy Orr-Ewing writes, "The Bible is a controversial book that evokes both devotion and derision. It has inspired some of the greatest thinkers this world has ever known and attracted the hostility of others. It takes a central role in any study of Western civilization and touches the most unlikely of souls."[1]

The godslayer attacks any belief and devotion to the Scriptures by saying that to do so evidences faulty logic that assumes its conclusions. He attacks the logic that the Bible is true because it says it is true and therefore it must be true. As previously noted, the Bible's claim to its own truthfulness is "one" evidence of many as to being the Word of God. It is not the only evidence cited in a previous chapter of this book, but it is the only one the godslayer addresses.

How does he deal with the Bible's claim that it is true? Does he set forth evidence that disputes such a contention? On the contrary, he makes claims that the Bible is full of contradictions, that it contains information contrary to popular science and contains obscure explanations. He seems to be arguing that the Bible is false because he says it is false and therefore it must be false.

In a previous chapter we addressed the Bible's complementary perspective to science as it pertains to the universe. The Bible does not contradict science; rather it seems to be that science, or certain scientists, seek to contradict the Bible.

Regarding the examples given concerning apparent contradictions found in the Scriptures, let us examine each of the passages he cites. Upon closer examination, they do not appear to be as difficult as one would think.

Acts 20:35 says, "In all things I have shown you that by working hard in this way we must help the weak and remember the words of the Lord Jesus, how he himself said, 'It is more blessed to give than to receive.'"[2] Luke records the person who is making these statements is the Apostle Paul.

Notice how the godslayer frames his statement. He says Acts 20:35 claims Jesus said it was "more blessed to give than receive" in the Scriptures. Sounds good doesn't it. The only problem he contends is that nowhere in the Scriptures does he say that.

The godslayer is correct. Nowhere in the Scriptures does Jesus say that. But Acts 20:35 does not say the Scriptures record the statement Paul attributes to Jesus. Rather, Paul refers to common knowledge that Jesus personally said "it was more blessed to give than to receive." There is no contradiction or inconsistency in this text.

In fact, the Apostle John alludes to many more statements and incidents in Jesus's life that the Scriptures do not record. John 21:25 says, "Now there are also many other things that Jesus did. Were every one of them to be written, I suppose that the world itself could not contain the books that would be written."[3] Is John exaggerating?

Perhaps! However, he makes his point. The Bible in general and the Gospels in particular, do not record everything Jesus said and did.

Let us now turn our attention to John 7:38, which says, "Whoever believes in me, as the Scripture has said, 'Out of his heart will flow rivers of living water.'" Now this he said about the Spirit, whom those who believed in him were to receive, for as yet the Spirit had not been given, because Jesus was not yet glorified."[4] The godslayer contends that nowhere in Scriptures does this phrase occur. Unlike Acts 20:35, Luke 7:38 uses the phrase "as the Scripture has said."[5] Therefore, it must be noted where in the Scriptures this phrase occurs of which Jesus makes reference.

The image is one of salvation and cleansing from sin. Jesus made reference to this metaphorical image in John 4 in His conversation with the woman at the well. Living water flowing from one's inner most being is symbolic of new life in Christ. It is also a reference to the Jewish tradition of water pouring, illustrating the eschatological (End Times) rivers of living water prophesied in Ezekiel 47:1–12 and Zechariah 13:1. Jesus's statement, and John's record of the same, is supported by these Scripture references.

Additionally, I will not reply to the godslayer's apparent sarcastic comments concerning Revelation 22:19, but I will respond to his question arising from Isaiah 9:6. He says that Jesus was not the messiah prophesized in Isaiah 9:6–7. He comments that the prince of peace messiah would bring with him endless peace (which coincidently contradicts Revelation that the messiah's return to wage terrible war). As we all know, after Jesus's reported appearance, there has never been an age of peace.

The title Prince of Peace alludes to the Millennial Kingdom, which will follow the second coming of Christ. The government of Emmanuel will perpetuate peace. This environment of peace and tranquility is also mentioned in Isaiah 2, 11:1–9 and in Micah 4. It will be a kingdom of peace and righteousness.

Yet that foretaste of the peace to which Isaiah refers is found in the sinner's justification by grace alone, through faith alone, in Christ alone. The Apostle Paul says in Romans 5:1, "Therefore, since we have been justified by faith, we have peace with God through our Lord Jesus Christ."[6] This is not a subjective peace but rather an objective and external reality here and now for every believer in Christ. Each converted sinner has come into a peace relationship with God through Jesus Christ, the Prince of Peace.

God is at war with every sinner because of their rebellion toward and hatred of God (Rom. 1:18; Exod. 22:24; Deut. 32:21–22; Ps. 7:1–11; John 3:36; Eph. 5:1–6). However, the first great result of God declaring the believing righteous through the imputed righteousness of Jesus Christ is peace. The war between God and the sinner is over. This is what the Bible calls reconciliation (Rom. 5:10–11; 2 Cor. 5:18–20).

This is the peace that is lacking in the lives of those who refuse to repent and believe in Jesus Christ. They may appear to have the world on a string. They may even say that they do. However, as you examine their lives more closely, you see an inner turmoil that drugs, alcohol, sex, money, and possessions cannot overcome. They have no peace because they do not know the Prince of Peace.

The godslayer finds fault with me, and I must assume with others, who think only from the Bible. I do not think only from the Bible, but I do hold to the presupposition, and supporting evidence, that the Bible is the Word of God. Therefore, it is the preeminent truth that fills my life as a Christian. Why should it not? I am a Biblicist. I am a Christian. I am a preacher of the gospel. It would be rather contradictory of me to preach from a book that I do not personally believe is true, and it is totally consistent to submit my life and living to the doctrines that are contained therein.

He says the Bible has no empirical verification to its claims. Empirical means experiential, observable, and practical. What about the countless lives that daily display empirical evidence to the Bible's veracity? Lives that I hear weekly that have been changed by the truth of the gospel.

I speak of those who minister to students, to unwed mothers, to the sick, and to the dying. I speak of those who display the Bible's truth in their marriages, to their children, and to those within their community. I speak of those who display biblical ethics in the most difficult of circumstances. I speak of employers who seek to be godly examples to their employees. I speak of employees who endeavor to be godly witnesses to their employers. I speak of those who serve in full-time ministry who not only talk the talk but also walk the walk.

Are there historical and present day examples of Christian failure, inconsistency, and hypocrisy? Of course there is! In fact, the Bible itself contains many examples of such. That is an evidence of the Bible being truth. The Bible presents people as they really are: sinners saved by God's grace. We should neither shy away from acknowledging those failures nor fail to acknowledge failures of our own. However, God forgives us of those sins even though we may still face the consequences of our sinful choices. We learn from those failures and seek to press on unto godliness and Christ-likeness in spite of failure.

These are but some of the hard issues to which the Bible speaks. These are not trivial issues of doctrine. Neither do the Scriptures give us trite and trivial answers. The doctrinal answers may not be acceptable to the godslayers in the world, but the Bible says they would not be (1 Cor. 2:14). The Christian's responsibility is to present the truth. It is God's responsibility to make that truth come alive within the soul of the unbeliever (1 Cor. 3:1–3).

What is the godslayers underlying worldview? There is an underlying perspective that frames the godslayer's thinking and conclusions: the way he looks at life. It is because of this pattern of thinking that the godslayer comes to the conclusions he holds. Unless we understand how the godslayers in our lives process their ideas, we will be hard-pressed to answer their objections.

The godslayer gives every evidence of being a naturalist. He rejects the belief in the One True God of the Bible; he refuses to submit to God's Word and its answers and believes that life and living must be figured out on the basis of man's human intelligence and logic. In his challenge to me at the conclusion of his letter concerning why do people have to die, he does so by imposing his own boundaries upon my answers.

He does not want me to respond by citing Adam and Eve and the events of Genesis 3. He does not accept what he refers to as the fiction of original sin. He will not consider as a legitimate answer the infinity of God or that believers must just accept what God says based upon, in his words, blind faith.

The godslayer not only wants to ask the questions, he gives the parameters regarding the answers. He gives the impression that instead of desiring a dialogue, he is content with a self-confident monologue. Why is this seemingly always the case with those who not only attack the Scriptures but also those who believe in the Bible? He is great at posing questions but does not seem interested in honest feedback. What is the godslayer afraid of?

Why do people die? The Bible gives ample instruction. The godslayers of this world will not like the answer, but here it is. People die because they are sinners and because they sin. Ezekiel 18:4 says, "Behold, all souls are mine; the soul of the father as well as the soul of the son is mine: the soul who sins shall die."[7] This is reiterated in Ezekiel 18:20.

The Apostle Paul writes in Romans 6:20–23:

> For when you were slaves of sin, you were free in regard to righteousness. But what fruit were you getting at that time from the things of which you are now ashamed? For the end of those things is death. But now that you have been set free from sin and have become slaves of God, the fruit you get leads to sanctification and its end, eternal life. For the wages of sin is death, but the free gift of God is eternal life in Christ Jesus our Lord.[8]

The godslayer will probably not accept this succinct answer, because it comes from the Bible. However, it is the truth. Does this reveal my lack of intelligence or naiveté? I believe not. Sinful people physically die. It is only through the death, burial, and resurrection of Jesus Christ that sinful people can be brought from death to life (John 5:24–25). This is the only hope for life beyond the grave.

I cannot make the godslayer believe this. Only God can. However, I am responsible to give an answer for the hope within me (1 Pet. 3:15). I am responsible to answer an atheist's questions. I hope that the Lord will enable the godslayer to hear, listen, and understand.

Letter Five

The Christian religion is a parody on the worship of the sun in which they put a man called Christ in the place of the sun and pays him the adoration originally paid to the sun.

—Thomas Paine

Since you choose the path of intellectual cowardice and refuse to consider the hard questions (which is no surprise since religion's responses are so disingenuous and illogical) and retreat back to the unoriginal Christian dogma of biblical inerrancy and resurrection mythology, I propose the following information for your consideration of the validity of your beliefs.

Born of a virgin on December 25, heralded by a bright star in the east, adored by three kings, a teacher at twelve, baptized and ministering by age 30, twelve disciples, did miracles like healing the sick and walking on water, called "lamb of God" and god's anointed one. Called a "good shepherd," betrayed, crucified, dead three days and resurrected. This was the sun god Horus of Egypt, 3,000 B.C.

Resurrected! This was the god Attis of Greece, 1,000 B.C.

Born of a virgin on December 25, signaled by a star in the east, performed miracles with his disciples, was crucified and resurrected. This was the god Krishna of India, 900 B.C.

Born of a virgin on December 25, performed miracles including changing water into wine, called "king of kings," the "alpha and omega," crucified and resurrected. This was Dionysus of Greece, 200 B.C.

Born of a virgin on December 25, had twelve disciples, did miracles, called the "truth and the light," crucified, dead three days, and resurrected. This was the god Mithra of Persia, 1,200 B.C.

Do you see a pattern here? Is there anything of the mythology that Christianity did not copy? Actually, there is. The only original contribution of Christianity to religious thought was that of an eternal hell where this "loving god" would torture forever those who did not blindly follow his nonsense.

Anyway, ancient man first worshipped the sun because to him it was life. He associated his gods with the sun, its movement and the stars and this astrological foundation became imbued with dogma. For example, 12 disciples, the 12 twelve tribes of Israel, the 12 signs of the Zodiac. So let us ponder this.

1. *The star of wonder. The brightest star in the east is Sirius which in the winter solstice on December 24 is in perfect alignment with the three stars on Orion's belt. These three stars in ancient times were known as the three kings. On December 25, they all point directly to the place of the sunrise; that is the birth of the sun god or the son of god.*

2. *Virgin Mary. The Virgin Mary was originally the constellation Virgo whose symbol is an altered M. Not surprisingly, the virgin mother of Buddha was Maya. Virgo was called "the loaf of bread" and was always pictured with a sheaf of wheat. The name of Bethlehem means "loaf of bread."*

3. *Dead three days. During the winter the sun moves south until December 22 and stays in the same spot for three days. On December 25, it moves north one degree and then moves northward. Hence, three days of death of the sun and then its resurrection. However, the ancients didn't actually have their celebration until Easter time because then the sun day is first longer than the night.*

4. *The Bible original? In the temple of Luxor in Egypt are images of Horus during the annunciation, the Immaculate Conception, the Holy Ghost impregnating the virgin mother, etc. The plagiarism is obvious and this was inscribed fifteen centuries before the asserted Christ.*

5. *The Ten Commandments. These were taken outright from the Spell 135 of the Egyptian Book of the Dead. Baptism afterlife, final judgment, virgin birth, crucifixion, resurrection, arc of the covenant, holy communion... all were Egyptian ideas long Christianity.*

6. *Jesus. Isn't it odd that a miracle worker who rose from the dead and ascended into the sky started a major religion...and that there is no non-biblical evidence of him? Of the 40 major historical writers of that age, none of them mentions him and the one that does, Josephus, has long since been discredited as a forgery.*

So Christianity is mere plagiarism and not based on truth but is rather a mere political establishment to hold man hostage through its borrowed superstition. After the Council of Nicaea, all Christianity has done for 1,600 years is to enter in Dark Ages and promote such "lofty" events as the crusades and the inquisition.

It empowers those who know truth but use myth to manipulate and control society and to extort from their believers their money knowing they profit from this lie. Consider this then as you live off the labor of others; you have betrayed us. You are a thief among us. You have deceived us and remember in a Dante like fashion, the lowest circles of hell are reserved for the traitors of man.

—The godslayer

The godslayer's skepticism toward the Scriptures is unpalatable. It is unpleasant, and it is conspicuous. The irony is that while he is skeptical toward biblical truth, he would have us believe his convictions and those of ancient myths. While he questions my commitment to God and His Word, he appears to want every person to unquestioningly believe his philosophy and that of ancient mythology. What is the godslayer's worldview? Why does he attack Christianity the way in which he does?

I submit the godslayer, along with being a naturalist, is also a postmodernist. Postmodernism is a contemporary worldview that is skeptical of any and all absolute truth. The postmodernist denies absolute truth. Postmodernism rejects the certainty of modernism. The postmodernist approaches life with a disillusioned and skeptical outlook. The postmodernist is suspicious of any and all who would question his beliefs while at the same time attacking others for their beliefs.

Amy Orr-Ewing writes, "That there is no ultimate meaning in any (biblical) text has become extremely powerful in a postmodern context, and it has enormous implications for any communication of the gospel."[1] Ewing continues by stating "the postmodern questioner is likely to operate from a base of suspicion and skepticism when presented with a text such as the Bible, which makes a clear claim to authoritative truth."[2]

The postmodern does not believe in an overarching system of truth within any cultural context. He rejects a meta-narrative that is "a large scale theory that seeks to make sense of the world, such as the onward and upward progress of the human race throughout history, the confidence that everything is explicable by science or the possibility of absolute freedom."[3]

For the postmodern, truth is only truth within a particular context of culture. You have your truth and I have my truth. However, in making such a claim, the postmodern is making an absolute truth statement. He says there is no such thing as absolute truth, and in making such a statement, he is affirming an absolute truth belief system.

Ewing summarizes the dilemma existing for the postmodernist. "The fundamental problem with this challenge to the Bible—this suspicion of authority and rejection of meta-narrative—is that it is essentially inconsistent. That is, we soon discover when probing this denial of overarching stories (*truth*) that an exception is made for the overarching idea that there are no overarching ideas! Postmodern skeptics critique all worldviews except their own."[4]

It should be noted that while the term postmodernism may be recent, its philosophy is as old as the Scriptures themselves. In fact, the Bible goes so far as to accurately articulate the doctrine of postmodernism. Where? The concept of postmodernism is found in the final verse of the final chapter the Old Testament Book of Judges.

Judges 21:15 states, "In those days there was no king in Israel. Everyone did what was right in his own eyes."[5]

During a particularly bleak time in Israel's history, before the monarchies of Saul, David, and Solomon, this concluding verse demonstrates how permeating sin can become within a culture and a country. The corresponding result of unchecked sin within society is the rejection of God's absolute truth. As was the case in Israel from 1398 BC–1043 BC, so it is today.

The godslayer packs an awful lot of information in one brief letter. On the surface, he seems to make a compelling argument attacking the historicity of Jesus Christ and Christianity. He refers to many mythological tales that seemingly parallels much that is contained in the conception, birth, earthly life, and ministry of Jesus Christ. However, while he does not find fault with these aforementioned myths, he finds great contention with the Bible. The only recourse that we have is to answer his contentions point by point.

However, the believer should not be intimidated by any godslayer's contentions and assertions. His line of reasoning may appear to be recent and contemporary, but the methodology behind his assertions are acknowledged by both the Apostle Peter and the Apostle Paul. They are ancient and have always been with us.

For example, Peter writes in 2 Peter 1:16–21 the following:

> For we did not follow cleverly devised myths when we made known to you the power and coming of our Lord Jesus Christ, but we were eyewitnesses of his majesty. For when he received honor and glory from God the Father, and the voice was borne to him by the Majestic Glory, "This is my beloved Son, with whom I am well pleased," we ourselves heard this very voice borne from heaven, for we were with him on the holy mountain. And we have the prophetic word more fully confirmed, to which you will do well to pay attention as to a lamp shining in a dark place, until the day dawns and the morning star rises in your hearts, knowing this first of all, that no prophecy of Scripture comes from someone's own interpretation. For no prophecy was ever produced by the will of man, but men spoke from God as they were carried along by the Holy Spirit.[6]

Peter's use of the Greek word for myths (μύθοις) refers to mythical stories about gods, goddesses, and miracles that existed during his lifetime. They were recognized as fictional false and inventions. He understood that false teachers would seek to discredit biblical truth by creating their own fanciful fairy tales. Some commentators contend that false teachers may have accused the apostle of fabricating false teachings about Jesus Christ. They might contend Peter was seeking fame, power, and fortune. Regardless, the myths Peter is referring to must be seeking to repudiate the historicity and authenticity of Jesus Christ, not only his person but also his ministry.

False prophets always seek to distort the gospel by fabricating myths of their own. What is a myth? As Simon Kistemaker explains, "A myth is a story which man has formulated to express his own desires without any reference to reality."[7] All myths are man-centered in their focus and therefore void of any life changing power. "By contrast, Scripture originates with God. The Bible is divinely inspired, rooted in history, and unquestionably true. The gospel message redeems man from sin and glorifies God."[8]

In his pastoral epistles, the Apostle Paul similarly reacts to the myths he encountered. In I Timothy 1:3–4 he says, "As I urged you when I was going to Macedonia, remain at Ephesus so that you may charge certain persons not to teach any different doctrine, nor to devote themselves to myths and endless genealogies, which promote speculations rather than the stewardship from God that is by faith."[9]

1 Timothy 4:1–2 states, "Now the Spirit expressly says that in later times some will depart from the faith by devoting themselves to deceitful spirits and teachings of demons, through the insincerity of liars whose consciences are seared."[10] Deceitful spirits may refer to the direct and indirect work of demons. The teachings of demons refer not necessarily to exclusively demons themselves but to the false teaching they propagate.

In 2 Timothy 4:3–4, the apostle acknowledges what often occurred in churches during his lifetime and what occurs during our own. He writes, "For the time is coming when people will not endure sound teaching, but having itching ears they will accumulate for themselves teachers to suit their own passions, and will turn away from listening to the truth and wander off into myths. As for you, always be sober-minded, endure suffering, do the work of an evangelist, fulfill your ministry." [11]

Finally, in Titus 1:10–14 the apostle says,

> For there are many who are insubordinate, empty talkers and deceivers, especially those of the circumcision party. They must be silenced, since they are upsetting whole families by teaching for shameful gain what they ought not to teach. One of the Cretans, a prophet of their own, said, "Cretans are always liars, evil beasts, lazy gluttons." This testimony is true. Therefore rebuke them sharply, that they may be sound in the faith, not devoting themselves to Jewish myths and the commands of people who turn away from the truth. [12]

King Solomon said in Ecclesiastes 1:9–10, "What has been is what will be, and what has been done is what will be done, and there is nothing new under the sun. Is there a thing of which it is said, 'See, this is new'? It has been already in the ages before us." [13] What was true for Solomon in his quest for ultimate meaning to life is applicable to those attacking the truth of God today. Those who seek to undermine the truth of God in general, and the incarnation of Jesus Christ in particular, have always been with us. The Scriptures do not shy away from this acknowledgement, and neither should we.

Pontius Pilate interrogated Jesus hours before He would be condemned and sentenced to die by the Roman governor. Pilate asked Jesus, "So, you are a king?" Jesus answered, "You say correctly that I am a king. For this I have been born and for this I have come into the world, to testify to the truth. Everyone who is of the truth hears my voice." Pilate said to him, "What is truth?"[14]

What is truth? The word generally used means "constant, permanent, faithful, reliable." God above all is true, that is, real and reliable (Isa. 65:16; Jer. 10:10); people are to seek God's truth (Ps. 25:5; 51:6; 86:11). People are admonished to judge truly, and the lack of truth is lamented (Zech. 8:16; Isa. 59:14–15). Prophecies may be true or false (1 Kings 10:6–7). In all these instances, the emphasis is upon reliability; something or someone true will stand up under testing. For the Jews, truth was moral and relational, but not intellectual.

However in the New Testament, the Greek word for truth is primarily concerned with the intellectual: truth is known, trusted, or relied upon. The New Testament draws on both Greek and Old Testament Jewish understandings for its definition and understanding of truth. The word is found mainly in the Pauline writings and especially the Gospel and Letters of John.

Paul uses the word in the Greek sense (Rom. 1:18), but he also uses it with Hebrew meanings: truth is to be obeyed (Rom. 2:8; Gal. 5:7); truth proves reliable (2 Cor. 7:14; 11:10); and its opposite is malice and evil (1 Cor. 5:8). One is to know the truth (1 Tim. 4:3; 2 Tim. 2:25) and avoid false beliefs (2 Tim. 2:18; 4:4).

The Apostle John builds on the Jewish understanding that God is true or real (John 3:33; 7:28). Christ reveals God and therefore reveals truth (John 8:26, 40; 18:37). Christ himself is full of grace and truth (John 1:14, 17). Indeed, he is "the way, and the truth, and the life" (John 14:6); he is the true light and the true vine (John 1:9; 15:1). Christ also sends the Counselor, the Spirit of truth (John 15:26). Thus, the Jewish understanding of God as truth extends to Christ and the Holy Spirit.

The Lord guides the believer into truth (John 16:13), and the believer is to worship God in spirit and truth (John 4:23–24). Having a personal relationship with Christ as Savior enables one to know the truth and so be free (John 8:32).

Regarding the existence of myths that seek to undermine or replace the gospel, what is the core message from the Word of God that the Holy Spirit of truth (John 14:16) communicates through the people of God? I respectfully submit the following as the core message of God's Word: the Gospel of truth.

1. God exists. Genesis 1:1.

2. God is holy (Father, Son, and Holy Spirit). Isaiah 6:1–7; Leviticus 11:44; 19:1–2; 20:1–7; 1 Peter 1:15–16.

3. Man or mankind is radically corrupted by sin: sinful by nature and behavior. Psalm 14; 36:1; 53:1–3; 140:1–3; Isaiah 59; Romans 3:8–20; Ephesians 2:1–3; Colossians 2:13–15.

4. God the Son was conceived and born a sinless man. Matthew 1:18–25; Luke 1:26–38; 2:8–14; John 1:14; Acts 2:22–36; Philippians 2:5–11; 1 John 4:1–3

5. God the Son, the God/Man, lived a sinless, righteous life while physically on earth. Acts 3:14; 2 Corinthians 5:21; Hebrews 4:15; 7:26; 1 Peter 2:22; 1 John 3:5.

6. God the Son died on the cross providing substitutionary atonement for sinners. Isaiah 52:13–53:12; John 10:15; Romans 3:21–26; Galatians 3:10–14; Colossians 2:13–15; Hebrews 9:11–14; 1 Peter 2:24.

7. God the Son rose from the dead conquering death, hell, and grave. John 2:13–22; 5:226–29; 14:19; Acts 2:22–24; Romans 1:1–4; 4:24–25; 6:5–10; 1 Corinthians 15:1–4; 20, 23.

8. God the Son ascended to the right hand of the Father. Matthew 28:6; Luke 24:38–39; Acts 2:30–31; Romans 4:25; 8:34; Hebrews 7:25; 9:24; 1 John 2:1.

9. God the Son will return to the earth in power, might, and glory. Acts 1:9–11; 1 Thessalonians 4:1318; Revelations 20.

10. Salvation for sinners, from the penalty, power and eventually the presence of sin and its corresponding judgment, is offered by God by grace alone, through faith alone in Christ alone and therefore the sinner is declared righteous, given eternal life, and adopted into the family of God. Romans 3:25; 5:1–9; 2 Corinthians 5:14–15; 1 Peter 2:24; 3:18.

11. As the mediator between God and man (1 Tim. 2:5), the head of His body the church (Eph. 1:22; 5:23; Col. 1:18), and the coming universal King who will reign on the throne of David (Isa. 9:6–7; Ezek. 37:24–28; Luke 1:31–33), He is the final judge of all who fail to place their trust in Him as Lord and Savior (Matt. 25:14–46; Acts 17:30–31).

One of the more increasingly imperative disciplines Christians must embrace is separating fact from fiction regarding the incarnation of Christ. Too many people, even believers, have difficulty distinguishing between the biblical truths of the birth of Jesus Christ from the fables that increasingly dominate the Christmas holiday season. More is known about Rudolph the Red Nose Reindeer than Jesus our Blessed Redeemer. Too often the birth of Christ is known more for a Little Drummer Boy than Mary's Little Boy Child. Christmas has become more about what Santa can give than the truth that God so loved the world that He gave His only begotten Son (John 3:16).

While admittedly there are similarities between Jesus's incarnation and non-Christian religions and mythology, the birth of Jesus Christ is uniquely different. Unlike the various myths the godslayer mentions, the Bible presents the incarnation as a real, historical event (John 1:1–18; Phil. 2:5–11). It also depicts Jesus's incarnation as permanent. He is the eternal God-Man (1 Tim. 2:5).

The godslayer accuses Christianity of being an example of plagiarism and not being based on truth. He contends that Christianity is rather all about being a mere political establishment to hold man hostage through its borrowed superstitions. However, does Christianity borrow all these so-called superstitions, or is it rather the other way around? Is it rather more probable that pagan societies have borrowed from biblical truth and perverted it for their own gains? It is more logical and historical to contend that rather than Christianity plagiarizing pagan myths, pagan societies have plagiarized biblical truth for their own intentions.

While evolutionists insist the earth is billions of years old, the biblical account of creation argues for a much later date. While the exact date of creation cannot be determined with any degree of finality, we can, through the genealogies listed in Genesis, come to a logical and biblically consistent conclusion.

The Genesis record contains a genealogy in chapters five, ten, and eleven. This record traces the development of the human race from Adam to Abram (Abraham). It contains the exact ages of those listed and when their children were born. "Archbishop James Ussher did a careful analysis of the genealogies and concluded that the date for Adam's creation was 4004 B.C."[15] This is also taking into account possible gaps, even though there is no evidence of such gaps existing in the Genesis genealogies of chapters five, ten, and eleven.

One secular Web site, not in any way a Christian sponsored resource, cites the following regarding the date of creation.

> Many efforts have been made to determine the Biblical date of creation, yielding a variety of results. Two dominant dates for creation using such models exist, about 5500 BC and about 4000 BC. These were calculated from the genealogies in two versions of the Bible, with most of the difference arising from two versions of Genesis. The older dates are based on the Greek Septuagint. The later dates are based on the Hebrew Masoretic text. The patriarchs from Adam to Terah, the father of Abraham, were often 100 years older when they begat their named son in

the Septuagint than they were in the Hebrew or the Vulgate (Genesis 5, 11). The net difference between the two genealogies of Genesis was 1466 years (ignoring the "second year after the flood" ambiguity), which is virtually all of the 1500–year difference between 5500 BC and 4000 BC. For example, the period of creation to the Flood is derived using the genealogical table of the ten patriarchs listed in Genesis 5, and 7:6, called the generations of Adam. According to the Masoretic Text, this period consists of 1,656 years, and this dating is also followed by Western Christian Bibles derived from the Latin Vulgate. However, according to the Samaritan texts the period is 1,307 years, and according to the Septuagint (Codex Alexandrinus, Elizabeth Bible) it is 2,262 years. [60] J. Usher agrees with the dating until the birth of Abraham, which he argues took place when Terah was 130, and not 70 as is the direct reading of Genesis 11:26, thus adding 60 years to his chronology for events postdating Abraham.[16]

Why is this information so important? The earliest date the godslayer submits in referring to the incarnation myths occurs in Egypt in 3000 BC. This is a thousand years after creation and God's subsequent promise to Adam and Eve of a Savior contained in Genesis 3:15: "I will put enmity between you and the woman, and between your offspring and her offspring; he shall bruise your head, and you shall bruise his heel."[17]

Even with this brief description called the *proto evangelium*, we witness the seeds of ancient nations borrowing from biblical truth for their doctrines, not only from the verbal transmission of God's revelation but also from the biblical recorded text rather than the Biblicist borrowing from theirs. Mankind to this day continues to question and doubt God's Word.

In addressing these ancient myths, we must ask whether Jesus was really born on December 25. No one truly knows but God when Jesus was born. There remains no historical record as to the exact day and date of His birth. According to some scholars, the possibility that He was born on December 25 is highly unlikely due to the fact that shepherds were abiding in the fields watching over their flocks of sheep by night (Luke 2:8–14) and they would not have done so during the winter. As Dr. William Hendrickson comments, "The sheep were at pasture and at this season of the year many roads in that region are impassable. No government would have forced people to travel then to the places where they must be registered."[18]

However, there are those who contend that sheep are found in the Judean fields even during the winter months. Additionally, there are those who argue that traveling in Israel during December can be accomplished if the winter is mild and rains are not torrential.

How then did December 25 come to be known and observed as Jesus's birthday? The decision to observe

December 25 as the birth date of Jesus Christ occurred in the fourth century during the reign of the Roman Emperor Constantine. He was the first Christian emperor and ruled AD 306–337. It was in AD 336 that Constantine decreed the birth date of Jesus Christ should coincide with the pagan festival Saturnalia. The festival celebrated the return of the sun after the increasing days of darkness.

Saturnalia was marked by gift giving, feasting, parades, special music, lighted candles, and green trees. Christians at this time, some commentators explain, reacted to the Christianized festival with equal parts of enjoyment and rejection. There probably were those who celebrated the birth of Christ during the festival while others would refrain from what they viewed as the paganizing of Jesus's incarnation. As one pastor writes, "Some church leaders, such as John Chrysostom (A.D. 347–407) rebuked Christians for adopting a pagan holiday."[19]

The first documented controversy regarding Christmas began in the 1640s when England was ruled by a Puritan Parliament. The Puritans sought to remove many elements of the holiday they believed were not biblical in origin. In 1647, Parliament banned the celebration of Christmas for a time of fasting and prayer. They believed the holiday was filled with immoral and lustful behavior. Scottish Presbyterians agreed. However, the edict was met with rioting by pro-Christmas protestors. The restoration of Charles II to the English throne effectively ended the ban.

The controversy over Christmas continued in the American colonies. Puritans in New England were not in favor of Christmas, and it was outlawed in Boston during 1659–1681. It would not be widely viewed as fashionable until the mid-1800s. It was relegated as a secondary religious holiday when compared to Epiphany and Easter.

Many believe Christmas' popularity is owed to Charles Dickens and his classic story *A Christmas Carol*. It is believed Dickens did much to convey the idea of Christmas as a time for family and generosity to the poor and destitute. Additionally, C. Clement Moore's poem "A Visit from St. Nicholas" remains for many the quintessential take on the image of Santa Claus, his eight tiny reindeer and Christmas being a time for receiving gifts from this jolly, old elf.

The debate concerning the Christmas holiday continues to this day. Certain religious groups continue to reject it outright. This includes certain reformed and fundamentalist churches along with other Protestant evangelicals. Others embrace it as an opportunity to share the gospel. Even so, December 25 remains the traditional date for the birthday of Christ.

Of the many essential doctrines contained in Scripture, few engineer such controversy as the virgin birth of Christ. It seems that whenever an attack upon the inerrancy of Scripture occurs, one of the first doctrines that come under particular attack is the doctrine of the virgin birth of Christ. Why?

Perhaps it is because the virgin birth points to the inherent need each sinner has for redemption and the reality that all are born in sin. The doctrine of the virgin birth assures us that Jesus Christ was conceived and born a sinless human being—the eternal God/Man. Conceived and born as such enabled him, along with a corresponding sinless and righteous life, to provide a substitutionary atonement on behalf of sinners.

Dr. James Montgomery Boice concluded that the virgin birth is significant in four major ways. First, it is significant because it is not some late addition to the Christian gospel but is present in its earliest sources. Genesis 3:15 and Isaiah 7:14 for example.

Secondly, the virgin birth was not invented by Luke, the writer of the gospel, which bears his name. Rather, Luke learned of it not only from biblical sources in the Old Testament but presumably from Mary herself.

Thirdly, it remains a fact of history in spite of people who would seek to deny it as such. Dr. Boice once commented, "We recognize that people do not like facts that fail to correspond with their own experience. If they fail to conform, these facts are presumed to have no basis and skeptics are ready to dispense with them as myth."[20]

Fourthly, the virgin birth points to the uniqueness of Jesus Christ. He was not only virgin born but was also one who resurrected from the dead. One solitary life bracketed by two great miracles. This is then the essential issue: do you believe in miracles? Yes!

Regarding the mythological treatment of the three wise men or three kings, there is so much misunderstanding regarding these mysterious visitors. Who exactly were they? Were they indeed kings from some far off land in the Orient? Did they have the names ascribed to them in various Christmas carols? Did they indeed come to the manger scene in Bethlehem the night Jesus was born? If not, where and when did they come upon the Christ child? Were there only three? We must separate biblical and historical fact from fiction.

The biblical account of the visit from these foreign visitors to Israel in the first century is found in Matthew 2. Even a superficial reading of the text dispels some of the mistaken speculations regarding their quest to worship He who was born King of the Jews.

> Now after Jesus was born in Bethlehem of Judea in the days of Herod the king, behold, wise men from the east came to Jerusalem, saying, "Where is he who has been born king of the Jews? For we saw his star when it rose and have come to worship him." When Herod the king heard this, he was troubled, and all Jerusalem with him; and assembling all the chief priests and scribes of the people, he inquired of them where the Christ was to be born. They told him, "In Bethlehem of Judea, for so it is written by the prophet: "'And you, O Bethlehem, in the land of Judah, are by

no means least among the rulers of Judah; for from you shall come a ruler who will shepherd my people Israel.'"

Then Herod summoned the wise men secretly and ascertained from them what time the star had appeared. And he sent them to Bethlehem, saying, "Go and search diligently for the child, and when you have found him, bring me word, that I too may come and worship him." After listening to the king, they went on their way. And behold, the star that they had seen when it rose went before them until it came to rest over the place where the child was. When they saw the star, they rejoiced exceedingly with great joy. And going into the house they saw the child with Mary his mother, and they fell down and worshiped him. Then, opening their treasures, they offered him gifts, gold and frankincense and myrrh. And being warned in a dream not to return to Herod, they departed to their own country by another way.[21]

The historical context of the wise men's visit is given two specific points of reference: (1) it was after Jesus was born in Bethlehem and (2) it was during the days of Herod the king. The location of Bethlehem is critical because Hebrew scholars understood that this was to be the birthplace of the coming Messiah (Micah 5:2; Matt. 2:5; John 7:42). Matthew refers to this historical and prophetical point because he was writing to Jews.

The identity of Herod was the ruler called Herod the Great. He was the first of a number of important rulers from the Herodian dynasty. This particular Herod ruled from 37–4 BC. He is believed to have been Idumean, a descendant of the Edomites, who were descendants of Esau, the eldest son of Isaac and grandson to Abraham.

Herod was a ruthless and shrewd king. He loved luxury and grand building projects. His most ambitious and well-known undertaking was the rebuilding of the temple in Jerusalem. See Matthew 24:1. That particular project alone took several decades to complete, and not until after Herod's death. See John 2:20.

It was within this historical context that wise men from the east came to Jerusalem. The word *east* must be understood in the geographical context of its relationship with Israel. Whoever these wise men were, they were coming from someplace east of Israel.

Who and what were these wise men? The word for wise men is the Greek word *magi*. The word is a name given by the Babylonians (Chaldeans), Medes, Persians, and others, to the wise men, teachers, priests, physicians, astrologers, seers, interpreters of dreams, soothsayers, and sorcerers. These oriental wise men (astrologers) came to Jerusalem.

The word *magi* (μάγοι) is in the plural form indicating to the reader that there was more than one of these wise men. However, while there was at least two, we do not with any certainty know that there were three. There may have been more than three. Also, there is no indication that they were kings, but rather men who specialized in astrology, medicine, and natural science.

They came to Jerusalem, saying, "Where is he who has been born king of the Jews? For we saw his star when it rose and have come to worship him."[22] The grammar indicates these wise men were persistently and continually asking anyone in Jerusalem the location of this one who was born king of the Jews. Why come to Jerusalem? Perhaps it is because Jerusalem was then the universally recognized capital of Israel and the logical location for a newborn king of Israel to reside.

However, there was another plausible reason for this particular location being their destination. The magi had witnessed a star rising in the east and this event prompted them to come to Jerusalem to worship the newborn monarch. Much speculation has been made as to the exact nature of this star. Was it a supernova or the alignment of several planets, which produced a particularly bright illumination in the night sky?

Could it conceivably have been the Shekinah glory of God leading and directing the magi as it led the children of Israel in the wilderness thousands of years earlier? How appropriate it seems for this to be the most logical explanation. The glory of God, which led Israel to the Promised Land, now leads the magi to the Promised Savior. This seems most plausible when the text later on says that the star led them to the exact place the child and his mother were residing (Matt. 2:9).

When Herod the king eventually heard about these foreign visitors and their inquiries, he was troubled and agitated by the news. Not only was Herod feeling threatened by a potential rival, but the citizens of Jerusalem were also concerned. They had witnessed what Herod would and could do for those he suspected of treachery. He was a murderous and ruthless man to any and all real and suspected challengers to the throne.

Herod did not know the exact location of where the newborn king could be found, but being the intelligent man that he was, he knew who to ask for such information. He assembled all the chief priests and scribes of the people, and he inquired of them where the Christ was to be born. Notice that Herod referred to the newborn as the Christ. This means the Messiah or the Anointed One of God. Herod knew who he was dealing with.

The scribes replied and told him from the Prophet Micah, "In Bethlehem of Judea, for so it is written by the prophet: And you, O Bethlehem, in the land of Judah, are by no means least among the rulers of Judah; for from you shall come a ruler who will shepherd my people Israel."[23] The scribes were the professional, biblical scholars of the day. They knew the Scriptures and found the exact Old Testament prophecy from the prophet Micah, which answered Herod's question. However, while they knew the answer to the propositional question they did not act on the information they knew. There is no biblical record of these scribes and scholars making the five mile journey from Jerusalem to Bethlehem to see if what Micah had prophesied had indeed been fulfilled. How tragic to have God's revelation and refuse to act upon it.

Before we judge the scribes too harshly, we must ask ourselves whether we fall into the same trap. Do we ever, or often, know the truth of God but fail to act or respond to the truth of God we know as truth.

Within the context of this particular chapter, and book wherein it is contained, is the more fundamental issue of responding, or not, to one who is antagonistic to the God and His truth. As a Christian, should I remain quiet and just let the godslayers I encounter stew in their own juices as it were? Or, do I respond to and act upon the truth of God when He says in 1 Peter 3:13–15, "Now who is there to harm you if you are zealous for what is good? But even if you should suffer for righteousness' sake, you will be blessed. Have no fear of them, nor be troubled, but in your hearts honor Christ the Lord as holy, always being prepared to make a defense to anyone who asks you for a reason for the hope that is in you; yet do it with gentleness and respect."[24]

This is but one example of many circumstances believers will face when we engage our minds, emotions, and wills to Gods' written revelation. Will God find us obedient or complacent? Will He find us passionate or ambivalent?

Will He find us as the wise men who actively searched and sought truth, or the scribes who knew where to look for truth but did not have the integrity of heart to personally encounter the truth they thought they knew?

The text goes on to explain that King Herod summoned the magi for a personal audience. The king was not the least bit interested in discussing international relations or domestic trade policies, but rather sought to discover how long the wise men had been on their journey. The reason for the inquiry becomes violently and tragically apparent later on in Matthew 2 when Herod, based upon that information, decrees all male children, two years old and younger in the surrounding areas of Bethlehem, to be killed (Matt. 2:16).

However, at this point in the narrative, Herod is charming and diplomatic to the magi. "And he sent them to Bethlehem, saying, 'Go and search diligently for the child, and when you have found him, bring me word, that I too may come and worship him.'"[25] I remain convinced, based upon what the text says Herod ultimately did to the many children, that he had no real intention to worship the Christ child. He shrewdly desired to find the information he sought in order to eliminate any and all potential threats to his throne and his power.

The wise men, not knowing any different, went on their way to Bethlehem. The text says, "And behold, the star that they had seen when it rose went before them until it came to rest over the place where the child was. When they saw the star, they rejoiced exceedingly with great joy."[26] This is a clear indication the uniqueness of this star. Whatever it was, it was not a fixed luminary in the galaxy or an alignment of three or more planets.

When the wise men arrived, they went into the house where the Christ child was residing. They encountered the child, not a baby, and Mary his mother. Nothing is said about Joseph being in the house at this time. Notice, that the wise men visited the family in a house and not at a stable and a manger scene surrounded by cattle and all.

Perhaps the reason for the traditional view of their being three wise men in attendance is due to the fact that they presented three types of gifts to the child. "And going into the house they saw the child with Mary his mother, and they fell down and worshiped him. Then, opening their treasures, they offered him gifts, gold and frankincense and myrrh."[26] The presenting of gifts coincided with their worship. Whoever these magi were and wherever they came from, perhaps Babylon or Persia, they acknowledged and esteemed the child in the house as one worthy of their honor and praise.

As an indication of God's sovereign leading, He warns the wise men to not return to Herod. As an indication of their acknowledgment of God, they obeyed and returned to their own country using another route that would not require them to journey into or near Jerusalem.

The final issue that needs addressing is the godslayer's contention that "there is no non-biblical evidence of Jesus Christ's existence. Of the 40 major historical writers of that age, none of them mentions him and the one that does, Josephus, has long since been discredited as a forgery." We already mentioned the number of secular historians existing during and immediately following Jesus's life on earth and their acknowledgment of His historical existence. This includes the Jewish historian Josephus.

In my research on Josephus, I have found no credible evidence that would in any way support the allegation that Josephus is discredited as a forger and his historical account a forgery. I cite but one example lauding Josephus's scholarship.

L. Michael White, Professor of Classics and Director of the Religious Studies Program at the University of Texas at Austin, in presenting the topic "Josephus, Our Primary Source," states the writings of this first-century Jewish historian are critical for reconstructing the world of Judaism into which Jesus was born. He indicates that Josephus is one of our most important sources for all the history of the time period of Jesus Christ. The primary complaint against Josephus is his tendency to insert himself into the narrative and to not keep strictly to the historical events and personalities he is documenting.

I find it interesting that the godslayer makes a pejorative statement about Josephus, along with many other subjects, but tends to not back it up with corroborating evidence. He simply expects the reader to accept his contention with no supporting evidence to give it credence.

We have sought to answer the objections the godslayer proposes against the birth narrative of Jesus Christ. While our responses may satisfy some, I realize it may not be sufficient for all. This may be due to a fundamental predisposition in whether or not the individual reading this response is wanting to know the truth concerning Jesus Christ's incarnation or not and to make a decision concerning the historicity of Christ based solely on the evidences presented.

We have continually sought to provide evidence that the Bible is a credible witness of written revelation from God. Does this extend to the Ten Commandments? This is what we will answer in our next chapter.

Letter Six!

If man was made in the image of a god, then it follows that god has man's attributes. So this god must dedicate and moreover has had an eternity to deposit his "largess" all over the heavens. So does this mean that when we go to our heavenly reward we may spend our time, since there will be nothing else to do, cavorting god's (expletive) and praising his holy stench? Maybe that's where the term "Holy (expletive)" arose.

—The godslayer

Greetings hypocrite, since you fail to lack the courage to answer any of the real questions but prefer to hide behind your bible to beguile the ignorance of the many for their money. Let me see if you are honest enough to acknowledge your own dogma…and its stupidity.

What is the last of the Ten Commandments? Don't boil a young goat in the milk of its mother. Believe it or not this prohibition from Exodus 34:26 is the official tenth commandment. From the only set of stone tablets that were called "the ten commandments." There were three sets of commandments.

The first time Moses came down from Mt. Sinai with commandments, he merely recited a list (Exodus 20:2–17), which is the version most churches today erroneously call the "Ten Commandments." Although they were not engraved on stone tablets and not called "the ten commandments."

The first set of stone tablets was given to Moses at a subsequent trip up the mountain (Exodus 31:18). In this farcical story, Moses petulantly destroyed those tablets when he saw the people worshipping the golden calf (Exodus 32:19).

So he (Moses) went back for a replacement. God told Moses, "Hew these two tablets of stone like unto the first; and I will write upon these tablets the words that were in the first tables, which thou brakest" (Exodus 34:1). Here is what was on the replacement tablets (from Exodus 34:14–26).

1. Thou shalt worship no other God.

2. Thou shalt make thee no molten gods.

3. The feast of unleavened bread shalt keep.

4. Six days you shalt work, but on the seventh day thou shalt rest.

5. Thou shalt observe the festival of weeks.

6. Thrice in the year shall all your men children appear before the Lord God.

7. *Thou shalt not offer the blood of my sacrifice with leaven.*

8. *Neither shall the sacrifice of the feast of the Passover be left until the morning.*

9. *The first of the first fruits of thy land shall thou bring unto the house of the* LORD *they God.*

10. *Thou shalt not seethe a kid in his mother's mile.*

Keep this in mind next time you are tempted to boil a goat. This list obviously differs from the one in Exodus 20 (was God's memory faulty)? But it is only this list that is called the "Ten Commandments." "And he wrote upon the tablets the words of the covenant, the Ten Commandments." (Exodus 34:28).

Ahhhhh, such relevance. Such wisdom. Such profundity. Do you still assert a divine origin of your bible? Now let us see if you have the courage to admit this divine truth before your congregation and still maintain your imaginary god had any rational validity. This is but one tiny example from the wholly babble.

—The godslayer

As previously mentioned, one of the characteristics of the postmodernist is a rejection of and distrust in any absolute truth claim. Therein is one of the reasons for their antagonism toward the Bible, God's Word. It makes the claim that it is absolute truth (John 17:17; 2 Tim. 3:16–17; 2 Pet. 1:20–21) and the postmodern theorist rejects this claim on the basis that there is no such thing as absolute truth. However, in holding such a position, the postmodernist is in effect making an absolute statement of what he considers truth. Apparently, only postmodernists who reject God's absolute truth can hold to an absolute truth system of their own making.

Regarding the Ten Commandments and exactly their specific content, the godslayer raises an interesting question. At the heart of what he is saying is whether or not the Bible can be trusted, or does it contain contradictions? If the Scriptures do indeed contain contradictions, then what portion of Scripture, if any, can indeed be trusted as truth? Or is the Bible nothing more than a book of contradictions? Does it contain errors?

The Ten Commandments that traditionally society and the church are most familiar with are found in Exodus 20:1–17. They include the following: (1) You shall have no other gods before me; (2) you shall not make for yourself a carved image, or any likeness of anything that is in heaven above, or that is in the earth beneath, or that is in the water under the earth; (3)you shall not take the name of the LORD your God in vain, for the LORD will not hold him guiltless who takes his name in vain; (4) remember the Sabbath day, to keep it holy; (5) honor your father and your mother, that your days may be long in the land that the LORD your God is giving you; (6) you shall not murder; (7) you shall not commit adultery; (8) you shall not steal; (9) you shall not bear false witness against your neighbor; and (10) you shall not covet your neighbor's house; you shall not covet your neighbor's wife, or his male servant, or his female servant, or his ox, or his donkey, or anything that is your neighbor's.

God verbally gave these words and many more in fact, when Moses encountered God on Mt. Sinai three days journey from Egypt as recorded in Exodus 19:18–25.

> Now Mount Sinai was wrapped in smoke because the LORD had descended on it in fire. The smoke of it went up like the smoke of a kiln, and the whole mountain trembled greatly. And as the sound of the trumpet grew louder and louder, Moses spoke, and God answered him in thunder. The LORD came down on Mount Sinai, to the top of the mountain. And the LORD called Moses to the top of the mountain, and Moses went up.
>
> And the LORD said to Moses, "Go down and warn the people, lest they break through to the LORD to look and many of them perish. Also let the priests who come near to the LORD consecrate themselves, lest the LORD break out against them." And Moses said to the LORD, "The people cannot come up to Mount Sinai, for you yourself warned us, saying, 'Set limits around the mountain and consecrate it.'" And the LORD said to him, "Go down, and come up bringing Aaron with you. But do not let the priests and the people break through to come up to the LORD, lest he break out against them." So Moses went down to the people and told them.[1]

It was within this context that God dictated the Ten Commandments to Moses. Known as the Decalogue, they are structured in two main categories: (1) man's vertical relationship to God (20:2–11) and (2) man's horizontal relationship within the community (20:12–17). The significance of these ten words is that "true theology and true worship, the name of God and the Sabbath, family honor, life, marriage, and property, truth and virtue are well protected."[2]

The godslayer is somewhat accurate in his accounting of not only what God gave Moses in the Ten Commandments in Exodus 20, but also when He gave them. God gave Moses His commandments, the most familiar being the ten known as the Decalogue, in Exodus 20:1–23:33. However, God did not cease to give His law following His initial utterance of the Ten Commandments. Exodus 20:18–23:23 contains many more stipulations and standards that God's people were expected to know, teach to their children and to live by them (Deut. 6:1–9). These so-called ordinances involved case law along with direct commands. They would be an expansion of the Decalogue. They would prove to be the framework for the resolution of civil disputes within the community of God's people.

These laws and ordinances addressed such subjects as personal injury (21:12–14), family relationships (21:15–17), the punishment of slaves (21:20–27), and damages to property and posterity along with appropriate compensation

(21:22–32). Other issues included personal oaths (22:11), the occult (22:18), widows and orphans (22:22), and interest loans (22:25).

Exodus 23 addressed various other laws including bribes, perjury, and any perversion of justice (23:1–9). Additionally God commanded that there be a national and annual observance of three major feasts (23:14–19). These included the Feast of the Unleavened Bread, the Feast of the Harvest (Weeks, Pentecost, or Firstfruits), and the Feast of the Ingathering (Tabernacles or Booths). Following this was God's promise that He would guarantee Israel's success as they entered the land He had prepared for them (23:20–33).

Moses recorded all these words in writing (24:1–4). This book came to be known as the Book of the Covenant (24:7a). Moses would take the book and read it aloud so all the people could hear what God had commanded. The people's response was a fervent desire to obey God's Word (24:7b).

Following Moses's ceremonial sprinkling of blood upon the people, which signified their heart obedience, Moses went up with Aaron, Nadab, Abihu (Aaron's sons), and seventy of the elders of Israel to come and meet God (24:1–2, 9–11). While there, the Lord said to Moses, "Come up to me on the mountain and wait there, that I may give you the tablets of stone, with the law and the commandment, which I have written for their instruction."[3]

It is important for us to understand that not only was there a book of the covenant, which Moses had recorded God's commandments in total, but there were also two tablets that God had given to Moses containing the Ten Commandments recorded in Exodus 20:1–17.

The godslayer's contention is whether this well-known list found in Exodus 20:1–17 is in fact the actual Ten Commandments? He states that it is not and that the actual Ten Commandments are found in Exodus 34:14–26, to which he makes reference in his letter. The question then is what exactly are the true Ten Commandments? In posing this question, the godslayer casts doubt upon the accuracy of the Bible and the believing community's understanding of it. If that is indeed his intention, then this is a question that must be answered.

Having recorded God's extensive commandments in the book of the covenant (Exod. 24:7), and having received two tablets from God containing the Ten Commandments (24:12), Moses then receives further instructions from God concerning plans for the Tabernacle (Exod. 25–27; 30) and the qualifications for the Levitical priesthood (Exod. 28–29).

It was during Moses's intimate encounter with the One True God and His law that the nation of Israel at the same time engaged in an intimate and wicked encounter with a mute idol of their desires, design, and making (Exod. 32). Upon hearing from God of this situation (Exod. 32:1–10), and entreating before God on the Israel's behalf (Exod. 32:11–14), Moses went down the mountain from the holy presence of God into the unholy presence of God's people (Exod. 32:15–18). As he does so, he carries with him the two tablets of the testimony in his hands. Written on both sides, the Bible says "the tablets were God's work, and the writing was God's writing engraved on the tablets."[4]

Upon seeing the debauchery of the Israelites and their unholy worship of the golden calf, he angrily threw down the two tablets and shattered them at the foot of the mountain (Exod. 32:19). He burned the golden calf with fire, ground it into powder, scattered it over the surface of the water, and made the Israelites drink the bitter brew (Exod. 32:20). Three thousand men forfeited their lives that day due to their persistent idolatry (Exod. 32:25–29).

Moses was not petulant and neither was God toward Israel's sin. They both took sin seriously. The Israelites, however, did not and would not throughout their Old Testament history. Their willingness to sin with utter abandonment parallels today's world and culture of unbridled sinfulness coupled with an unwillingness to repent of, or own up to, the consequences of their sin.

Moses then interceded on behalf of the nation before God (Exod. 32:30–35). As a type of Christ, Moses was willing to be judged for Israel's sin in order for the people to avert condemnation. God tells Moses that He will judge those who sinned (Exod. 32:33) and that He wanted Moses to lead the people where He told him to take them (Exod. 32:34). As the journey to the Promised Land continued, Moses continued to intercede on behalf of God's people before the One True God.

However, what became of the tablets? Moses shattered the two that God had provided and which contained the Ten Commandments. How would they be replaced?

Exodus 34 provides the answer. It is within this written account we read that the LORD told Moses to cut out two new stone tablets and that God would write on them the same words that were on the previous tablets (Exod. 34:1). Moses obeyed the LORD and did as instructed (Exod. 34:4). Moses went back up to the mountain to once again encounter the LORD. He carried with him the two new tablets (Exod. 34:4). This would be Moses's second forty-day period of time with God on Mt. Sinai.

Following the Lord's self-discloser regarding His character (Exod. 34:5–9), He renews the covenant with Israel. It is at this time the Lord not only restates previously given commandments contained in the book of the covenant, but also makes new ones (Exod. 34:10–26). It is these statements to which the godslayer makes reference. These were extensive commandments God gave in addition to the Ten Commandments list in Exodus 20:1–17.

As before, the Lord directs Moses to write down these covenant words (Exod. 34:27). As before, it is reasonable to conclude that the extensive new revelation God gave Moses was recorded in the Book of the Covenant. However, the Ten Commandments that God previously gave in Exodus 20:1–17 and that were contained on the first set of tablets are now written down by Moses on the new set of tablets (Exod. 34:28). "So he was there with the LORD forty days and forty nights. He neither ate bread nor drank water. And he wrote on the tablets the words of the covenant, the Ten Commandments" (Exod. 34:28, ESV). The Ten Commandments given and listed in Exodus 20:1–7 are to what Moses refers. Moses wrote down the ceremonial and judicial commands (Exod. 34:11–26) while at the same time rewriting the Ten Commandments on the newly prepared slabs.

Therefore, there is no contradiction between what God gave Moses in Exodus 20 and what Moses received in Exodus 34. The ten words contained on the two tablets were consistently the same commandments on both occasions and on both sets of tablets. Additionally, there were the words and commands God subsequently gave to Moses. There is no contradiction and no hypocrisy.

This is not the first attempt to take a seemingly obscure passage and events recorded in Scripture and turn it on its head to make it mean something it was never intended to mean. However, with each attempt, the student of Scripture comes away with a better understanding of God's Word and a stronger trust in its veracity. Thank you, godslayer.

Letter Seven!

My dear deluded Thomas.

Well, well, well. After months of meandering, you finally get around to a semi-intelligent excuse for your monster god's evil. According to your contention, he creates evil just so our faith can be tested? And to think you advance that rationalization with an apparent straight face. I do wish we could debate publically so I could show the intellectual fallacies and shallow emptiness of your faith. It is not that I have anything against you. No, I do pity you for you seem to believe the nonsense you are spouting. No, it is not you I hate; it is your god I despise. But enough of this ranting let us consider your argument.

So evil is god's way of testing faith? Doesn't that beg the question of why there even needs to be a test? Is your "perfect" god incompetent to make a perfect world? Assuming he is rational, then he either couldn't, or in the exercise of discretion has determined that he shouldn't.

But remember, your god is allegedly omniscient. Therefore, he knows all that will happen. Therefore, he knows the result of any faith test before it ever happens. Of what use is a test where the result is foreordained? It is like your god, a fraud.

And what of those who pass this test? What if they fail the next one? And if they do pass, does this assure them any benefit? Even retreating into Nietzschean "what doesn't-kill-us-makes-us-stronger" claptrap doesn't explain why he still needs to test those who accept his tyranny.

And what of those who are doomed to fail? Why test them if they are going to fail anyway? Isn't a more sensible answer that god is a sadist? Why else would a "loving," "perfect," god of forgiveness (who just can't seem to bring himself to forgive those who fail) have created a hell for eternal torment? Oh yes, I forgot: Jesus loves us.

So what is the purpose of testing faith at all? Those who fail did so because their faith wasn't strong enough? And those who pass can then gloat over how more-holy-than-thou-you I am?

And doesn't your theory ignore those whose tests end in death or suicide? I have known two friends who did commit suicide and I can tell you from personal observation that it wasn't because of any lack of faith. As a child, I was told that god never tempts anyone beyond what they could endure. I have learned this is pure movie (expletive) else there would never be any suicides at all.

I realize that "faith" is your bread and butter and that without this mental opium people would see your religion for the farce it really is and, heaven knows, you might be forced to get a real job.

Anyway, perhaps then you can explain to me your god's allegedly rational reason for tsunamis, earthquakes, floods, or other natural disasters? Do you seriously contend the millions killed all lacked the requisite faith? Are you saying there is a purpose to these "acts of god?" No! Your excuses in no way rationalize the existence of random acts of natural disasters.

Also, let us consider the acts of this loving mass murder of a god. 24,000 people die every day from starvation; many of these are children below the requisite age of discretion. Are you telling us that they all died, and are dying even now, merely to see if they had faith?

I know that you would never have the courage to publish my letter verbatim in the paper. The gullible need their mental drugs, but at least you will know the transparency of your ideas.

Hopefully you can now realize how vaporous your excuse is for the god of evil. I suppose you will continue vomiting out your religious stupidity, but be aware that it is recognized for the emptiness it really is by anyone of intelligence.

—The godslayer

This particular letter perhaps is the most provocative, intense, and revealing of all the correspondences the godslayer has written thus far. The passion and transparency he exhibits says as much perhaps about who he is as well as what he believes. Therefore, any biblical response must display a Holy Spirit fueled understanding of both the

Bible's content and compassionate emotions in order for the biblical answers to glorify the Lord and perhaps minister to this individual and others like him.

The godslayer reveals several aspects of his life and character in his letter. Perhaps he did not intend to, but he does. He allows his personal veneer to fall away and he gives us a glimpse into his true identity. This statement is not intended as a criticism but rather as an observation.

To begin with, the godslayer is not an atheist. He is not one who ultimately believes God does not exist. He acknowledges God's existence and he hates the One True God who exists. As he writes, "No, it is not you I hate; it is your god I despise." A true atheist would not waste their time expending this type of emotion toward a God they regard as a nonexistent being. However, one who does acknowledges God's existence, and loathes it, would. Therefore, the godslayer's atheism is a farce.

The existence of God, and correspondingly the subject of evil, is not just a philosophical topic for the godslayer but rather a deeply personal one. As it is for many people. It is equally apparent the godslayer blames God for evil and holds Him responsible for the pain he and others have encountered in this life. He makes reference to two friends who committed suicide. He describes them as people who did not lack faith. In the godslayer's attempt to understand why his friends ended their lives, he holds God responsible. I do not know the depth of despair the godslayer feels because of the death of his friends, but it is real, and he blames God for their past pain as well as presently his own.

The godslayer in his own mind and reasoning has a sense of right and wrong, a sense of good and evil. A true atheist, or naturalist or nihilist, who does not believe in the existence of God, does not believe there is an ultimate purpose to life, and that any and all ultimate purposes to life and living must be discovered by the individual. They do not believe there is an ultimate good or an ultimate evil. For the godslayer to be so angry at what he perceives as evil must presume an opposite concept of an ultimate good which contrasts and defines evil.

By this very insistence in addressing the issue of good and evil and why bad things happen, this presupposes an objective standard by which good and evil can be determined, defined, and evaluated. If there is no ultimate good, if there is no God who is the ultimate good, then how can good and evil be objectively understood and recognized? How, therefore, can evil, any kind of evil, exist if there is no definition of goodness by which evil can and may be compared and defined?

That is why there are no true atheists. They live, as do theists, from a paradigm that insists on a standard of right and wrong. This sense does not come from society as much as it does from within each individual's intellect, emotions, and will. In short, from the image of God stamped upon each human being. All humans have an inherent sense of what is right and what is wrong. Do you doubt that? Are you skeptical? Then please note the reaction you have upon seeing that your brand new car has just been keyed.

Consequently, there must be someone who has established this sense of an ultimate right and an ultimate wrong or evil. That person is God. If this is not so, then why expend so much energy on arguing about God not doing what is right, when at the same time denying God's very existence. Would it not make better sense to acknowledge that God does exist, and then begin the quest of discovering and understanding why God allows evil to exist?

The godslayer also refers to the time when as a child he learned that God never tempts anyone beyond what they could endure. Ever so briefly the godslayer pulls back a curtain of his life to let us know that he received some degree of biblical instruction as a youth. We can only speculate when he began to reject what he had learned. Did he learn about God at a church? If so, what church? How long did he attend? Were his parents believers? What became of his parents? Does he have any brothers or sisters? Are they believers? He does not tell us. We do not know.

The godslayer's personal references express deep sorrow and disillusionment. His sorrow is over those he loved who have died. His disillusionment is that God has not conducted Himself in the way the godslayer believes He should have. The result is a deep-seated hatred for God who he blames for these situations and who he accuses of being a fraud.

Therein lies the core issue of the godslayer's correspondence to me. He attempts to mask a deep-seated pain, for which he holds God responsible, with philosophical meanderings and attempts to discredit those who follow the Lord as His disciples. For if he cannot discredit God's existence as holy, righteous, sovereign, and just, he then faces a huge dilemma of being in opposition to the One True God who loves him and created Him. Faced with such a problem, the godslayer would rather shake his fist in anger at God than confess and repent of his rebellion and submit his life to God.

This the godslayer will not do. The risk is too great in his mind. It is too costly. It will involve acknowledging the pain he would rather bury. Yet the irony is that a simple column by me in a local newspaper causes the pain to rise up with such a vengeance from its grave deep in the center of his soul. He cannot escape it. He cannot deny its existence. So he attacks. He attacks God, and he attacks those who follow God. He attacks me!

Several years ago, author Phillip Yancey wrote a book entitled *Disappointment with God.* It was modern day examination of those who encounter "Job like" experiences. In his ministry, Yancey explored the reactions people have to the evil they have faced and how this affected their relationship with God. Obviously, there were several Yancey wrote of who were disappointed with the Lord.

It must again be noted that the godslayer is not disappointed with God, but rather he is angry. His anger is not superficial. It is deep, bitter, and has become entrenched into his soul.

Dr. J. I. Packer, in his book *Knowing God,* shares the following insights.

> Two facts about the triune Jehovah are assumed, if not actually stated, in every single biblical passage. The first is that He is king—absolute monarch of the universe, ordering all its affairs, working out His will in all that happens within it. The second fact is that he speaks—uttering words that express His will in order to cause it to be done. God's relations with His world have to be understood in terms of His sovereignty, so His sovereignty is to be understood in terms of what the Bible tells us about His word.[1]

The Bible reveals that the One True God is sovereign Lord of the universe. He is in absolute control of all things that occur. He is in charge!

Therefore, the ultimate issue at hand is a subject that has concerned and perplexed believers and unbelievers for centuries: how do we reconcile the existence of evil in light of the Bible's teaching that God is holy, loving, sovereign, and just? The question is whether the Bible is false and God is not who He reveals Himself to be, or there is a biblical explanation for the problem and the existence of evil. Why indeed do bad things happen, not only to so-called good people, but to anyone? The matter at hand is known as a theodicy. It is a complex subject that has elicited a variety of perspectives: both current and historical.

Theodicy (from the Greek *Theos* "God" and *dike* "justice") is the attempt to resolve the righteousness and justice of God with the conspicuous reality of evil. The term was invented by Gottfried Leibniz in his work *Theodice.* A theodicy seeks to vindicate the Bible's teaching that God is holy, righteous, sovereign, and just in the wake of all manner of evil in the world, which would appear to deny such a biblical claim about God.

A theodicy is not a defense of, nor an argument for, understanding God's existence and purpose for permitting evil. Rather, a theodicy proposes that rational creatures can understand why God permits evil to exist, even when He remains untarnished by the evil He permits to exist. A theodicy contends that we can believe in God even in the face of all manner of evil.

A theodicy is a complex subject with several traditions of thought seeking to explain it. There are the historical traditions based upon the writings of Augustine of Hippo and St. Irenaeus. There are also the more contemporary writings of such individuals as German philosopher Max Weber who saw theodicy as a social problem, sociologist Peter Berger who believed religion arose from a need to explain evil, and many Jewish theologians who sought to formulate a number of new perspectives regarding theodicy in the aftermath of the Holocaust. For many Jews, like Elie Wiesel in his book *Night*, the idea of anti-theodicy took hold maintaining that the concept and reality of God cannot be meaningfully justified.

There are a number of Christian writers who deny theodicies. They contend they are destructive, contribute to the world's evils, are unhelpful, and seek to legitimize evil and suffering. Some argue for some form of justice, anger, and pity rather than just a cool, detached philosophical speculation. However, nineteenth-century theologian Karl Barth believed that human suffering was ultimately in the "control of divine providence."[2]

The issue at hand is not one that is examined in the objective setting of a scientific laboratory. The problem of evil cannot be placed into a test tube and all manner of experiments conducted in order to arrive at a scientific conclusion. There is nothing sterile about the subject of evil and pain. It is not a subject in which one can be detached with disinterest.

Rather, the subject of evil's existence is emotional, personal, and dirty. There are no easy answers to the hard questions evil's existence poses. The questions are all too real and the appropriate biblical answers are all too often in short supply. These questions of where God is when it hurts and why does evil happen so randomly to so many people are faced in a children's cancer ward and a cardiac care unit of any major hospital. It is witnessed in the scene of a horrific traffic accident as well as in a behavioral health center wherein people "at risk" are seeking and needing help as they battle personal and psychological demons. It is seen in the aftermath of a tornado or hurricane ravaged town.

While some debate and doubt the existence of God, very few people and philosophical systems deny the existence of evil. There are a few, Christian Scientists for example, but they are the exception rather than the norm. With every random act of violence, such as a shooting at a school, news commentators, and politicians, atheists and agonistics deride the incident and the perpetrator as being the embodiment of evil. Yet, what does this mean?

What is evil, and can we truthfully understand it when at the same time the culture is all too prone to deny the existence of the ultimate good: God? You would be hard-pressed to deny the one and embrace the other. The two go hand in hand. Yet, that is what the current culture endeavors to do. However, in order to grasp the reality of evil, one must also grasp the reality of God. For in so doing, evil can eventually be evaluated by He who is inherently and intrinsically good.

First of all, evil exists. We may not at first be able to verbalize a definition, but we know evil when we see it. In the Old Testament, the biblical word for evil comes from the Hebrew word *Ra*. It means "to spoil," "to break in pieces," and to be made worthless. It is unpleasantness, disagreeableness, offensiveness. *Ra* refers to not only the evil act but also its consequences.

In the New Testament the Greek word for evil is *Kakos*, *Ponēros*, and *Phaulos*. *Kakos* and *Ponēros* refer to the quality of evil in its essential character. It also addresses evil's hurtful effects or influences.

What kind of evil exists? Are their various categories of evil? The Bible submits there are.

One of the most recognizable categories of evil is natural evil. This is disease, disasters, and other catastrophes that occur within the natural universe. This ranges from viruses to the violent force of a hurricane. People become sick, injured, hurt, and killed.

Other examples of natural evil include cancer, birth defects, typhoons, earthquakes, tsunamis, and other so-called acts of God. Often these occurrences have no observable corresponding good. Therefore, natural evil is impersonal. It is no respecter of persons.

A second type of evil is moral evil. While natural evil is impersonal, moral evil is not. It is personal, prevalent, and pernicious. Synonyms include wickedness, sin, and transgressions. It is evidenced in how people think, feel, speak, and act. Moral evil is clearly explained by the Apostle Paul in Romans 3:10–20.

> What then? Are we Jews any better off? No, not at
> all. For we have already charged that all, both Jews

and Greeks, are under sin, as it is written: "None is righteous, no, not one; no one understands; no one seeks for God. All have turned aside; together they have become worthless; no one does good, not even one." "Their throat is an open grave; they use their tongues to deceive." "The venom of asps is under their lips." "Their mouth is full of curses and bitterness." "Their feet are swift to shed blood; in their paths are ruin and misery, and the way of peace they have not known." "There is no fear of God before their eyes." Now we know that whatever the law says it speaks to those who are under the law, so that every mouth may be stopped, and the whole world may be held accountable to God. For by works of the law no human being will be justified in his sight, since through the law comes knowledge of sin.[3]

The reality of moral evil is everywhere. However, many still hold to the false concept of mankind's inherent goodness. This is in spite of overwhelming evidence to the contrary.

Thirdly, there is supernatural evil. This involves what is referred to as spiritual warfare. It is the conflict followers of Jesus engage involving demons and the devil himself, Satan.

The Apostle Paul describes this conflict in several of his epistles. 2 Corinthians 10:1–6 says,

I, Paul, myself entreat you, by the meekness and gentleness of Christ—I who am humble when face to face with you, but bold toward you when I am away!—I beg of you that when I am present I may not have to show boldness with such confidence as I count on showing against some who suspect us of walking according to the flesh. For though we walk in the flesh, we are not waging war according to the flesh. For the weapons of our warfare are not of the flesh but have divine power to destroy strongholds. We destroy arguments and every lofty opinion raised against the knowledge of God, and take every thought captive to obey Christ, being ready to punish every disobedience, when your obedience is complete.[4]

Paul further describes the weapons believers in Christ need with such a conflict in Ephesians 6:10–20.

Finally, be strong in the Lord and in the strength of his might. Put on the whole armor of God that you may be able to stand against the schemes of the devil. For we do not wrestle against flesh and blood, but against the rulers, against the authorities, against the cosmic powers over this present darkness, against the spiritual forces of evil in the heavenly places. Therefore take up the whole armor of God that you may be able towithstand in the evil day, and having done all, to stand firm. Stand therefore, having fastened on the belt of truth, and having put on the breastplate of righteousness, and, as shoes for your feet, having put on the readiness given by the gospel of peace. In all circumstances take up the shield of faith, with which you can extinguish all the flaming darts of the evil one; and take the helmet of salvation, and the sword of the Spirit, which is the word of God, praying at all times in the Spirit, with all prayer and supplication. To that end keep alert with all perseverance, making supplication for all the saints, and also for me, that words may be given to me in opening my mouth boldly to proclaim the mystery of the gospel, for which I am an ambassador in chains, that I may declare it boldly, as I ought to speak. [5]

In writing to his young protégé Timothy, Paul describes the reality of supernatural evil and its corresponding conflict in 1 Timothy 1:18. "This charge I entrust to you, Timothy, my child, in accordance with the prophecies previously made about you, that by them you may wage the good warfare."[6]

Paul additionally encouraged Timothy in 2 Timothy 2:1–4 regarding his role as a soldier engaged in spiritual conflict. Paul said, "You then, my child, be strengthened by the grace that is in Christ Jesus, and what you have heard from me in the presence of many witnesses entrust to faithful men who will be able to teach others also. Share in suffering as a good soldier of Christ Jesus. No soldier gets entangled in civilian pursuits, since his aim is to please the one who enlisted him." [7]

In 1 John 5:18–20, the Apostle John warns the recipient of his letter to be aware of the culture of corruption surrounding them in the fallen world. John explains, "We know that everyone who has been born of God does not keep on sinning, but he who was born of God protects him, and the evil one does not touch him. We know that we are from God, and the whole world lies in the power of the evil one."[8]

John even records how this ongoing supernatural evil affected the abode of God: heaven. In Revelation 12:7–12, John records the follow account:

> Now war arose in heaven, Michael and his angels fighting against the dragon. And the dragon and his angels fought back, but he was defeated, and there was no longer any place for them in heaven. And the great dragon was thrown down, that ancient serpent, who is called the devil and Satan, the deceiver of the whole world—he was thrown down to the earth, and his angels were thrown down with him. And I heard a loud voice in heaven, saying, "Now the salvation and the power and the kingdom of our God and the authority of his Christ have come, for the accuser of our brothers has been thrown down, who accuses them day and night before our God. And they have conquered him by the blood of the Lamb and by the word of their testimony, for they loved not their lives even unto death. Therefore, rejoice, O heavens and you who dwell in them! But woe to you, O earth and sea, for the devil has come down to you in great wrath, because he knows that his time is short!"[9]

Finally, there is eternal evil. This is hell. It is eternal, and there will be a great many individuals existing for eternity in hell. The godslayer hates the teaching that there is a literal hell. He is not alone. Many people, including Christians and so-called evangelical pastors, deny the biblical teaching and existence of hell. Yet the Bible makes clear mention of it.

Hell is the place of disembodied spirits (Acts 2:31), a place Christ visited (Acts 2:31; 1 Pet. 3:19), and a place of torment (Luke 16:23). It is the place of future punishment and destruction from the presence of God (2 Thess. 1:9).

Hell is described as everlasting punishment (Matt. 25:46), everlasting fire (Matt. 25:41), everlasting burnings (Isa. 33:14), a furnace of fire (Matt. 13:42, 50), a lake of fire (Rev. 20:15), fire and brimstone (Rev. 14:10), unquenchable fire (Matt. 3:12), and devouring fire (Isa. 33:14). It is a placed prepared for the devil and his angels (Matt. 25:41; 2 Pet. 2:1–4; Jude 6).

The Bible says that the punishment of hell is eternal (Isa. 33:14; Rev. 20:10) in which not only the body suffers (Matt. 5:29; 10:28) but also the soul (Matt. 10:28). No human power can preserve someone from the reality of hell (Ezek. 32:27).

The wise man is one who avoids hell (Prov. 15:24) and also seeks to keep others from it (Prov. 23:14; Jude 23). The powers of hell cannot overcome the church (Matt. 16:18). God uses the illustration of Gehenna, the place of refuse for the ancient city of Jerusalem, as a vivid picture of hell (Isa. 30:33).

The Bible does not ignore the reality of evil and suffering. Rather, God clearly communicates throughout the Scriptures that evil and suffering exists. In fact, there are some 164 references alone to the word *suffering*, and its variants, in the Old and New Testaments. Here is but a sampling from the Scriptures regarding the subject of suffering, trials, and trouble.

1. Job 5:6–7—"For affliction does not come from the dust, nor does trouble spring from the ground; yet man is born to trouble as the sparks fly upward."[10]

2. Job 7:1–2—"Is there not a time of hard service for man on earth? Are not his days also like the days of a hired man? Like a servant who earnestly desires the shade, and like a hired man who eagerly looks for his wages."[11]

3. Job 14:1–2—"Man who is born of woman is of few days and full of trouble. He comes forth like a flower and fades away; He flees like a shadow and does not continue."[12]

4. Psalm 9:9–10—"The LORD also will be a refuge for the oppressed, a refuge in times of trouble. And those who know your name will put their trust in You; For You, LORD, have not forsaken those who seek You."[13]

5. Psalm 22:10–11—"I was cast upon You from birth. From my mother's womb You have been my God. Be not far from me for trouble is near; for there is none to help."[14]

6. Psalm 32:7—"You are my hiding place; you shall preserve me from trouble; You shall surround me with songs of deliverance. Selah!"[15]

7. Psalm 46:1–3—"God is our refuge and strength, a very present help in time of trouble. Therefore we will not fear, even though the earth be removed, and thought the mountains be carried into the midst of the sea; though its waters roar and be troubled, though the mountains shake with its swelling. Selah!"[16]

8. Ecclesiastes 2:22–23—"For what has man for all his labor, and for the striving of his heart with which he has toiled under the sun? For all his days are sorrowful, and his work burdensome; even in the night his heart takes no rest."[17]

9. Luke 13:1–5—"There were some present at that very time who told him about the Galileans whose blood Pilate had mingled with their sacrifices. And he answered them, 'Do you think that these Galileans were worse sinners than all the other Galileans, because they suffered in this way? No, I tell you; but unless you repent, you will all likewise

perish. Or those eighteen on whom the tower in Siloam fell and killed them: do you think that they were worse offenders than all the others who lived in Jerusalem? No, I tell you; but unless you repent, you will all likewise perish."[18]

10. John 16:33—"I have said these things to you, that in me you may have peace. In the world you will have tribulation. But take heart; I have overcome the world."[19]

We conclude with the obvious: evil exists. It is huge and all-pervasive within the world. There is no escaping it. It is real, and it is relevant.

The second truth we must consider is that not only does evil exist, but God also exists. The Scriptures contain many references to not only the existence of God but also to the sovereignty of God. God is in complete control of everything that occurs. He is all-powerful and all-knowing. The following citations are but a sampling of this divine truth.

1. 1 Chronicles 29:10–13—"Therefore David blessed the Lord in the presence of all the assembly. And David said: "Blessed are you, O Lord, the God of Israel our father, forever and ever. Yours, O Lord, is the greatness and the power and the glory and the victory and the majesty, for all that is in the heavens and in the earth is yours. Yours is the kingdom,

O Lord, and you are exalted as head above all. Both riches and honor come from you, and you rule over all. In your hand are power and might, and in your hand it is to make great and to give strength to all. And now we thank you, our God, and praise your glorious name."[20]

2. Psalm 115:1–3—"Not to us, O Lord, not to us, but to your name give glory, for the sake of your steadfast love and your faithfulness! Why should the nations say, 'Where is their God?' Our God is in the heavens; he does all that he pleases."[21]

3. 1 Timothy 6:13–16—"I charge you in the presence of God, who gives life to all things, and of Christ Jesus, who in his testimony before Pontius Pilate made the good confession, to keep the commandment unstained and free from reproach until the appearing of our Lord Jesus Christ, which he will display at the proper time—he who is the blessed and only Sovereign, the King of kings and Lord of lords, who alone has immortality, who dwells in unapproachable light, whom no one has ever seen or can see. To him be honor and eternal dominion. Amen."[22]

4. Revelation 4:11. "Worthy are you, our Lord and God, to receive glory and honor and power, for you

created all things, and by your will they existed and were created." [23]

Evil exist! God exists! The third truth that the Bible holds to regarding the reality of evil and at the same time the reality of a just and holy God is that God permits or wills evil to exist. This is a troubling truth for many people, but if we are to be biblically consistent, it is the only conclusion we can draw when honestly considering the two preceding points.

1. Exodus 4:10–11—"But Moses said to the LORD, 'Oh, my Lord, I am not eloquent, either in the past or since you have spoken to your servant, but I am slow of speech and of tongue.' Then the LORD said to him, 'Who has made man's mouth? Who makes him mute, or deaf, or seeing, or blind? Is it not I, the LORD?'" [24]

2. Deuteronomy 32:39—"'See now that I, even I, am he, and there is no god beside me; I kill and I make alive; I wound and I heal; and there is none that can deliver out of my hand.'" [25]

3. 1 Samuel 2:6–8—"The LORD kills and brings to life; he brings down to Sheol and raises up. The LORD makes poor and makes rich; he brings low and he exalts. He raises up the poor from the dust; he lifts the needy from the ash heap to make them sit with princes and inherit a seat of honor.

For the pillars of the earth are the LORD's, and on them he has set the world."[26]

4. 2 Samuel 10:9–12—"When Joab saw that the battle was set against him both in front and in the rear, he chose some of the best men of Israel and arrayed them against the Syrians. The rest of his men he put in the charge of Abishai his brother, and he arrayed them against the Ammonites. And he said, 'If the Syrians are too strong for me, then you shall help me, but if the Ammonites are too strong for you, then I will come and help you. Be of good courage, and let us be courageous for our people, and for the cities of our God, and may the LORD do what seems good to him.'"[27]

5. 2 Kings 17:24–25—"And the king of Assyria brought people from Babylon, Cuthah, Avva, Hamath, and Sepharvaim, and placed them in the cities of Samaria instead of the people of Israel. And they took possession of Samaria and lived in its cities. And at the beginning of their dwelling there, they did not fear the LORD. Therefore the LORD sent lions among them, which killed some of them."[28]

6. 2 Samuel 12:15—"And the LORD afflicted the child that Uriah's wife bore to David, and he became sick."[29]

7. Psalm 33:10–12—"The Lord brings the counsel of the nations to nothing; he frustrates the plans of the peoples. The counsel of the Lord stands forever, the plans of his heart to all generations. Blessed is the nation whose God is the Lord, the people whom he has chosen as his heritage!" [30]

8. Psalm 103:15–19—"As for man, his days are like grass; he flourishes like a flower of the field; for the wind passes over it, and it is gone, and its place knows it no more. But the steadfast love of the Lord is from everlasting to everlasting on those who fear him, and his righteousness to children's children, to those who keep his covenant and remember to do his commandments. The Lord has established his throne in the heavens, and his kingdom rules over all." [31]

9. Isaiah 14:24–27—"The Lord of hosts has sworn: 'As I have planned, so shall it be, and as I have purposed, so shall it stand, that I will break the Assyrian in my land, and on my mountains trample him underfoot; and his yoke shall depart from them, and his burden from their shoulder.' This is the purpose that is purposed concerning the whole earth, and this is the hand that is stretched out over all the nations. For the Lord of hosts has purposed, and who will annul it? His hand is stretched out, and who will turn it back?" [32]

10. Isaiah 46:8–11—"Remember this and stand firm, recall it to mind, you transgressors, remember the former things of old; for I am God, and there is no other; I am God, and there is none like me, declaring the end from the beginning and from ancient times things not yet done, saying, 'My counsel shall stand, and I will accomplish all my purpose,' calling a bird of prey from the east, the man of my counsel from a far country. I have spoken, and I will bring it to pass; I have purposed, and I will do it." [33]

11. Daniel 4:34–35—"At the end of the days I, Nebuchadnezzar, lifted my eyes to heaven, and my reason returned to me, and I blessed the Most High, and praised and honored him who lives forever, for his dominion is an everlasting dominion, and his kingdom endures from generation to generation; all the inhabitants of the earth are accounted as nothing, and he does according to his will among the host of heaven and among the inhabitants of the earth; and none can stay his hand or say to him, 'What have you done.'"[34]

12. Amos 4:3–6—"Do two walk together, unless they have agreed to meet? Does a lion roar in the forest, when he has no prey? Does a young lion cry out from his den, if he has taken nothing? Does a bird fall in a snare on the earth, when there is no trap for it? Does a snare spring up from the ground, when it

has taken nothing? Is a trumpet blown in a city, and the people are not afraid? Does disaster come to a city, unless the LORD has done it?"[35]

13. Matthew 10:28–29—"And do not fear those who kill the body but cannot kill the soul. Rather fear him who can destroy both soul and body in hell. Are not two sparrows sold for a penny? And not one of them will fall to the ground apart from your Father."[36]

While God did not actively create evil, He did create the potential for evil to exist and in His sovereign will permits evil to exist and to accomplish His purpose. Admittedly, this is hard for many people to grasp, but what other options are there? Do we believe in a God who is all-knowing but not all-powerful? Or do we embrace the other possibility that God is all-powerful but not all-knowing. Either perspective fails to honestly consider the biblical text that affirms that God is both omniscient and omnipotent.

Where does that leave us when we consider the reality of evil? It drives us to the biblical text that affirms that God is sovereign, all-powerful, all-knowing, holy, and just and that He uses each and every event in this world to accomplish His will. Nowhere does it say in the Bible that God is obliged to tell us why He uses and permits the evil that occurs in our lives. Nor does the Bible communicate that believers will always understand God's purposes and plans.

What the Bible does command us to do is to trust God. Believers are to trust the LORD with all their heart (Prov. 3:5–6). This means to trust with one's intellect, emotions, and will. At the same time, believers are commanded to trust in the LORD; they are also commanded to not depend or "lean" on their own understanding as their foundation for getting through the day. Rather, believers are to acknowledge God's sovereign control in all things knowing that God has led, is leading, and will lead His redeemed and adopted children through the storms of life and living.

The prophet Isaiah as God's herald explains this exact point regarding God willing evil to exist. Isaiah 45:5–7 says, "I am the LORD, and there is no other, besides me there is no God; I equip you, though you do not know me that people may know, from the rising of the sun and from the west, that there is none besides me; I am the LORD, and there is no other. I form light and create darkness, I make well-being and create calamity, I am the LORD, who does all these things."[37] If you recall, the godslayer said this is the only verse in the Bible that is true in his opinion.

The context is God's prophetic word to Cyrus, the King of Persia, who God would raise up to conquer the Babylonians. See Daniel 5. Even though the king did not know God, God knew him and would use this king to destroy the rule and reign of Nebuchadnezzar's Babylonian empire. The reason God could announce this with such confidence is because He is the LORD, and there is no other.

He forms light and creates darkness, He makes well-being and creates calamity. He is the LORD, who does all these things. All people are to recognize that God is ultimately responsible for life (light), death (darkness), prosperity, and disaster. As sovereign LORD of all, He does everything that is in keeping with His righteous and holy character. This includes permitting and willing evil to exist.

The New American Standard Bible's translation of Romans 8:28 says, "And we know that God causes all things to work together for good to those who love God, to those who are called according to His purpose."[38] God orchestrates each and every thing that occurs in this world for a good purpose to those who God loves and who love Him in return because of His love.

When the believer who stares evil in the face, whether it is natural, moral, supernatural, or eternal, trusts that God has a divine purpose and plan for all that occurs, then God is truly glorified in that believer's life. Job rightly concluded when he said, "Naked I came from my mother's womb, and naked shall I return. The LORD gave, and the LORD has taken away; blessed be the name of the LORD."[39] and "Shall we receive good from God, and shall we not receive evil?" In all this, Job did not sin with his lips."[40]

In our predominant, humanistic culture, humanity recoils at the notion that they are not in control and that someone else, namely God, is. However, if we are honest with ourselves, we realize how little of life we do control.

In fact, when evil occurs, in whatever its forms, our lack of control over events, incidents, situations, and circumstances is glaringly apparent. We may shake our fist with a poignant cry of "why," but we still remain powerless to prevent further such tragedies from occurring in the future.

One of the most endearing texts of Scripture regarding the God's purpose in permitting evil in people's lives is found in 2 Corinthians 1:3–4. It is relevant and real. The text states, "Blessed *be* the God and Father of our Lord Jesus Christ, the Father of mercies and God of all comfort, who comforts us in all our tribulation, that we may be able to comfort those who are in any trouble, with the comfort with which we ourselves are comforted by God."[41]

In this text, we read that God is described as the Father of mercies. This means that He is a God of compassion and pity. Within Him resides a heart of compassion to the plight of the suffering.

Additionally, He is described as the God of all comfort. Comfort means consoling. God not only is known as the God of all comfort, but He also comforts, brings consolation, in all our tribulations or afflictions, distresses, and oppressions. There is nothing that happens in our lives in which He is does not care or is not concerned.

However, since we conclude that God is ultimately responsible for permitting tribulations in our lives, what possible motive may He have in doing so? The answer is found not only in the comfort we discover in Him during difficult days, but also in us having the opportunity to comfort other people. How? We comfort people with the same comfort we have received from God when He comforted us; perhaps through friends and family. The comfort God freely give us is the comfort we freely give to others in their time of need.

Think about it! Who best to comfort someone suffering from cancer than a cancer survivor? Who best to comfort a person who has seen their home destroyed by a tornado than someone who has lived through the same tragedy? Who better to comfort someone going through a divorce than one who has endured the painful death of a marriage? For those who have encountered sufferings, and who among us has not, we also have the opportunity and privilege to be a minister of mercy to those who are hurting. Let us begin!

I submit that the view presented of the existence of evil, and God's ultimate purpose in using it, is the best explanation available for why bad things happen in this world. God uses natural, moral, supernatural, and eternal evil for His ultimate glory. This perspective will either be accepted and embraced or rejected by individuals possessing a prior perspective, either negative or positive, regarding God. The one who loves God knows that God has our ultimate good in mind. This is ultimately displayed on the cross wherein God was reconciling all things unto Himself through the substitutionary atonement and resurrection of Jesus Christ from the dead (2 Cor. 5:18–19). It is through the cross and the empty tomb that evil and suffering are overcome and may and can be therefore used for good.

The one who does not love God will not accept anything from Him: whether it is good or evil. Therein is the greater tragedy.

Letter Eight!

Christian nation? I frequently hear Christians claim that the United States is a Christian nation, or that the Founding Fathers intended us to be a Christian nation. When they bother to offer evidence, it's usually some McCarthy-era addition to our pledge or our money or some quote (often bogus) from a speech or a letter by one of the Founding Fathers.

Think about this for a second. If you were starting a Christian nation, how would you go about it? Would you make oblique references to "great powers" and "guiding hands" in obscure speeches and letters or would you fill your foundational documents with references to Jesus Christ and the Bible?

The Founding Fathers were brilliant men. They spent months and months working on the Constitution. They were very, very careful about what they wrote, discussing and debating every passage at great length. It seems to me that if they had intended this to be a Christian nation, they would have said so somewhere in the Constitution. The Founding Fathers had no reason to be vague. There

> *was no American Civil Liberties Union (ACLU) and no*
> *activist judges. If they had wanted a Christian nation,*
> *they could have written:*
>
> *God Almighty, in order to form a true Christian*
> *nation, establish divine justice, insure adherence to His*
> *laws, provide for the defense of His church, promote His*
> *Word, and secure His blessings of liberty to ourselves*
> *and our posterity, has led us to ordain and establish this*
> *Constitution of the United States of America.*
>
> *Instead they wrote:*
>
> *We the People of the United States, in Order to form*
> *a more perfect Union, establish Justice, insure domestic*
> *Tranquility, provide for the common defense, promote*
> *the general Welfare, and secure the Blessings of Liberty to*
> *ourselves and our Posterity, do ordain and establish this*
> *Constitution for the United States of America.*
>
> *The words "Jesus," "Christ," "Bible," "God," and even*
> *"Creator," appear nowhere in the Constitution. (Endowed*
> *by their creator is in the Declaration of Independence).*
> *Just how stupid would someone have to be to create a*
> *Christian nation and then forget to mention "Christ" in*
> *the Constitution?*
>
> —*The godslayer*

I agree with the godslayer that the Founding Fathers were, in his words, "brilliant men." The godslayer is absolutely correct when he says that our nation's founders "spent months and months working on the Constitution." I again concur that our founders were "very, very careful about what they wrote, discussing and debating every passage at great length."

Why then did the members of the Constitutional Convention, (also known as the Philadelphia Convention, the Federal Convention, or the Grand Convention at Philadelphia) which took place from May 25 to September 17, 1787, in Philadelphia, Pennsylvania, not specifically mention and use the words *Jesus, Christ, Bible, God,* and *Creator* within what would be later known as the Constitution of the United States of America? They could have. Many people believe that should have? Why did they not?

The answer is not that these founders were stupid. Again, they were brilliant. They understood what their fellow countrymen had left behind in England in the early seventeenth century. They understood the reasons for fighting a war for independence. They understood that independence from England was not just about political freedom or governmental freedom. It was also about religious freedom: freedom from the state mandating what religion was deemed legal.

The seeds of America's Christian heritage are not necessarily found in the resulting documents that fostered a revolution and solidified thirteen colonies, but rather in the impetus that drove these people, and their immediate ancestors, to settle an untamed wilderness and to establish colonies based upon biblical truth and principles. In order to identify those particular seeds, we must journey from the events of the mid-to-late eighteenth century to the early days of the seventeenth century. It is there we will find the evidence to answer the godslayer's questions. My primary source of evidence is the United States Library of Congress. It is here that ample evidence exists to more than suggest the predominant Christian influence in the settlement of America.

Many of the North American Colonies settled in the seventeenth century were established as "plantations of religion." Those who settled within the colonies of New England, New Jersey, Pennsylvania, and Maryland did so due to religious persecution, which caused them to flee Europe. While it is true that there were colonists who came to the New World to "catch fish," the majority left Europe to worship the One True God according to their conscience and their commitment to the Bible. The ideas of a "city on a hill" or a "holy experiment" were enthusiastically supported. Even so-called secular colonies, such as Virginia, contained entrepreneurs who regarded themselves as "militant Protestants."

The European persecution that precipitated the mass exodus to North America was founded on the idea that religion must play a role in society. The conflict arose as to what religion best represented the Bible: Catholicism or Protestantism. While it is true the Catholics persecuted Protestants during this period, it is equally true the

Protestants returned the favor. It is also true that Catholics and Protestants alike persecuted members within their own denominations among others. While England denounced religious persecution in 1689, it continued unabated in Europe. It was often bloody and sparked ongoing resentment, which continues to the present day.

Various groups that encountered religious persecution during this time included Mennonites, Jesuits, Austrian Lutherans, Huguenots (French Protestants), and Catholics. Various individuals who suffered include Jesuit priests like Brian Cansfield (1581–1643) who was imprisoned, and Ralph Corbington (Corby) (1599–1644) who was hanged by the English government for professing his faith. There was also the martyrdom of Protestant John Rogers (1500–1555) who was burned alive under the authority of England's Catholic Queen Mary. Roger's crime was denying the actual presence of Christ in Communion as per Catholic doctrine. As a result, he became the first Protestant martyr.

It should be duly noted that this atmosphere of persecution by professing believers in Christ among themselves and against their opponents does not do much for a strong biblical witness to loving God and loving one another. On the contrary, it is these examples, among many I acknowledge throughout history and even within our present day, that damage the very gospel these presumed followers of Christ indicated they believed. The tragic irony is that their fervency in what they believed carried them to these erroneous and violent behaviors. It was a belief system not founded upon Scripture, but rather founded upon a misguided understanding of Scripture, or church teachings independent and contradictory of Scripture.

A shining example of a commitment to biblical truth in this particularly dark period was a group known as the Puritans. While admittedly not perfect, they proved to be a movement known for their "concern to search the Scriptures, collate their findings, and apply them to all areas of life."[1]

They were passionate about the biblical doctrine of the Trinity, the electing grace of God, the substitutionary atonement of Jesus Christ on the cross, and the sanctifying work of the Holy Spirit in the lives of followers of Christ. They also believed in fervent and biblically centered worship as an expression of one's love for Christ. Additionally, the Puritans looked to Scripture for their theology regarding church and state, the role and authority of kings, Parliament and the citizenry.

Most importantly, the Puritans emphasized personal conversion and faith in Jesus Christ as Savior and Lord. They taught that "except a man be born again, he cannot see the kingdom of heaven."[2] They shined in preaching the gospel, calling sinners to repentance and faith in Christ, leading them to saving knowledge in Christ and teaching them once conversion occurred.

The Puritans worked to reform the church from within. They rejected any and all movements and decrees that sought to implement teachings by the government and the Church of England they believed were contrary to the Puritans commitment to Scripture alone as their ultimate authority. Theologian J. I. Packer comments that "Puritanism was an evangelical holiness movement seeking to implement its vision of spiritual renewal, national and personal, in the church, the state, and the home; in education, evangelism, economics; in individual discipleship and devotion and in pastoral care and competence."[3]

With the increasing conflict in the seventeenth century between the Puritans and the Church of England, by 1630 some twenty thousand Puritans immigrated to America to gain the ability to worship God according to their biblical convictions. Most settled in New England. Some settled as far south as the West Indies.

Arguably, the most famous and revered contingent of Puritans were the Pilgrims who established their colony in what became known as Plymouth. They established one of the most memorable documents establishing their purpose of existence and government. They entitled it the Mayflower Compact.

While current revisionist historians seek to eliminate its clear Christian overtones, the Mayflower Compact's original text and wording is overtly Christian. The original document no longer exists, but copies in William Bradford's journal entitled *Of Plymouth Plantation* is in agreement to the original and accepted by historians as accurate. The handwritten manuscript is kept in a special vault at the State Library of Massachusetts. Bradford's text of the Mayflower Compact is as follows:

> In the name of God, Amen. We whose names are underwritten, the loyal subjects of our dread (awe and reverence) Sovereign Lord King James, by the Grace of God of Great Britain, France and Ireland, King, Defender of the Faith, etc.
>
> Having undertaken, for the Glory of God and advancement of the Christian Faith and Honour of our King and Country, a Voyage to plant the First Colony in the Northern Parts of Virginia, do by these presents solemnly and mutually in the presence of God and one of another, Covenant and Combine ourselves together into a Civil Body Politic, for our better ordering and preservation and furtherance of the ends aforesaid; and by virtue hereof to enact, constitute and frame such just and equal Laws, Ordinances, Acts, Constitutions and Offices, from time to time, as shall be thought most meet and convenient for the general good of the Colony, unto which we promise all due submission and obedience. In witness whereof we have hereunder subscribed our names at Cape Cod, the 11th of November, in the year of the reign of our Sovereign Lord King James, of England, France and Ireland the eighteenth, and of Scotland the fifty-fourth. Anno Domini 1620.[4]

Notable Puritan pastors and leaders included Richard Mather (1596–1669), his son Increase (1639–1723), and grandson Cotton (1663–1728). Cotton Mather was one of the best known New England Puritans of his generation. He was a prodigious writer, he authored and published over 450 books and pamphlets, and was at the center of all of the major political, theological and scientific controversies of the day. He has been unfairly accused of instigating the Salem Witchcraft Trials.

It was during this period of time that two significant publications of the Bible occurred. First, the Geneva Bible was published in 1560 by English Puritans. It is regarded by biblical historians as the first study Bible. The Geneva Bible was used not only by the Puritans but also by the Pilgrims. Between 1560 and 1630, it was the predominant Bible in existence and was used by William Shakespeare, John Bunyan (Pilgrim's Progress), and English Puritan leader Oliver Cromwell.

The second Bible publication of lasting significance was the King James Bible, otherwise known as the "Authorized Version." Composed from 1607–1611 by biblical scholars commissioned by King James I of England, it eventually surpassed the Geneva Bible in popularity. It remains a popular translation even to this day.

As the North American colonies took shape within the seventeenth century, many laws were established on biblical principles. Criminal laws within the early New England colonies were taken directly from Scripture. Additionally, in order to sing the Psalms during Massachusetts' church worship services, Richard Mather and other ministers transformed the Psalms into verse and published the Bay Psalm Book (1640). It was the first book published in North America.

Evangelism of the Native Americans also occurred during this time. While not always successful, one of the most effecting ministers to the Algonquin Indians was John Elliot (1604–1690). A Massachusetts minister, he translated the Bible into the Algonquin language and pastored up to 1,100 praying Indians.

As the seventeenth century gave way to the eighteenth century, the fervency for the spread and proclamation of Christianity in the North American Colonies did not dissipate. Rather, it grew at an accelerated rate. The current cultural view is that Christianity was nominal at best within the English settlements up and down the eastern coast of North America. However, Christianity ascended and displayed great vitality and feverish growth during the 1700s.

It was during the midpoint of the century that America experienced its first, if not its greatest, religious revival: the Great Awakening. The Great Awakening swept not only through the English Colonies of North America but also in England, Scotland, and Wales. It took place during 1730–1740.

The singular emphasis in what was preached was the biblical doctrine of the new birth: conversion by grace alone, through faith alone in Jesus Christ alone. The Great Awakening proved to be an extension of the Protestant Reformation, which occurred in Europe during the sixteenth century. Leading figures during this spiritual phenomenon included Charles and John Wesley, Evangelist George Whitfield, and Theologian and Pastor Jonathan Edwards.

As it was with the Reformation, the movement had its supporters as well as its detractors. Those supporting the "Awakening" included Presbyterians, Baptists, and Methodists. Opponents included Anglicans, Quakers, and Congregationalists.

Ironically, it was also during this historical period that the religious movement known as "Deism" arose with some degree of acceptance and approval. Its emphasis was on human morality. However, it rejected the divinity of Jesus Christ, and while such noted figures as Thomas Jefferson and John Adams are said to be advocates, it never really supplanted or equaled biblical evangelicalism. Others leaders of Deism included John Toland (1670–1722), John Locke (1632–1704), and Lord Viscount Bolingbroke (1678–1751).

Colonists built church edifices or facilities with great regularity at this time. The structures came in all shapes and sizes. Many church buildings constructed during this period of America's history remain to this day. One such example is Christ Church in Philadelphia, PA, which I have visited. Belying the notion of America's religious indifference or ambivalence to evangelical Christianity, historical church structures dot the American landscape as a visible and lasting testimony of the faith of our fathers.

Another movement that also occurred in America due to the Great Awakening was that evangelical Christians began founding colleges to train men for the gospel ministry. Following in the shadow of Harvard College (1636), the College of New Jersey (later known as Princeton University) began in 1746 by Presbyterians.

The events of the early eighteenth century would mold and form the circumstances that shaped the American Revolution in the latter portion of these same one hundred years. America's fight for independence from England was as much about religious freedom as it was about economic freedom. Unless that is understood, America's story is only partially understood.

Christianity offered a moral compass for the colonists in their opposition to England's king and ministers. Pastors not only preached from the pulpit, they also served in many other roles during the Revolution. This included serving as military chaplains, as secretaries for committees of correspondence, and as members of state legislatures, constitutional conventions, and the national Congress. Some even, by taking up arms, led Continental troops in battle.

Not all Christians were united during America's struggle for independence. The Revolution caused splits between denominations. Members of the Church of England contained pastors who were bound by oath to serve the King. Quakers were pacifists. Additionally, regular church attendance for worship and instruction was hindered by the absence of ministers and the destruction of church facilities.

In spite of the ravages of war, the Revolution increased the Millennialist perspective in American theology. Pastors preached that an American victory over the British would result in the establishment of a literal Kingdom of God in which Christ would rule. This perspective of America's theological uniqueness was felt even by secularists as American territory increased under the Jeffersonian presidency in 1801.

The major point of discussion and dispute to the current day is whether the American Colonists were right in revolting against English rule, in all its forms. Joseph Galloway (1731–1803), a former speaker of the Pennsylvania Assembly and close friend of Benjamin Franklin, opposed the Revolution and fled to England in 1778. He believed that at best the Revolution was a religious quarrel, caused by Presbyterians and Congregationalists.

Pastor Jonathan Mayhew (1720–1766), at Old West Church, Boston, Massachusetts, was an eloquent proponent that God ordained civic and religious liberty. He considered the Church of England a dangerous, and an almost diabolical, enemy of the colonies. Mayhew asserted that resistance to England was in fact a religious duty. Most colonial ministers during this time agreed and argued that the war was approved by God.

Patriotic fervency resulted in many mistaken notions of British plots to supplant American clergy with those loyal to England. Additionally, the idea that the British would persecute Americans for their biblical convictions further poisoned relations between the two factions.

Peter Muhlenberg (1746–1807) was a prime example of a "fighting parson" during the Revolutionary War. The eldest son of the Lutheran pastor Henry Melchoir Muhlenberg, he threw off his clerical robes at the conclusion of a sermon in January 1776 to his congregation in Woodstock, Virginia, to reveal the uniform of a Virginia militia officer. He served with distinction throughout the war, Muhlenberg commanded a brigade that successfully stormed the British lines at Yorktown. He retired from the army in 1783 as a major general.

During the war, chaplains were appointed to serve and minster to those in the armed forces. They were paid at the rate of a major in the Continental Army. James Caldwell (1734–1781), a Presbyterian minister at Elizabeth, New Jersey, was one of the many ministers who served as chaplains during the Revolutionary War. "At the battle of Springfield, New Jersey, on June 23, 1780, when his company ran out of wadding, Caldwell was said to have dashed into a nearby

Presbyterian Church, scooped up as many Watts hymnals as he could carry, and distributed them to the troops, shouting, "Put Watts into them, boys." Caldwell and his wife were both killed before the war ended."[5]

Arguably, one of the most important pastors during this period was John Witherspoon (1723–1794). He represented New Jersey in the Continental Congress from 1776 to 1782. As such, he signed the Declaration of Independence and served on more than one hundred committees. As president of Princeton, he was accused of turning the institution into a "seminary of sedition."

The one denomination most adversely affected by the war was the Church of England. This was because the King of England was the head of the church. At their ordination, Anglican clergy swore allegiance to the King. The Book of Common Prayer offered prayers for the monarch, beseeching God "to be his defender and keeper, giving him victory over all his enemies."[6]

Many Anglican priests relinquished their pulpits because of the conflict. Others argued for an American Episcopal Church independent from the Church of England. This perspective also spread to Methodist and Presbyterian congregations.

In the aftermath of the Revolutionary War and following America's independence from England, the Continental-Confederation Congress became the legislative body governing the United States. It did so from 1774–1789.

While the Congress did contain many deeply religious men, it did not officially authorize any specific religion. However, it did encourage the practice of the Christian religion throughout the new nation to a degree unparalleled by any future American governments.

The Congress appointed chaplains, not only for itself, but it also continued to do so for the armed forces following the war. It additionally sponsored the publication of a Bible, imposed Christian morality in the armed forces, granted public lands to promote Christianity among the Indians, and observed national days of thanksgiving and prayer. The Congress embraced covenant or reformed theology, which taught that the One True Sovereign God covenanted with a nation and its people.

Congress' initial meeting began in prayer led by Reverend Jacob Duche (1738–1798), who at the time served at the rector of Christ Church, Philadelphia, PA. He was the first chaplain of the Congress, appointed in 1776. Following his defection to England, Duche was succeeded by William White (1748–1836) and George Duffield (1732–1790).

The Congressional Bible was called Aiken's Bible. This was because printer Robert Aiken (1734–1802) petitioned Congress to officially sanction a Bible to be distributed to the citizens of the United States. This became imperative due to the restriction of imported Bibles from England because of the war.

The most familiar public land grant authorized by Congress was the Northwest Ordinance of 1787. The document stressed that religion, morality, and knowledge was necessary to good government. This was compatible to Congress granting land in Delaware for the religious purposes. Congress allocated ten thousand acres on the Muskingum River to be vested for the Moravian Brethren for the civilizing of Indians and the promotion of Christianity.

As the United States continued to develop and grow under the Articles of Confederation (1777–1788) structure of government, the relationship between the church and state was harmonious. Unlike the ongoing and increasing tension between the American Colonies and England, colonial churches and their respective states were mutually cooperative and supportive.

The Massachusetts Constitution of 1780 declared that "the happiness of a people, and the good order and preservation of civil government, essentially depend on piety, religion and morality."[7] This perspective formed the basis for many decisions affecting the relationship of the church and the state.

Church denominations, such as Congregationalists and Anglicans, received public or government financial support. These respective church organizations began calling their government benefactors "nursing fathers" from Isaiah 49:23.

This concept was taught in the Westminster Confession of Faith (1646).

In order to be egalitarian and not accused of favoritism of one religious denomination over another, many state governments assessed "religious taxes" on all its citizens. However, the citizenry could designate their tax money be given to the church of their choice. Such laws were established in Massachusetts, Connecticut, and New Hampshire. Maryland and Georgia passed similar laws but they were never implemented.

Due to the growing perspective the United States needed a stronger federal government, a convention was convened in Philadelphia during the summer of 1787. On September 17, the convention delegates ratified the Constitution of the United States of America. In spite of America's documented Christian heritage and culture, the Constitution said little if anything about religion. The only religious reference that is directly found within the Constitution is Article VI, which states, "No religious test shall ever be required as qualification" for federal office holders.[8]

This conspicuous absence of any religious reference troubled two particular groups: those who wanted the Constitution and the federal government to give religion a larger role and those who believed it would do so. The latter group exerted pressure upon the delegates, which eventually resulted in the adoption, in September 1789, of the First Amendment to the Constitution. When ratified by the required number of states in December 1791, the First Amendment prohibited Congress to make any law "respecting the establishment of religion." In short, this meant there would be no tax supported churches as there had been under the Articles of Confederation.

When the American public first became aware of the content of the Constitution, many Christians were troubled by the absence of any reference to God, or even of His existence. Unlike the Declaration of Independence, there was no reference at all in the Constitution to God as Creator and the dispenser of law.

Why? The godslayer contends that it is because the United States was never a Christian nation to begin with and any insinuation to the contrary is misguided. The absence of any mention of God in the Constitution he believes evidences this perspective. However, the aforementioned evidence for biblical Christianity within the colonies, and then states, clearly says otherwise. So why did the delegates to the Constitutional Convention refuse to make any reference to God in the Constitution?

There are two reasons for this glaring omission of God within the Constitution. First, many delegates to the Constitutional Convention were committed Federalists. They believed that the power to regulate religion, if any such power to regulate religion existed within the power of government at all, ultimately lay within the domain of the individual states and not the national government. Second, the delegates believed that it would be a mistake to make reference to such a controversial issue as religion into the Constitution.

As one historian explains, "That religion was not otherwise addressed in the Constitution did not make it an 'irreligious document' any more than the Articles of Confederation was an 'irreligious document.' The Constitution dealt with the church precisely as the Articles had, thereby maintaining, at the national level, the religious status quo."[9]

Neither in the Articles of Confederation, nor in the Constitution of the United States, did the citizenry yield any explicit power to the federal government for the purpose of either sponsoring or eliminating organized religion and the church in general, and the gospel of Jesus Christ in particular.

However, it should be noted that even though the God of the Bible is not explicitly mentioned in the United States Constitution, the many unique ideas for the governing of the United States originated not with the Founding Fathers, as intelligent as they were, but rather from the Bible: the Word of God. The Bible is the underlying foundation for America: the Constitution. Let us examine some examples from the Constitution.

Article I, Section 8 says, "The Congress shall have power to establish a uniform rule of naturalization."[10] Leviticus

19:34 says, "The alien living with you must be treated as one of your native born. Love him as yourself, for you were aliens in Egypt. I am the LORD your God."[11]

Article II, Section 1 says, "No person, except a natural born citizen, or a citizen of the United States, at the time of the adoption of this Constitution, shall be eligible to the office of President."[12] Deuteronomy 17:15 says, "Be sure to appoint over you the king the LORD your God chooses. He must be from among your own brothers. Do not place a foreigner over you."[13]

Article III, Section 3 says, "No person shall be convicted of treason unless on the testimony of two witnesses to the same overt act, or on confession in open court."[14] Deuteronomy 17:6 says, "On the testimony of two or three witnesses a man shall be put to death, but no one shall be put to death on the testimony of only one witness."[15]

Article III, Section 3 says, "The Congress shall have power to declare the Punishment of Treason, but no Attainder of Treason shall work Corruption of Blood, or Forfeiture, except during the life of the person attainted."[16] Ezekiel 18:20 says, "The soul who sins is the one who will die. The son will not share the guilt of the father, nor will the father share the guilt of the son."[17]

Article IV, Section 4 says, "The United States shall guarantee to every State in this Union a Republican Form of Government, and shall protect each of them against Invasion; and on Application of the Legislature, or of the

Executive (when the Legislature cannot be convened) against domestic Violence."[18] Isaiah 33:22 says, "For the LORD is our Judge, the LORD is our Lawgiver, the LORD is our King; he will save us."[19]

It is apparent in even a quick reading of the Constitution that its contents originated from another source. That source being the Word of God: the Bible.

Aside from the brilliant minds of America's Founding Fathers, the roots of America's public school system are found in the Christian religion. In early colonial America, and even following the Revolutionary War, ministers were not only filling the pulpits of their respective churches, but they were also filling the classrooms as schoolteachers. The primary textbooks included not only the Bible but also the New England Primer and the Bay Psalm Book.

The New England Primer contained the names of the all the books of the Bible, the Lord's Prayer, the Apostle's Creed, the Ten Commandments, the Westminster Catechism, and Reverend John Cotton's own publication *Spiritual Milk for American Babes, Drawn out of the Breasts of Both Testaments for their Soul's Nourishment.*

The New England Primer was the first reading grammar textbook designed for the American Colonies. It became the most successful educational textbook published in eighteenth century America and it became the foundation of most schooling prior to the 1790s.

Prior to the seventeenth century, the schoolbooks used in colonial America had been brought over from England. By 1690, Boston publishers were reprinting the *English Protestant Tutor* under the new title of The New England Primer. The Primer included additional material that made it widely popular with colonial schools until Noah Webster's *Blue Back Speller* superseded it after 1790.

The primer's contents for beginning instruction included the alphabet, vowels, consonants, double letters, and syllables. The ninety–page work contained religious maxims, woodcuts, alphabetical assistants, acronyms, catechism answers, and moral lessons. It was made with a thin sheet of paper shellacked to a wooden board. The board was transfixed with a handle.

The New England Primer was in print well into the nineteenth century and was even used until the twentieth century. A reported two million copies were sold in the eighteenth century. No copies of editions before 1727 are known to survive; earlier editions are known only from publishers' and booksellers' advertisements.

Many of the primer's selections were drawn from the King James Bible while others were original. It reflected the dominant Puritan perspective and biblical worldview of the day. Among the topics discussed are respect to parental figures, sin, and salvation. Some versions contained the Westminster Shorter Catechism; others contained John

Cotton's shorter catechism, known as *Spiritual Milk for Boston Babes*; and some contained both.

Correspondingly, the Bay Psalm Book was the first book actually printed in British North America. The book is a metrical psalter and was first printed in 1640 in Cambridge, Massachusetts. Its publication, just twenty years after the Pilgrim's arrival at Plymouth, Massachusetts, represents a considerable accomplishment. It went through several editions and remained in use for well over one hundred years.

The Scriptures clearly indicate that the state is one of God's created social institutions along with the family, work, the significance of man, the church, and community. Here is but a sampling of biblical truth regarding the state and its rulers.

1. Psalm 22:27–28. "All the ends of the earth shall remember and turn to the LORD, and all the families of the nations shall worship before you. For kingship belongs to the LORD, and he rules over the nations."[20]

2. Daniel 4:34–37. "At the end of the days I, Nebuchadnezzar, lifted my eyes to heaven, and my reason returned to me, and I blessed the Most High, and praised and honored him who lives forever, for his dominion is an everlasting dominion, and his kingdom endures from generation to generation; all the inhabitants of the earth are accounted as

nothing, and he does according to his will among the host of heaven and among the inhabitants of the earth; and none can stay his hand or say to him, 'What have you done?' At the same time my reason returned to me, and for the glory of my kingdom, my majesty and splendor returned to me. My counselors and my lords sought me, and I was established in my kingdom, and still more greatness was added to me. Now I, Nebuchadnezzar, praise and extol and honor the King of heaven, for all his works are right and his ways are just; and those who walk in pride he is able to humble."[21]

3. Daniel 2:20–21. "Let the name of God be blessed forever and ever, for wisdom and power belong to Him. It is He who changes the times and the epochs; He removes kings and establishes kings. He gives wisdom to wise men and knowledge to men of understanding."[22]

4. Romans 13:1. "Every person is to be in subjection to the governing authorities. For there is no authority except from God, and those which exist are established by God."[23]

These truths are not relegated to just old and dusty preserved documents from long years past and which are apparent to only the interested few, or to the intellectual. These self-evident truths, so predominant to our founding fathers, are conspicuously apparent to everyone and anyone who travels to Washington, DC, the United States capital. They are a part of the monumental landscape that marks the city and which correspondingly expresses the nation's spiritual and biblical foundation.

Unfortunately, many American citizens are unaware of these testimonials to the biblical foundation of the American experiment. The low information voter seems content to allow their view of America to be framed and formed by popular politicians, media moguls, and antagonistic atheists.

What are these monument testimonials of which I speak and which can be observed even today for the sensitive of heart and sight? They include the following.

The National Archives Building houses several testimonials to America's biblical heritage. There is the image of the Ten Commandments engraved in bronze on the archive's floor signifying that our legal system had its origin in the Ten Commandments God gave to Moses on Mount Sinai. The archives also houses the original Declaration of Independence. The Declaration of Independence holds as an incontrovertible truth that our rights as human beings come from God, not from the king or the state. God is referred to in the Declaration as "lawgiver," "Creator," "Supreme Judge," and "Protector." Finally, the entrance to the National Archives holds a bronze medallion containing the Ten Commandments. Clearly, a reference not only to the Bible but also to the foundation of America's laws.

The Washington Monument, a tribute obelisk to America's first president George Washington, also contains several biblical references. The east side of the aluminum capstone reads the Latin inscription *Laus Deo*, which means "praise be to God." The cornerstone of the monument contains a Bible along with copies of the Declaration of Independence and the Constitution of the United States. Inside the monument is a memorial plaque from the Free Press Methodist-Episcopal Church. On the twelfth landing is a prayer offered by the City of Baltimore. There is a memorial from Chinese Christians located on the twentieth landing. There is a presentation made by Sunday school children from New York and Philadelphia on the twenty-fourth landing. Other carved tribute blocks include these statements: "Search the Scriptures," "Holiness to the Lord," "In God We Trust," and "Train up a child in the way he should go, and when he is old, he will not depart from it" (Prov. 22:6).[24]

The Jefferson Memorial is located near the Tidal Basin in Washington, DC. It resembles Jefferson's Virginia home, Monticello, and features several interior panels for viewing. Panel One in the memorial contains this reference from the Declaration of Independence: "We hold these truths to be self-evident: that all men are created equal, that they are endowed by their Creator with certain unalienable rights, that among these are life, liberty, and the pursuit of happiness." Panel Two says, "Almighty God hath created the mind free…" Panel Three states, "God who gave us life gave us liberty…"

One of the most familiar and visited memorials in our nation's capital is the Lincoln Memorial. Dominated by an imposing statue of America's sixteenth president, Abraham Lincoln, it also contains the text of two of the president's speeches. On the left side of the statue is the Gettysburg Address. While only 267 words, it concludes with Lincoln's view of America's relationship to God: "We here highly resolve that these dead shall not have died in vain, that this nation, under God, shall have a new birth of freedom." On the right side of the statue is Lincoln's Second Inaugural Address. Containing only 703 words, Lincoln refers to God fourteen times and quotes the Bible twice.

Another familiar building within the nation's capital is the United States Capitol Building in which both the United States Senate and the House of Representatives meet to make and pass laws. There are many overtly Christian testimonials within the capitol building that many citizens may be unaware.

Each day while in session, both the House of Representatives and the Senate open their session with the Pledge of Allegiance, which continues to include the phrase "One Nation under God." Various paintings are on display in the rotunda depicting prayer, fasting, the Bible, and God's divine protection.

In the Cox Corridor in the House wing is this saying carved into the wall; "America! God shed His grace on thee." Also in the House chamber is the inscription "In God We Trust." In the east entrance to the Senate chamber are the inscribed words in Latin *Annuit Coeptis*, which means "God has favored our undertakings." Also engraved are the words "What hath God Wrought!"

In the House chamber is a full face relief of Moses. Other leaders depicted in statues include many Christians, among whom were ministers. These include George Washington, James Garfield, Samuel Adams, Reverend Peter Muhlenerg, Reverend Roger Williams, Reverend Marcus Whitman, Daniel Webster, Lew Wallace, Reverend Jason Lee, John Winthrop, Reverend Jonathan Trumbull, Roger Sherman, and Francis Willard.

The capital also has a chapel. The capital's chapel contains a stained glass window of George Washington praying under the inscription "In God We Trust." The prayer inscribed in the window says "Preserve me, God, for in Thee do I put my trust." The United States Capital was the setting for church services through the vice presidency and presidency of Thomas Jefferson.

Across the street from the United States Capitol Building is the United States Supreme Court Building. The nine justices who meet there are responsible for interpreting the constitutionality of our nation's laws. While their decisions carry great weight and impact, so too does the building in which they gather.

Over the east portico of the Supreme Court building is a depiction of Moses and the Ten commandments. This scene is also depicted in the actual courtroom and engraved over the chair of the Chief Justice. It is also found on the bronze door of the Supreme Court itself. It is interesting to note that while plaques depicting the Ten Commandments are removed from courtrooms, city halls and schools throughout the country, the Supreme Court building prominently displays them.

The Library of Congress is the research library that officially serves the United States Congress, but which is the *de facto* national library of the United States. It is the oldest federal cultural institution in the United States. It is one of the largest and most international libraries in the world. President Thomas Jefferson called the concept of the Library of Congress a national institution that should be universal in scope and widely and freely available to everyone. Located in four buildings in Washington, DC, as well as the Packard Campus in Virginia, it is the second largest library in the world by number of items catalogued.

On permanent display is the Giant Bible of Mainz. It is a handwritten and illustrated version of the Bible. There is also a Guttenberg Bible on permanent display. Inscribed on the walls of the Great Hall are: "The light shinneth in darkness, and the darkness comprehendeth it not" (John 1:5),[25] and "Wisdom is the principle thing; therefore get wisdom and with all thy getting, get understanding" (Prov. 4:7).[26]

In the main reading room is a bronze statue of Moses holding the Ten Commandments. Also inscribed on the walls of the main reading room are the following engraved verses from the Bible: "What doth the Lord require of thee, but to do justly, and to love mercy, and to walk humbly with thy God" (Micah 6:8),[27] and "The heavens declare the glory of God and the firmament showeth His handiwork" (Ps. 19:1).[28]

Finally, the residence of the American President, known as the While House, contains one notable reference to the One True God. The fireplace mantle in the state dining room contains the following prayer by President John Adams. "I pray to heaven to bestow the best of blessings on this house and all that hereafter inhabit it. May none but the honest and wise men ever rule under this roof."

Historical revisionists, and so-called atheists like the godslayer, would have American citizens believe that America was never founded and conceived upon biblical principles. The historical record proves otherwise.

In his primer on America, entitled *The American Cause*, author Russell Kirk offers the following perspective regarding America's inception and its uniqueness that is being threatened by its enemies at worst, and ignored by its citizens at least.

He argues that America was founded upon three basic groups of ideas. While he believes all civilizations can claim these ideas as their own, America has uniquely embraced and embodied them. These three groups of ideas are (1) a set of moral convictions that America holds, preeminent being its belief in God and the subsequent issues between virtue and vice, honesty and dishonesty, honor and dishonor; (2) a set of political convictions it holds regarding justice and injustice, freedom and tyranny, personal rights and power along with living together as a community; and (3) a set of economic convictions about wealth and property, public and private ownership, labor and the distribution of goods and services.

Out of all three of these principles of ideas comes forth the idea known as the American experience. Kirk maintains that, "Most Americans are convinced that certain of these enduring truths were revealed to humankind by God: among these principles are the necessity for worshipping the Creator, the essence of private morality, and the nature of love which teaches us our duties toward other men and women. The powers and the limits of human nature, Americans have felt, have been implanted in our minds by divine revelation"[29]

Because of this foundation, Kirk believes America is a Christian nation. Kirk did not write that America was a Christian nation or had been founded as a Christian, all of which is arguably true. He wrote "America is a Christian nation." What did he mean by this statement originally written in the 1950s and in the immediate aftermath of his greatest literary work *The Conservative Mind* and the conclusion of the Korean War? Kirk explains:

> The United States is a Christian nation. This is a simple statement of fact, not an argument to advance the American cause. With the exception of the five and half million American Jews, Christians or people strongly influenced by Christian beliefs make up the great majority of our population. The ideas of freedom, private rights, love, and duty and honesty, for instance, all are beliefs religious in origin. These ideals also are discussed and advanced by philosophers, or course, but the original impulse behind them is religious. And in America, it is the Christian religion, some two thousand years old (or much older when one includes the Jewish source of Christianity) and now worldwide in influence, which ultimately affects our actions.[30]

Kirk goes on to say that at the heart of the American cause are the beliefs in the fatherhood of God, the brotherhood of man, and the dignity of man. He explains that from these beliefs there has developed conviction of how Americans are to conduct their lives, how we are to treat our fellow human beings, and what makes life worth living.

This is the self-evident truth the founders understood. What we consider oblique language to us was normal speech to them. When they referred to the "laws of nature" and "natures God" in the Declaration of Independence, they were referring to the God of the Bible.

The God of the Bible was the dominant focus on the establishment of the United States government. This is evident by the many existing quotes from our Founding Fathers.

America is not the Kingdom of God. America is not a substitute for heaven. America is not perfect. However, God has established America in time and history, has worked through its leaders and citizens to bring Him glory, and is calling His chosen people to repent of their sins and be the salt and light that America desperately needs.

14

Letter Nine!

With or without religion you would have good people doing good things and evil people doing evil things...but for good people to do evil things, that takes religion.

—*Steven Weinberg*

I just finished reading your insipid newspaper similar. Not surprisingly, your facts are misleading. You forgot to mention how these bucolic pilgrims refused community food to any who were not submissive to their "inspired" interpretation of the scriptures, or of murdering Indians because they followed a different god or of course laying the framework to burn and drown thousands of witches to show their Christian love.

So let me challenge you, Why not try and answer a real question. I assure you that not all who read your pabulum are mindless sheep that cannot, or will not, think for themselves.

Questions:

1. *Why does your god allow evil, illness or poverty?*

2. *Why does your god never cure amputees?*

3. *Why did your god not make people incapable of sin?*

4. *Why did your god not assure man of paradise?*

Choose any of the above but please do not insult my intelligence by coping out with the myth of transferred liability from Adam/Eve or the idiotic claptrap of original sin.

I wait to see your responses...if you have the courage. Or perhaps you are such a slave to your delusions that you are just another charlatan for Christianity.

Let us see if you are, or are not, a phony.

—The godslayer

Why does the godslayer, and others like him, lack faith in God? I submit it is not because of a lack of answers to their questions. Neither is it because of a lack of evidence to their skepticism. Lack of faith in the God of the Scriptures is not the result of the lack of answers or the lack of evidence. Rather, it is due to the absence of the Holy Spirit within their deadened soul.

1 Corinthians 2:14 says, "The natural person does not accept the things of the Spirit of God, for they are folly to him, and he is not able to understand them because they are spiritually discerned."[1] The text is saying that anyone who

is dead in their trespasses and sins (the natural person) does not accept the truth originating from the Holy Spirit and found in Scripture. They regard biblical truth as foolishness.

The text also says that neither do they accept the truths belonging to nor emanating from the Spirit of God, but they also do not understand the biblical truths they reject. The only way biblical truth can be understood by anyone is for that individual in question to be indwelt by the Holy Spirit. In other words, the individual needs to be converted unto Christ in order to understand the truths regarding Christ. The person must be born again (John 3:1–3) or regenerated by the Holy Spirit (Titus 3:1–7). Regeneration results in the individual being indwelt by the Holy Spirit (Rom. 8:1–9) and therefore one result of this miracle is being able to understand biblical truth (1 Cor. 2:1–14).

Followers of Jesus are not mindless sheep who cannot think for themselves. Rather, they are individuals who now possess the Holy Spirit and who view life and living, its origin and its purpose, from a completely different mindset than the world. They are not called or commanded to hate the people of the world, but rather to show God's love for those who belong to the fallen, ungodly world.

On the other hand, the world hates the follower of Jesus. Jesus said this would happen, so his disciples today should not be surprised when this hatred occurs. John the apostle wrote in 1 John 3:13–15:

> For this is the message that you have heard from
> the beginning, that we should love one another. We
> should not be like Cain, who was of the evil one and
> murdered his brother. And why did he murder him?
> Because his own deeds were evil and his brother's
> righteous. Do not be surprised, brothers, that the
> world hates you. We know that we have passed out of
> death into life, because we love the brothers. Whoever
> does not love abides in death. Everyone who hates his
> brother is a murderer, and you know that no murderer
> has eternal life abiding in him.[2]

Jesus said in Matthew 5:11–12, "Blessed are you when others revile you and persecute you and utter all kinds of evil against you falsely on my account. Rejoice and be glad, for your reward is great in heaven, for so they persecuted the prophets who were before you"[3] Jesus also said in John 15:18–25:

> If the world hates you, know that it has hated me
> before it hated you. If you were of the world, the world
> would love you as its own; but because you are not of
> the world, but I chose you out of the world, therefore
> the world hates you. Remember the word that I said
> to you: "A servant is not greater than his master." If
> they persecuted me, they will also persecute you. If
> they kept my word, they will also keep yours. But all
> these things they will do to you on account of my
> name, because they do not know him who sent me. If
> I had not come and spoken to them, they would not

have been guilty of sin, but now they have no excuse for their sin. Whoever hates me hates my Father also. If I had not done among them the works that no one else did, they would not be guilty of sin, but now they have seen and hated both me and my Father. But the word that is written in their Law must be fulfilled: "They hated me without a cause."[4]

In facing the obvious challenge the godslayer lays before me, Proverbs 26:4–5 comes to mind. The text says, "Answer not a fool according to his folly, lest you be like him yourself. Answer a fool according to his folly, lest he be wise in his own eyes."[5]

On the surface, these two verses seem to be contradictory. I am surprised the godslayer has not brought this to my attention earlier as an example of an apparent contradiction within the Bible. However, there are wise principles in these verses, lessons to help followers of Jesus be much more effective in countering false arguments and in witnessing to people with the gospel.

Let us begin by looking at verse 4: "Do not answer a fool according to his folly, lest you also be like him." A "fool" is an individual who is an unbeliever who rejects God's truth. David writes in Psalm 14:1 that, "The fool says in his heart, 'There is no God.' They are corrupt, they do abominable deeds, there is none who does good."[6]

Proverbs 26:4 is saying that the follower of Christ should not respond to an unbeliever's objections to biblical truth by agreeing with a particular individual's ideas and presuppositions. If one does this, they will think they are right.

Rather, he should be rebuked, which is the substantive meaning of Proverbs 26:5, "Answer a fool according to his folly, lest he be wise in his own eyes."[7] The unbelieving fool should be confronted with his own foolishness and shown the truth in order to see how truly foolish he is.

Therefore, with Proverbs 26:4–5 in mind, I will biblically respond to the godslayer's challenge. I pray the Holy Spirit will persuade him of the truth. All four of are worthy of a biblical answer. While the godslayer may not accept the answers provided, it is a responsible thing to answer the questions he has posed.

The godslayer asks, "Why does your god allow evil, illness or poverty?" Since I have already answered the problem of evil from a Scriptural perspective, I will not repeat myself. I would refer the reader to the earlier chapter where this subject is addressed. However, I would pose a question back to the godslayer in light of the question he poses to me.

Why would a free thinker like the godslayer have a problem with evil in the first place? How does he define evil? What standard does he possess in which he can comprehend and define what exactly is evil since in order to do this you must have a corresponding standard of goodness for comparison?

The believer's standard of goodness is God. However, the godslayer objects to the very idea of God's existence and His goodness. Therefore, how then does he define what is evil? Is it a personal opinion? Will everyone agree with his personal opinion regarding what is evil?

In a worldview in which there is no God, or a rejection of the one, true God, what can really be identified as evil? For many, child abuse, rape, murder, war, disease, etc., may be viewed in a humanistic, atheistic system of thought as good and not evil. Again, there must be a standard for goodness in order for any deviation from that standard to be identified as evil.

The godslayer offers no alternative, objective standard for goodness. Therefore, his question concerning evil's existence betrays his atheistic worldview. He is revealing a latent theistic worldview in which he objects to evil's existence in light of God's existence. The godslayer, and others like him, are not the atheistic free thinkers they portray themselves to be since they continue to operate from an inherent system of thought that evidences the existence of God (Rom. 1:18–23).

The other questions are "Why does your God never cure amputees?" "Why did your god not make man incapable of sin?" "Why did your god not assure man of paradise?"

The godslayer says to not respond to his questions by insulting his intelligence by coping out with the so-called myth of transferred liability from Adam/Eve or the idiotic claptrap of original sin. It seems that the godslayer is not only intending to control the questions that are posed but also the answers that are given. He desires an answer from me, except the answer that he does not want to hear from me.

When my children were younger, they would ask me questions regarding an issue they were dealing with, at school for example. Often they would want me to side with their point of view. Many times I did. Sometimes I did not. When I did not agree with them, they became upset. In those moments, it was apparent they wanted my input just as long as my input was agreeable to them and what they wanted.

The godslayer wants me to answer his questions, but he does not want to hear my answers if they are what he does not want to hear. In that context, it becomes a no-win situation. The answer has to be biblical. It will not be what he wants to hear but it is what he, and others like him, needs to hear.

Why does God never cure amputees? Aside from the obvious reason that it would relieve the amputee's difficulty in presently functioning without the use of a limb(s), what is the purpose for a question such as this? It reminds me of those who ask the question of whether God could make a rock so heavy He could not lift it.

Would God curing an amputee create belief within people who witness such an event? All we have to do is go to Scripture and discover the reaction of people who witnessed many miracles performed by Jesus. More often than not the crowds were not persuaded to believe in Jesus. Often the result of Jesus's miracles, take the Feeding of the 5,000 from John 6 for example, resulted in the crowd only wanting to see another miracle. They wanted to be entertained. They wanted the miraculous as long as the miraculous made no demands upon them. They wanted the sensational but did not want any such event to occur within their soul resulting in a changed life or lifestyle. They wanted God on their terms, failing to understand that God brings sinners to Himself on His terms alone.

In Matthew 12:38–40 Jesus said, "Then some of the scribes and Pharisees answered him, saying, 'Teacher, we wish to see a sign from you.' But he answered them, 'An evil and adulterous generation seeks for a sign, but no sign will be given to it except the sign of the prophet Jonah. For just as Jonah was three days and three nights in the belly of the great fish, so will the Son of Man be three days and three nights in the heart of the earth.'"[8]

Jesus reiterated this statement in Matthew 16:1–4 when responding to the religious leaders He said,

> And the Pharisees and Sadducees came, and to test him they asked him to show them a sign from heaven. He answered them, "When it is evening, you say, 'It will be fair weather, for the sky is red.' And in the morning, 'It will be stormy today, for the sky is red

and threatening.' You know how to interpret the appearance of the sky, but you cannot interpret the signs of the times. An evil and adulterous generation seeks for a sign, but no sign will be given to it except the sign of Jonah." So he left them and departed.[9]

Luke 6:6–11 records an incident during Jesus's ministry to this pertinent question from the godslayer.

On another Sabbath, he entered the synagogue and was teaching, and a man was there whose right hand was withered. And the scribes and the Pharisees watched him, to see whether he would heal on the Sabbath, so that they might find a reason to accuse him. But he knew their thoughts, and he said to the man with the withered hand, "Come and stand here." And he rose and stood there. And Jesus said to them, "I ask you, is it lawful on the Sabbath to do good or to do harm, to save life or to destroy it?" And after looking around at them all he said to him, "Stretch out your hand." And he did so, and his hand was restored. But they were filled with fury and discussed with one another what they might do to Jesus.[10]

The word *withered* (ξηρός) means a paralyzed and shrunken hand. It was a hand that could not move was not useable. The text does not tell us how this man came to be in this condition, only that he was truly in this condition. Jesus healed this man in a public setting. It was a miracle that was undeniably real. Yet the response from the religious leaders was not belief or worship, but rather scorn and fury.

Jesus cured many diseases and infirmities when He was on earth. Sometimes those events solicited belief and faith in Christ. Many times, those miraculous events invited scorn and ridicule from Jesus's enemies. Does Jesus still possess the ability to heal disease and restore lost limbs? Yes! However, He does not do so like a marionette who jumps at creation's beck and call. He is the sovereign Lord, not us. Everyone, including the godslayer, will eventually realize this: either in salvation or judgment.

The godslayer asks, "Why did your god not make man incapable of sin?" God promises to make man incapable of sin, but that is not the present existence of redeemed man as of now. Believers struggle and fight sin (Gal. 5:16–23) and sometimes they gives into temptation (2 Sam. 11). Ultimately, God will redeem them completely. Romans 8:18–25 says,

> For I consider that the sufferings of this present time are not worth comparing with the glory that is to be revealed to us. For the creation waits with eager longing for the revealing of the sons of God. For the creation was subjected to futility, not willingly, but because of him who subjected it, in hope that the creation itself will be set free from its bondage to corruption and obtain the freedom of the glory of the children of God. For we know that the whole creation has been groaning together in the pains of childbirth until now.

> And not only the creation, but we ourselves, who have the first fruits of the Spirit, groan inwardly as we wait eagerly for adoption as sons, the redemption of our bodies. For in this hope we were saved. Now hope that is seen is not hope. For who hopes for what he sees? But if we hope for what we do not see, we wait for it with patience.[11]

The believer's original state in Adam was the power to not sin but still possessing the ability to sin. This evoked a complete freedom of the will in Adam and Eve. They truly had a free choice to either obey God or to disobey. How unlike them we are.

The fallen state of all sinners is the power only to sin. No longer free to obey God, the sinner is locked in a complete bondage of the will. This is what is meant by the phrase "total depravity." This means that sin affects fallen man in every area of his being: intellect, emotions, and will. All those in Adam experience this bondage. They are known as the lost. Each and every Christian were lost at some time in their past. The "freedom" fallen, sinful man possesses is the freedom to sin, but not to please and serve God. Deliverance from this bondage is only through Jesus Christ. This deliverance is called salvation.

The third state of man is the redeemed state. The present condition for those in Christ is the power to not sin but still retaining the ability to sin. This is the state of the freed will. This is the existence of those known as the justified. The process of sanctification, which follows justification, is the cooperative effort by the redeemed and the Holy Spirit, unlike justification, which is solely the work of God, to grow in personal holiness and to truly become what the redeemed is before God in position: glorified.

The final state of the Christian's redeemed condition will be the ability to not sin. The redeemed in everlasting covenant with God in heaven will not be able to sin. This is a total and complete freedom of the will. This is what is known as glorification. It is this fourth and final state that the redeemed anxiously anticipate.

The fourth question the godslayer poses is "Why did your god not assure man of paradise?" God has. The particular occasion is found in Luke 23:39–43. What was true for the thief on the cross is also true for all types of sinners who place faith in Christ.

> Two others, who were criminals, were led away to be put to death with him. And when they came to the place that is called the Skull, there they crucified him, and the criminals, one on his right and one on his left. And Jesus said, "Father, forgive them, for they know not what they do." And they cast lots to divide his garments. And the people stood by, watching, but the rulers scoffed at him, saying, "He saved others; let him save himself, if he is the Christ of God, his Chosen One!" The soldiers also mocked him, coming up and offering him sour wine and saying, "If you are the King of the Jews, save yourself!" There was also an inscription over him, "This is the King of the Jews."

> One of the criminals who were hanged railed at him, saying, "Are you not the Christ? Save yourself and us!" But the other rebuked him, saying, "Do you not fear God, since you are under the same sentence of condemnation? And we indeed justly, for we are receiving the due reward of our deeds; but this man has done nothing wrong." And he said, "Jesus, remember me when you come into your kingdom." And he said to him, "Truly, I say to you, today you will be with me in Paradise."[12]

The same meaning for paradise is also found in 2 Corinthians 12:1–3, "I must go on boasting. Though there is nothing to be gained by it, I will go on to visions and revelations of the Lord. I know a man in Christ who fourteen years ago was caught up to the third heaven—whether in the body or out of the body I do not know, God knows. And I know that this man was caught up into paradise—whether in the body or out of the body I do not know, God knows."[13]

A final occurrence of the word *paradise* is found in Revelation 2:7. "He who has an ear, let him hear what the Spirit says to the churches. To the one who conquers I will grant to eat of the tree of life, which is in the paradise of God."[13]

God promises paradise for all who believe in the Lord Jesus Christ as Savior and Lord. The assurance is found in God's Word and is given to us by God. God has clearly promised paradise to all believers in Jesus Christ. No exceptions! Paradise is synonymous with heaven.

Only God and the godslayer know whether or not the godslayer's questions are sincere and reflect a person who truly wants answers, or his letters are just a posturing for the purpose of articulating his prejudiced propositions against biblical Christianity.

Letter Ten!

Here it is, another Christmas and a year of hate, pain, horrors, death and desolation. Another year of subject silence from an allegedly "loving god." But it does make one think: what is the real meaning of Christmas?

Visions of a soft cuddly baby surrounded by adoring parents, dozing animals, friendly shepherds and the rest of the mythological crèche are everywhere obscured with the sedative strains of Silent Night. But are these visions real?

Christmas means the birth of Christ. But why was he born? The party line is that he was born to save man from sin…but what sin? Why the "adopted" sin of someone centuries ago eating a piece of fruit, or course. Although this speaks volumes about a deity who would damn an entire race for this symbolic wrong, one wonders why this god who touted "forgiveness" just couldn't forgive.

No, the only way this evil monster of a god could be placated was by the torture and murder of His son. Was this the act of a loving father or one of an insane psychopath, while all the time demanding that we love him and shower him with all of the credit and none of the blame? Perhaps, the only "saving" we need is to be saved from this god.

To make matters worse, even this evil wrath didn't do what he was supposed to. This monster, even after having enjoyed the agony and death of his son, still demanded we acknowledge his asserted superiority, symbolically consume his flesh, be born in the right time into the right religion, die free from any transgressions for acting the way he made us. And even then most people would find themselves tortured in the hell created by this bastard.

Still this monster god claims he has the ONLY proper moral values. Let us consider this, assuming that god was Jesus and is rational and knows what he is doing:

1. *Mary was married to another man at the time god impregnated her; therefore god is an adulterer.*

2. *Mary was a minor at the time of conception; therefore god was a child molester.*

3. *Mary did not consent to have intercourse with god (and being a minor could not give consent anyway); therefore god was a rapist.*

4. *If god was Jesus and Jesus had sexual relations with his mother, then god committed incest.*

5. *After the birth of Jesus, god was nowhere to be found and left it to others to raise the child he fathered. Therefore, god was a deadbeat dad.*

6. *God supposedly has a purpose in life and that was to
    kill his own son; therefore god is a murderer.*

    *So, at this time of year we must reflect "what does
    this make god?" God is obviously an adulterer, child
    molester, rapist who committed incest and abandoned his
    responsibilities and is a murderer to boot. Can one honestly
    say such a psychopath is not insane? Isn't it obvious that
    this capricious monster is severely mentally ill?*

    *May this monster rot in his own hell, in his own
    pathetic blood. Season's greetings to god in his hell.*

    —*The godslayer*

Just when I think the godslayer could not become any
more blasphemous than what he already has been, I read
another letter from him. I not only consider the content
of what he writes, but also the anger and wrath with
which he writes it. This appears to be a tortured soul who
apparently seeks to relieve his agony by attacking God and
others who God has delivered through Jesus Christ from
their own personal condemnation before God. I so want
to know the circumstances that perhaps resulted in this
person who has written to me. A person who has reached
out with such hatred for God, His followers in general and
me in particular.

However, I believe I know this man all too well. I know
the anger that fills his being and the void within his soul
that cannot be comforted by the hateful venom with which
he spews. The very God he hates with such passion is the

only one who can overcome his deepest need. He is like the woman at the well (John 4:1–42) who sought to fill the deepest need of her soul with multiple men and marriages. He is like the prodigal sons (Luke 16) who filled the void of their souls with respectively riotous living and rigid self-righteousness.

How do I know this man who calls himself a godslayer with such confidence? It is because I once was like this man, as is every sinner without Christ. The fallen sinner detests the very one who created him and who offers the only hope for one's eternal soul's greatest need: recreation and regeneration by the Holy Spirit based upon the substitutionary atonement gospel of Jesus Christ (John 3:1–8; Titus 3).

As in previous chapters of this book, let me address the godslayer's comments point by point. I do so not only to respond to his statements, but also to equip believers to appropriately respond to similar statements when, or if, they ever encounter such contempt.

The godslayer's venom does not extend to just the Christmas season, but also to the One True God of which the season is predominately focused. This is not the place to comment on the commercialism of the Christmas season, but the godslayer describes the holidays as the culmination of another year of hate, pain, horrors, death, and desolation. I do not discount or deny the reality of hate, pain, horror, death, and desolation in this world throughout any given year. Why then did God enter into this world, if not to finally deal with the source of hate, pain, horrors, death, and desolation?

There is no question that these problems exist and are huge. However, no matter how impassioned the godslayer is about these issues, and his critique that God is not sufficient to address them, he as of yet offers no solutions to these pressing problems. As is his practice, he passionately criticizes God, and bemoans the human condition, but is strangely silent in offering "any" alternative answers or solutions. It is not enough to complain about societies' ills and then fail to offer any constructive answer to address those ills.

Ironically, the godslayer acknowledges the truth of the Bible contained in Ephesians 2:1–3. While on one hand he mentions the tragic plight of man's fallen condition, he fails to recognize that man is ultimately responsible for the inevitable evidence of his fallen condition.

> And you were dead in the trespasses and sins in which you once walked, following the course of this world, following the prince of the power of the air, the spirit that is now at work in the sons of disobedience— among whom we all once lived in the passions of our flesh, carrying out the desires of the body and the mind, and were by nature children of wrath, like the rest of mankind.[1]

He echoes the words of American poet Henry Wadsworth Longfellow in the familiar Christmas carol "I Heard the Bells on Christmas Day." The song is based upon his 1863 poem "Christmas Bells," which was written Christmas Day 1863 during the height of the American Civil War. The song tells of the poet's despair upon hearing Christmas bells, because "hate is strong and mocks the song of peace on earth, good will to men." The carol concludes with the bells carrying renewed hope for peace from God among men because the right will prevail. As one Longfellow biographer explains,

> During the American Civil War, Longfellow's oldest son Charles Appleton Longfellow joined the Union cause as a soldier without his father's blessing. Longfellow was informed by a letter dated March 14, 1863, after Charles had left. "I have tried hard to resist the temptation of going without your leave but I cannot any longer," he wrote. "I feel it to be my first duty to do what I can for my country and I would willingly lay down my life for it if it would be of any good." Charles soon got an appointment as a lieutenant but, in November, he was severely wounded in the Battle of New Hope Church (in Virginia) during the Mine Run Campaign. Coupled with the recent loss of his wife Frances, who died as a result of an accidental fire, Longfellow was inspired to write "Christmas Bells."[2]

I recently reviewed the lyrics Longfellow wrote two centuries ago. They strangely echo the words recently written to me by my anonymous adversary. However, where the godslayer continues to wallow in despair, Longfellow, while in the midst of his misery, clings to the truth of God's faithfulness and sovereign and righteous providence.

> I heard the bells on Christmas Day
> Their old, familiar carols play,
> and wild and sweet
> The words repeat
> Of peace on earth, good-will to men!
>
> And thought how, as the day had come,
> The belfries of all Christendom
> Had rolled along
> The unbroken song
> Of peace on earth, good-will to men!
>
> Till ringing, singing on its way,
> The world revolved from night to day,
> A voice, a chime,
> A chant sublime
> Of peace on earth, good-will to men!
>
> Then from each black, accursed mouth
> The cannon thundered in the South,
> And with the sound
> The carols drowned

Of peace on earth, good-will to men!

It was as if an earthquake rent
The hearth-stones of a continent,
And made forlorn
The households born
Of peace on earth, good-will to men!

And in despair I bowed my head;
"There is no peace on earth," I said;
"For hate is strong,
And mocks the song
Of peace on earth, good-will to men!"

Then pealed the bells more loud and deep:
"God is not dead, nor doth He sleep;
The Wrong shall fail,
The Right prevail,
With peace on earth, good-will to men."[3]

The godslayer complains that God is silent; this God who he attacks and denies even exists. Yet, this holy God of the Scriptures is not silent as the godslayer contends. On the contrary, He speaks long and loud; not only through His creation but also in His Word. He has revealed Himself and His will. Here is what the psalmist King David says in Psalm 19 regarding God's general revelation of Himself through creation and His specific revelation through Scripture. It is a psalm addressed to the choirmaster.

The heavens declare the glory of God,
And the sky above proclaims his handiwork.
Day to day pours out speech,
And night to night reveals knowledge.
There is no speech, nor are there words,
Whose voice is not heard?
Their voice goes out through all the earth,
And their words to the end of the world.
In them he has set a tent for the sun,
Which comes out like a bridegroom leaving his
chamber,
And, like a strong man, runs its course with joy.
Its rising is from the end of the heavens,
And its circuit to the end of them,
And there is nothing hidden from its heat.
The law of the LORD is perfect,
Reviving the soul;
The testimony of the LORD is sure,
Making wise the simple;
The precepts of the LORD are right,
Rejoicing the heart;
The commandment of the LORD is pure,
Enlightening the eyes;
The fear of the LORD is clean,
Enduring forever;
The rules of the LORD are true,
And righteous altogether.
More to be desired are they than gold,
Even much fine gold;
Sweeter also than honey

And drippings of the honeycomb.
Moreover, by them is your servant warned;
In keeping them there is great reward.
Who can discern his errors?
Declare me innocent from hidden faults.
Keep back your servant also from presumptuous sins;
Let them not have dominion over me!
Then I shall be blameless,
And innocent of great transgression.
Let the words of my mouth and the meditation of
my heart
Be acceptable in your sight,
O Lord, my rock and my redeemer.[4]

Not only does God continually reveal Himself to humanity each and every day through His creation and through the Word of God, but he has revealed Himself most significantly through the historical God-man Jesus Christ (Heb. 1:1–4). Creation and the Bible are God's self-revelation. The reason why man perceives that God is silent is because man has rejected the revelation God has provided (Rom. 1:18–32).

God reveals Himself and is not silent, and what He reveals is truth. We are to submit to the revelation of God because His revelation discloses His character. He is the God of truth (Ps. 31:5; Isa. 65:16). He is abundant in truth (Exod. 34:6). His truth reaches to the highest clouds (Ps. 108:4). Finally, His word is truth (2 Sam. 7:28; Ps. 119:160; John 17:17). Truth means stability, reliability, firmness, and trustworthiness. Therefore, God cannot lie (Num. 23:19; 1 Sam. 15:29; Titus 1:2; Heb. 6:18).

God not only reveals His true character but also our own. Romans 3:10–19 reveals the character of fallen, sinful mankind.

> What then? Are we Jews any better off? No, not at all. For we have already charged that all, both Jews and Greeks, are under sin, as it is written: "None is righteous, no, not one; no one understands; no one seeks for God. All have turned aside; together they have become worthless; no one does good, not even one." "Their throat is an open grave; they use their tongues to deceive." "The venom of asps is under their lips." "Their mouth is full of curses and bitterness." "Their feet are swift to shed blood; in their paths are ruin and misery, and the way of peace they have not known." "There is no fear of God before their eyes." Now we know that whatever the law says it speaks to those who are under the law, so that every mouth may be stopped, and the whole world may be held accountable to God. For by works of the law no human being will be justified in his sight, since through the law comes knowledge of sin.[5]

God's indictment against sinful humanity is not just a New Testament concept, but rather one that is consistent throughout the Scriptures. Within the previously quoted section of his Epistle to the Romans, the Apostle Paul extensively quotes from the Old Testament verifying his inspired words in what would become the New Testament as God revealed truth.

God does not deny the reality of pain and suffering. In fact, the Scriptures fully reveal the reality of what life and living is like in this sin-filled world. What the godslayer fails to acknowledge is that this hate, pain, horror, death, and desolation mankind experiences is sourced in people not unlike himself.

Why not place the responsibility for the world's problems on the doorstep of the guilty: sinners like him and me. The difference between the godslayer and me, and others like me, is that God has shown His love abundantly into our souls and has rescued us from the despondency of life without Him and the just condemnation of our sins before Him. It is because of the realization of that deliverance that the believer in Christ praises God for His great salvation. The sinner exclaims "salvation is of the LORD" (Jonah 2:9, ESV).[6] This is the message the follower of Christ is to communicate to those who are still bound in sin.

True, Christians experience pain, suffer horrors, encounter death and perhaps even desolation. However, while the godslayer has nothing to cling to during those experiences but his incalculable hatred toward God, the disciple of Jesus rests upon the Lord's sustaining grace. Hebrews 4: 14–16 says,

> Since then we have a great high priest who has passed through the heavens, Jesus, the Son of God, let us hold fast our confession. For we do not have a high priest

who is unable to sympathize with our weaknesses, but one who in every respect has been tempted as we are, yet without sin. Let us then with confidence draw near to the throne of grace, that we may receive mercy and find grace to help in time of need.[7]

The psalmist David declares similar sentiments in Psalm 27. He acknowledges the reality of real pain and suffering. However, he also offers the eternal hope found in the One True God who has chosen to reveal Himself.

> The LORD is my light and my salvation;
> Whom shall I fear?
> The LORD is the stronghold of my life;
> Of whom shall I be afraid?
> When evildoers assail me
> To eat up my flesh,
> My adversaries and foes,
> It is they who stumble and fall.
> Though an army encamp against me,
> My heart shall not fear;
> Though war arise against me,
> Yet I will be confident.
> One thing have I asked of the LORD,
> That will I seek after:
> That I may dwell in the house of the LORD
> All the days of my life,
> To gaze upon the beauty of the LORD
> And to inquire in his temple.
> For he will hide me in his shelter

In the day of trouble;
He will conceal me under the cover of his tent;
He will lift me high upon a rock.[8]

The hymn, "My Hope Is Built on Nothing Less," or its more familiar title "The Solid Rock," was written by Edward Mote, who served as a pastor at Rehoboth Baptist Church in Horsham, West Sussex. Pastor Mote wrote around one hundred hymns. "The Solid Rock" was written in 1834 and is his best known work. The hymn writer describes the difficulties of life this way.

My hope is built on nothing less
Than Jesus' blood and righteousness;
I dare not trust the sweetest frame,
But wholly lean on Jesus' name.

Refrain:
On Christ, the solid Rock, I stand;
all other ground is sinking sand,
all other ground is sinking sand.

When darkness veils His lovely face,
I rest on His unchanging grace;
in every high and stormy gale,
my anchor holds within the veil.

His oath, His covenant, His blood
Support me in the whelming flood;

when all around my soul gives way,
He then is all my hope and stay.

When He shall come with trumpet sound,
Oh, May I then in Him be found;
dressed in His righteousness alone,
Faultless to stand before the throne.[9]

Let me not be guilty of dismissing all the questions the godslayer poses. He does present a legitimate question when he asks "what is the real meaning of Christmas?" This continues to be annually asked by, and to, saints and sinners. However, his answers are blasphemously sad and contemptuously inaccurate. He describes the visions of a soft cuddly baby surrounded by adoring parents, dozing animals, friendly shepherds, and the rest of the serene crèche obscured with the sedative strains of Silent Night as mythological. Are these pastoral scenes that are all too frequently seen on annual Christmas cards and during many a church Christmas program real? Or was the incarnation of Jesus Christ far more crude and rustic than believers are often willing to acknowledge?

Jesus was born outside an inn in a small Jewish village called Bethlehem. It was during the days of the Roman Empire. Jesus was more than likely born in a stable where He was placed in an animal's feeding trough (manger), which would serve as a His first crib.

How then do we respond to the godslayer's attempt to once again place believers in Christ on the defensive? Why was Jesus born? Why can't the Father just forgive? Did God the Father torture and murder His Son, and if so, is He an insane psychopath? Does the cross effectively accomplish what God determined before the foundation of the world? What about the claims that God is an adulterer, a child molester, a rapist, incestuous, irresponsible, and a murderer?

Once again, we must look at the revelatory record contained in the Scriptures to ascertain what really happened over two thousand years ago. It is from this trustworthy account that God reveals the truth of Jesus's ignoble birth, righteous life, violent death, but also His glorious resurrection. The biblical record tells us the truth, which strips away the all too familiar fables surrounding the birth of Christ.

The first biblical account, of many, comes from Paul's Epistle to the Galatians. In Galatians 1:1–5 the apostle writes,

> Paul, an apostle—not from men nor through man, but through Jesus Christ and God the Father, who raised him from the dead—and all the brothers who are with me, To the churches of Galatia: Grace to you and peace from God our Father and the Lord Jesus Christ, who gave himself for our sins to deliver us from the present evil age, according to the will of our God and Father, to whom be the glory forever and ever. Amen.[10]

Why was Jesus born? To begin with, Paul says that Jesus came to earth as the incarnation of God's grace and peace. "Grace and peace from God our Father and the Lord Jesus Christ."[11] Grace is defined as "unmerited favor." It is the "bestowing of pleasure, delight, or favorable regard." It is God's loving-kindness to those who deserve judgment. Peace is "the resulting harmony, on the basis of grace, between God and man." Peace is accomplished through the gospel. Peace is also the rest and consequential contentment, which is the result of God's grace.

Romans 5:6–8 says, "For while we were still helpless, at the right time, Christ died for the ungodly. For one will hardly die for a righteous man; though perhaps for the good man someone would dare even to die. But God demonstrates His own love toward us, in that while we were yet sinners, Christ died for us."[12] This predominant theme is echoed also in Psalm 116:5, Psalm 111:4, Psalm 112:4, John 3:16, Ephesians 1:7, and Romans 16:20.

The reason Jesus came is that as sinners we were helplessly dead in our trespasses and sins. Yet, in spite of this contemptible and condemnable condition, God pursued sinners like you and me in order to deliver us from this dead state of existence. Even though sinners dismiss, denounce, and degrade God's great love.

Paul continues by saying that Jesus was born to be the atoning sacrifice, or propitiation, for sinners. "Who gave Himself for our sins."[13] This was done in order to satisfy the righteous wrath of God against sin and sinners. The phrase "Who gave" refers to a complete and total surrender. What did Jesus surrender? Himself. This one word refers to the great doctrine of substitutionary atonement. For whom was this atonement made? It was done on behalf of sinners; those who are missing the mark of God's perfect righteousness. The following texts reiterate this truth.

1. Galatians 3:13. "Christ has redeemed us from the curse of the law, having become a curse for us (for it is written, 'Cursed is everyone who hangs on a tree'), that the blessing of Abraham might come upon the Gentiles in Christ Jesus, that we might receive the promise of the Spirit through faith."[14]

2. 1 John 4:7–10. "Beloved, let us love one another, for love is of God; and everyone who loves is born of God and knows God. He who does not love does not know God for God is love. In this the love of God was manifested toward us, that God has sent His only begotten Son into the world, that we might live through Him. In this is love, not that we loved God, but that He loved us and sent His Son to be the propitiation for our sins."[15]

3. 1 John 2:1–2. "My little children, these things I write to you, so that you may not sin. And if anyone sins, we have an Advocate with the Father, Jesus Christ the righteous. And He Himself is the propitiation

for our sins, and not for ours only but also for the whole world."[16]

4. Hebrews 2:14–18. "Inasmuch then as the children have partaken of flesh and blood, He Himself likewise shared in the same, that through death He might destroy him who had the power of death, that is, the devil, and release those who through fear of death were all their lifetime subject to bondage. For indeed He does not give aid to angels, but He does give aid to the seed of Abraham. Therefore, in all things He had to be made like *His* brethren, that He might be a merciful and faithful High Priest in things *pertaining* to God, to make propitiation for the sins of the people. For in that He Himself has suffered, being tempted, He is able to aid those who are tempted."[17]

5. Romans 3:25a. "…whom God set forth as a propitiation by His blood, through faith, to demonstrate His righteousness.[18]

Jesus was born to be the atoning sacrifice for sinners in order to cancel the legal demands of the law condemning sinners. The godslayer repeatedly asks why God does not just forgive since He is the God of forgiveness and forgiving. God does forgive, but at the same time he cannot forsake His righteous standard: the Law. The Law of God is a reflection of the person of God. God is holy and just.

God is the supreme ruler who rules on the basis of the rule of law. Whose law? His law.

Colossians 2:13–15 says, "And you, who were dead in your trespasses and the uncircumcision of your flesh, God made alive together with him, having forgiven us all our trespasses, by canceling the record of debt that stood against us with its legal demands. This he set aside, nailing it to the cross. He disarmed the rulers and authorities and put them to open shame, by triumphing over them in him"[19] (ESV). We should duly note the significant meaning of the phrase "record of debt."

This refers to the handwritten certificate of debt by which a debtor acknowledged his indebtedness. All people (Rom. 3:23) owe God an unpayable debt for violating his law (Gal. 3:10; James 2:10; cf. Matt. 18:23–27), and are thus under sentence of death (Rom. 6:23). Paul graphically compares God's forgiveness of believers' sins to wiping ink off a parchment. Through Christ's sacrificial death on the cross, God has totally erased our certificate of indebtedness and made our forgiveness complete nailing it to the cross. This is another metaphor for forgiveness. The list of the crimes of a crucified criminal was nailed to the cross with that criminal to declare the violations he was being punished for (as in the case of Jesus, as noted in Matt. 27:37). Believers' sins were all put to Christ's account, nailed to his cross as he paid the penalty in their place for them all, thus satisfying the just wrath of God against crimes requiring punishment in full.[20]

In the Greco-Roman world, the "record of debt" (*Gk. cheirographon)* was a written memorandum of indebtedness. The Apostle Paul uses this as an illustration to describe each person's indebtedness to God because of their sin. God has personally and mercifully solved this problem for all who put their faith in Jesus by taking this record of condemnation and nailing it to the cross, wherein Jesus paid the debt. The image comes from the notice being fastened to a cross by the Roman authorities, declaring the crime for which the criminal was being executed (John 19:19–22). The Apostle Paul also speaks of this reality in Galatians 3:10–14 when he says,

> For all who rely on works of the law are under a curse; for it is written, "Cursed be everyone who does not abide by all things written in the Book of the Law, and do them." Now it is evident that no one is justified before God by the law, for "The righteous shall live by faith." But the law is not of faith, rather "The one who does them shall live by them." Christ redeemed us from the curse of the law by becoming a curse for us—for it is written, "Cursed is everyone who is hanged on a tree"—so that in Christ Jesus the blessing of Abraham might come to the Gentiles, so that we might receive the promised Spirit through faith.[21]

Due to the sinner's inability to perfectly keep the perfect law of God, the sinner stands condemned as one spiritually separated from God. However, Jesus not only came to rescue sinners from the condemnation of God, but also from the evil of this world.

Therefore, Jesus was born "that He might rescue us from the present evil age."[22] The word *that* refers the reader to a purpose clause. God's purpose in sending Jesus Christ to earth was that He would, or could, rescue and deliver sinners from the condemnation of their sin and set them free. The word *rescue* refers to those who are in great danger from which they are unable to extricate themselves. Those who are rescued originally were by nature enemies, and this rescue is accomplished by the death of the rescuer.

This rescue is progressive in character and will not be complete until all believers are glorified. However, it is being accomplished whenever a sinner is brought out of darkness into the light and whenever a saint gains a victory in his struggle against sin.

The "present evil age" is the non-religious world system—a world in motion. It is a world that is transient and that is hastening to its close and in which, in spite of all its pleasures and so-called treasures, abides nothing of lasting value. This is the world many evangelicals say we must embrace and use in order to win people to Christ. The Bible offers no such methodology.

Jesus was also born to carry out the Father's will. He came "according to the will of our God and Father."[23] This means that the fulfillment of the Father's purpose and intent to redeem fallen sinners was the focus of Jesus Christ. He could accomplish this task because He was the perfect and obedient substitute (2 Cor. 5:21; Isa. 53:1–12) who alone was able to provide justification and redemption (Rom. 5:8–9; Rom. 3:21–24; Gal. 2:16), by becoming the elect's righteousness (Rom. 5:19; 2 Cor. 5:21; Phil. 2:5–8; Phil. 3:4–9), to reconcile sinners to God (Rom. 5:10; 2 Cor. 5:17–20; Col. 1:20–22), thereby providing the only hope for eternal life (John 3:16; John 3:36; John 17:3; John 20:30–31; 1 John 5:20–21).

As a result, Jesus Christ, along with God the Father, deserves all the glory. For salvation is truly of God, from first to last. "To whom be glory forever and ever. Amen."[24] Glory refers to praise and honor. This is going to occur forever and ever, unto the end of the ages. This refers to a period of indefinite duration (Phil. 2:10–11; Rom. 11:33–36; 1 Tim. 1:15–17; 2 Tim. 4:16–18; 2 Pet. 3:18; Rev. 1:4–7; Rev. 4:11; Rev. 5:11–14).

Jesus Christ was also born to fulfill the multiple prophecies made about the coming Messiah. Throughout the Old Testament, even the minutest detail was completed regarding the first coming of the Messiah. What remains to be fulfilled Jesus Christ will complete when He returns in power, might, and glory.

There are many within our world, culture, neighborhoods, schools, places of employment, and even churches that possess mistaken notions and ideas as to the characters, scenes, settings, and incidents that occurred that first Christmas. Many in our world would rather focus their attention on a variety of other sights, sounds, and characters. Others would even regulate Jesus Christ to the status of myth and attempt to banish and ban the very word *Christmas* from the holiday season.

Among religious people, and I use this term to refer to those who call themselves people of faith regardless of whatever object their faith may be centered in, there is rarely little debate that Jesus Christ was born. The debate centers on who Jesus Christ is? Is He the Messiah? Some say that He is just a man. Others would acknowledge that He is at least a prophet, and perhaps a good, moral teacher.

What does the Bible say about whom the Messiah would be, His credentials, and how He would come to earth and how we would recognize Him? Most significantly, does Jesus Christ fulfill the qualifications of the Messiah? If He does not, then He is not Messiah no matter how much people revere Him. However, if He does fulfill the qualifications of the Messiah, then the believer must be committed to this truth and at the same time be prepared (1 Pet. 3:15) to share this truth so the unbeliever is challenged to consider this truth. What are the prophetical qualifications surrounding the birth of the Messiah, and does Jesus Christ fulfill these qualifications?

First of all, the Messiah was to be born from the seed of a woman: He was to born of a virgin. Genesis 3:14–15 states, "So the LORD God said to the serpent: Because you have done this, you are cursed more than all cattle, and more than every beast of the field; on your belly you shall go, and you shall eat dust all the days of your life. And I will put enmity between you and the woman, and between your seed and her Seed; He shall bruise your head, and you shall bruise His heel."[25]

The "seed/offspring" mentioned in this verse became the root from which the tree of the OT promise of a Messiah grew. This, then, was the "mother prophecy" that gave birth to all the rest of the promises. Genesis 3:15 was the origin of assurance, which unfolds in the drama of salvation. Strange as it may seem, the history of the human race begins with the sin of our first parents and their expulsion from the Garden of Eden. But that is not where it ended, for in the middle of the bleakness and the dark tragedy of God's curse on the tempter, the woman, and the man came the first rays of light and hope embodied as the gospel of the grace of our God.

This initial prophecy would be reiterated by the Prophet Isaiah. He writes in Isaiah 7:13–14, "Hear now, O house of David! Is it a small thing for you to weary men, but will you weary my God also? Therefore, the Lord Himself will give you a sign: Behold the virgin shall conceive and bear a Son, and shall call His name Immanuel."[26] He also states in Isaiah 9:1–2, "Nevertheless the gloom will not be upon her who is distressed, as when at first He lightly esteemed the land of Zebulun and the land of Naphtali, and afterward more heavily oppressed her, by the way of the sea beyond the Jordan, in Galilee of the Gentiles. The people who walked in darkness have seen a great light; those who dwelt in the land of the shadow of death, upon them a light has shined."[27]

The New Testament gospels indicate that Jesus Christ fulfills this qualification of being virgin born. Matthew 1:18–25 states,

> Now the birth of Jesus Christ was as follows: After His mother Mary was betrothed to Joseph, before they came together, she was found with child of the Holy Spirit. Then Joseph her husband, being a just *man,* and not wanting to make her a public example, was minded to put her away secretly. But while he thought about these things, behold, an angel of the Lord appeared to him in a dream, saying, "Joseph, son of David, do not be afraid to take to you Mary your wife, for that which is conceived in her is of the Holy Spirit. And she will bring forth a Son, and you shall call His name JESUS, for He will save His people from their sins." So all this was done that it might be fulfilled which was spoken by the Lord through the prophet, saying: *"Behold, the virgin shall be with child, and bear a Son, and they shall call His name Immanuel,"* which is translated, "God with us." Then Joseph, being aroused from sleep, did as the angel of the Lord commanded him and took to him his wife, and did

not know her till she had brought forth her firstborn Son. And he called His name Jesus.[28]

Luke 1:26–38 recounts the same information but from the perspective of Mary, the mother of Jesus. Luke records:

> Now in the sixth month the angel Gabriel was sent by God to a city of Galilee named Nazareth, to a virgin betrothed to a man whose name was Joseph, of the house of David. The virgin's name *was* Mary. And having come in, the angel said to her, "Rejoice, highly favored *one,* the Lord *is* with you; blessed *are* you among women!" But when she saw *him,* she was troubled at his saying, and considered what manner of greeting this was. Then the angel said to her, "Do not be afraid, Mary, for you have found favor with God. And behold, you will conceive in your womb and bring forth a Son, and shall call His name Jesus. He will be great, and will be called the Son of the Highest; and the Lord God will give Him the throne of His father David. And He will reign over the house of Jacob forever, and of His kingdom there will be no end." Then Mary said to the angel, "How can this be, since I do not know a man?" And the angel answered and said to her, "The Holy Spirit will come upon you, and the power of the Highest will overshadow you; therefore, also, that Holy One who is to be born will be called the Son of God. Now indeed, Elizabeth your relative has also conceived a son in her old age; and this is now the sixth month for her who was called

barren. For with God nothing will be impossible."
Then Mary said, "Behold the maidservant of the
Lord! Let it be to me according to your word." And
the angel departed from her.[29]

Not only was the Messiah to be from the seed of a
woman, i.e. virgin born, but also from the seed of Abraham.
On five different occasions, God indicated that the Messiah
would be a descendant of Abraham. These five statements
are as follows:

1. Genesis 12:3. "And in you all the families of the
   earth shall be blessed."[30]

2. Genesis 18:1–18. "Abraham shall surely become a
   great and mighty nation, and all the nations of the
   earth shall be blessed in him."[31]

3. Genesis 22:18. "In your Seed all the nations of the
   earth shall be blessed, because you have obeyed My
   voice."[32]

4. Genesis 26:4–5. "I will multiply your offspring as
   the stars of heaven and will give to your offspring all
   these lands. And in your offspring all the nations of
   the earth shall be blessed, because Abraham obeyed
   my voice and kept my charge, my commandments,
   my statutes, and my laws."[33]

5. Genesis 28:13–14. "And behold, the LORD stood
   above it and said, "I am the LORD, the God of
   Abraham your father and the God of Isaac. The

land on which you lie I will give to you and to your offspring. Your offspring shall be like the dust of the earth, and you shall spread abroad to the west and to the east and to the north and to the south, and in you and your offspring shall all the families of the earth be blessed."[34]

God made eight promises to Abraham. These include the following: (1) He would make Abraham into a great nation; (2) He would bless him; (3) He would make his name great; (4) Abraham and his seed would be a blessing to others; (5) God would bless those who blessed him; (6) God would curse those who cursed him; (7) Through Abraham and his "seed" (or "offspring") God would be the channel of blessing to all the peoples on earth; and (8) God would give to Abraham's "seed" the land he had entered after leaving Ur of the Chaldeans. The first seven promises appeared in his "call" in Genesis 12:2–3, while the eighth was added when he arrived at Shechem in Palestine (v. 7). Does Jesus Christ meet these qualifications in fulfilling the promises given to Abraham?

Matthew 1:1 says, "The book of the genealogy of Jesus Christ, the Son of David, the Son of Abraham."[35] The genealogy in Luke 3:23–38 also states that Jesus was related to Abraham through His mother's lineage. A third statement is made in Galatians 3:16 where the Apostle Paul writes, "Now to Abraham and his Seed were the promises made. He (God) does not say, and to seeds, as of many but as of one, and to your Seed, who is Christ."[36]

The description of the Messiah and His qualifications continue to be narrowed. He is to not only be from the seed of a woman, and the seed of Abraham, but also from the tribe of Judah.

Genesis 49:10 says, "The scepter shall not depart from Judah, nor a lawgiver from between his feet, until Shiloh comes; and to Him shall be the obedience of the people."[37] Shiloh is best understood as a cryptic but shorthand form of a personal name for the Messiah. The one to whom belongs the true kingship of Israel.

Numbers 24:17 also says, "I see Him, but not now; I behold Him, but not near; A Star shall come out of Jacob; A Scepter shall rise out of Israel, and batter the brow of Moab, and destroy all the sons of tumult."[38] Star and scepter speak of royalty. The ruler of Israel will come from the family of Jacob, and more specifically, Judah.

The terms *star* and *scepter* certainly speak of the promise of a king like David, Israel's greatest king in the historical period. But ultimately these words reach beyond him. The setting of the text is "in the days to come." It reaches all the way to the Savior."

Israel has a coming deliverer. This verse has been debased by some, devalued by others, and allegorized by others still. However, this text speaks unmistakably of the coming of the Messiah. That this prophecy should come

Answering a Godslayer

from one who was unworthy (Balaam) makes the prophecy all the more dramatic and startling. Does Jesus Christ meet this qualification?

Matthew says Jesus was the "son of Judah."[39] The visitors from the east said to anyone who would listen, "Where is He who has born King of the Jews? For we have seen His star in the East and have come to worship Him."[40] Luke identifies Jesus as the "the son of Judah."[41] John does the same. "Behold, the Lion from the Tribe of Judah, the Root of David has prevailed to open the scroll and to loose its seven seals."[42]

Not only was Messiah to be from the seed of a woman, the seed of Abraham, and the tribe of Judah, but also to be from the family of King David. Psalm 89: 27 says, "Also I will make him My firstborn, the highest of the kings of the earth."[43] In addition, Psalm 132:11 says, "The LORD has sworn in truth to David; He will not turn from it: I will set upon your throne the fruit of your body."[44] 2 Samuel 7:12–16 also states,

> "When your days are fulfilled and you rest with your fathers, I will set up your seed after you, who will come from your body, and I will establish his kingdom. He shall build a house for My name, and I will establish the throne of his kingdom forever. I will be his Father, and he shall be My son. If he commits iniquity, I will chasten him with the rod of men and with the blows of the sons of men. But My mercy shall not depart

> from him, as I took *it* from Saul, whom I removed
> from before you. And your house and your kingdom
> shall be established forever before you. Your throne
> shall be established forever." According to all these
> words and according to all this vision, so Nathan
> spoke to David. [45]

Jeremiah 23:5–6 says, "Behold the days are coming, says the LORD that I will raise to David a Branch of righteousness; A King shall reign and prosper, and execute judgment and righteousness in the earth. In His days Judah will be saved, and Israel will dwell safely; Now this is His name by which He will be called: THE LORD OUR RIGHTEOUSNESS."[46] Finally, Isaiah 11:1–2 states, "There shall come forth a Rod from the stem of Jesse, and a Branch shall grow out of his roots. The Spirit of the LORD shall rest upon Him, the Spirit of wisdom and understanding, the Spirit of counsel and might, the Spirit of knowledge and of the fear of the LORD."[47] A shoot coming up from the stump of Jesse. This branch (Messiah) will bear fruit; He will prosper and benefit others. He will come directly from the lineage of David and will fulfill God's promises in the Davidic Covenant.

Does Jesus Christ meet this qualification? Once again, the New Testament gospels indicate that He does. Matthew 1:1 says, "The book of the genealogy of Jesus Christ, the Son of David, the Son of Abraham."[48] Luke 1:31–33, "And behold, you will conceive in your womb and bring forth a Son, and shall call His name JESUS. He will be great, and will be called the Son of the Highest; and the LORD God will give Him the throne of His father David. And He will reign over the house of Jacob forever, and of His kingdom there will be no end."[49], and Luke 3: 31, "...the son of David..."[50]

Not only was Messiah to be from the seed of a woman, the seed of Abraham, the tribe of Judah, and the family of David, but also Messiah is to Born in Bethlehem. Micah 5:2 says, "But you, Bethlehem Ephrathah, though you are little among the thousands of Judah, yet out of you shall come forth to Me. The One to be Ruler in Israel, whose goings forth are from of old, from everlasting."[51]

Does Jesus Christ meet this qualification? There are three references supporting the contention that Jesus Christ does fulfill this requirement.

1. Matthew 2:1. "Now after Jesus was born in Bethlehem of Judea in the days of Herod the king..."[52]

2. Luke 2:1–7. "And it came to pass in those days *that* a decree went out from Caesar Augustus that all the world should be registered. This census first took place while Quirinius was governing Syria. So all went to be registered, everyone to his own city. Joseph also went up from Galilee, out of the city of Nazareth, into Judea, to the city of David, which

is called Bethlehem, because he was of the house and lineage of David, to be registered with Mary, his betrothed wife, who was with child. So it was, that while they were there, the days were completed for her to be delivered. And she brought forth her firstborn Son, and wrapped Him in swaddling cloths, and laid Him in a manger, because there was no room for them in the inn."[53]

3. John 7:40–42."Therefore many from the crowd… said, truly this is the Prophet. Others said, this is the Christ! But some said, Will the Christ come out of Galilee? Has not the Scripture said that the Christ comes from the seed of David and from the town of Bethlehem, where David was."[54]

Not only was the Messiah to be from the seed of a woman, the seed of Abraham, the tribe of Judah, the family of David, to be born in Bethlehem, but also He is to have a threefold mission. First, He is to be prophet like Moses, a discloser of God's revelation to God's people. This requirement is found in Deuteronomy 18:15–22.

"The LORD your God will raise up for you a Prophet like me from your midst, from your brethren. Him you shall hear, according to all you desired of the LORD your God in Horeb in the day of the assembly, saying, 'Let me not hear again the voice of the LORD my God, nor let me see this great fire anymore, lest I die.'" And the LORD said to me: "What they have spoken is good. I will raise up for them a Prophet like you from among their brethren, and will put My words in His mouth, and He shall speak to them all that I command Him. And it shall be *that* whoever will not hear My words, which He speaks in My name, I will require *it* of him. But the prophet who presumes to speak a word in My name, which I have not commanded him to speak, or who speaks in the name of other gods, that prophet shall die." And if you say in your heart, "How shall we know the word which the LORD has not spoken?" When a prophet speaks in the name of the LORD, if the thing does not happen or come to pass, that *is* the thing which the LORD has not spoken; the prophet has spoken it presumptuously; you shall not be afraid of him.[55]

Second, the Messiah is to be a King like David—A ruler of the Kingdom of God consisting of God's people. As previously noted, this criteria is found in Genesis 49:10, Numbers 24:17, 2 Samuel 7:12–16 along with Psalm 2, Psalm 110, Matthew 2:1–2 and Luke 1:31–33.

Thirdly, Messiah is to be a priest like Melchizedek, an intercessor before the throne of God on behalf of God's people. Psalm 110:1–4 says,

The LORD said to my Lord, "Sit at My right hand, till I make your enemies Your footstool." The LORD shall send the rod of our strength out of Zion. Rule in the midst of Your enemies! Your people *shall be* volunteers in the day of Your power; In the beauties of holiness, from the womb of the morning, You have the dew of Your youth. The LORD has sworn And will not relent, "You *are* a priest forever. According to the order of Melchizedek."[56]

Does Jesus Christ meet this qualification? The writer of the Epistle to the Hebrews indicates that He does.

1. Hebrews 2:17–18."Therefore, in all things He had to be made like His brethren, that He might be a merciful and faithful High Priest in things pertaining to God, to make propitiation for the sins of the people. For in that He Himself has suffered, being tempted, He is able to aid those who are tempted."[57]

2. Hebrews 4:14–15. "Seeing then that we have a great High Priest who has passed through the heavens, Jesus the Son of God, let us hold fast our confession. For we do not have a High Priest who cannot sympathize with our weaknesses, but was in all points tempted as we are, yet without sin. Let us therefore come boldly to the throne of grace that we may obtain mercy and fine grace to help in time of need."[58]

3. Hebrews 5:1–6. "…a priest forever according the order of Melchizedek…"[59]

4.   Hebrews 7:26–27. "For such a high priest was fitting for us, who is holy, harmless, undefiled, separate from sinners, and has become higher than the heavens; who does not need daily, as those high priests, to offer up sacrifices, first of His own sins and then for the people's, for this He did once for all when He offered up Himself."[60]

Not only was the Messiah to be from the seed of a woman, from the seed of Abraham, the tribe of Judah, the family of David, born in the town of Bethlehem, to have a threefold mission in being the Prophet, Priest, and King, but also He is to be Son of God as indicated in Psalm 2:1–12.

> Why do the nations rage, and the people plot a vain thing? The kings of the earth set themselves, and the rulers take counsel together, Against the LORD and against His Anointed, *saying,* "Let us break their bonds in pieces and cast away their cords from us." He who sits in the heavens shall laugh; The LORD shall hold them in derision. Then He shall speak to them in His wrath, and distress them in His deep displeasure: "Yet I have set My King on My holy hill of Zion." "I will declare the decree: The LORD has said to Me, 'You *are* My Son, Today I have begotten You. Ask of Me, and I will give *You* The nations *for* Your inheritance, And the ends of the earth *for* Your possession. You shall break them with a rod of iron; You shall dash them to

pieces like a potter's vessel.'" Now therefore, be wise, O kings; Be instructed, you judges of the earth. Serve the LORD with fear, And rejoice with trembling. Kiss the Son, lest He be angry, And you perish *in* the way, When His wrath is kindled but a little. Blessed *are* all those who put their trust in Him.[61]

This requirement is also mentioned by Isaiah the prophet. "Unto us a Child is born, unto us a Son is given; And the government will be upon His shoulder. And His name will be called Wonderful Counselor, Mighty God, Everlasting Father, Prince of Peace" (Isa. 9:6, ESV). Does Jesus Christ meet this qualification? The following texts indicate that He does.

1. Matthew 1:18–25. "Now the birth of Jesus Christ was as follows: After His mother Mary was betrothed to Joseph, before they came together, she was found with child of the Holy Spirit. Then Joseph her husband, being a just *man,* and not wanting to make her a public example, was minded to put her away secretly. But while he thought about these things, behold, an angel of the Lord appeared to him in a dream, saying, "Joseph, son of David, do not be afraid to take to you Mary your wife, for that which is conceived in her is of the Holy Spirit. And she will bring forth a Son, and you shall call His name JESUS, for He will save His people from their sins." So all this was done that it might be fulfilled

which was spoken by the Lord through the prophet, saying: *"Behold, the virgin shall be with child, and bear a Son, and they shall call His name Immanuel,"* which is translated, "God with us." Then Joseph, being aroused from sleep, did as the angel of the Lord commanded him and took to him his wife, and did not know her till she had brought forth her firstborn Son. And he called His name Jesus."[62]

2. Luke 1: 31–35."And behold, you will conceive in your womb and bring forth a Son, and shall call His name Jesus. He will be great, and will be called the Son of the Highest; and the Lord God will give Him the throne of His father David. And He will reign over the house of Jacob forever, and of His kingdom there will be no end." Then Mary said to the angel, "How can this be, since I do not know a man?" And the angel answered and said to her, "The Holy Spirit will come upon you, and the power of the Highest will overshadow you; therefore, also, that Holy One who is to be born will be called the Son of God."[63]

3. John 1:1–5. "In the beginning was the Word, and the Word was with God, and the Word was God. He was in the beginning with God. All things were made through Him, and without Him nothing was made that was made. In Him was life, and the life was the light of men. And the light shines in the darkness, and the darkness did not comprehend it."[64]

4. John 20:30–31. "And truly Jesus did many other signs in the presence of His disciples, which are not written in this book, but these are written that you may believe that Jesus is the Christ, the Son of God, and that believing you may have life in His name."[65]

The time has come to specifically respond to the godslayer's heretical and blasphemous conclusions regarding the incarnation of Jesus Christ. In his letter to me, he downgraded the birth, life, and death of Christ as something sordid and disgusting.

He called God an adulterer in choosing Mary and using her as a virgin, to conceive and eventually bear the Son of God. Attacks upon the virgin birth of Jesus Christ are not new. They range from the notion that Mary was impregnated by a Roman soldier, or a neighbor of hers from Nazareth came in the dark of night and had sex with her and she assumed it was Joseph, to the idea that Jesus was the natural biological son of Joseph and Mary.

These attacks, including that God the Father was an adulterer are from unbelievers who possess no shame in mocking the God who created them and who came to earth to provide redemption for many like them. However, to even call God a pedophile, a rapist, and incestuous goes beyond the pale or natural boundary of what can even be defined as a logical disagreement.

God the Father is neither a deadbeat dad nor a murderer. God entrusted His only begotten Son to a couple who would raise Jesus in the nurture and admonition of the Lord. God the Father watched over Jesus as He watches over every human being. The truth of Psalm 139 rings true: not only in the life of Jesus Christ but also in our own.

Jesus's death on the cross was a substitutionary atonement on behalf of sinners. No one took Jesus's life, not even God the father. Jesus offered up His life willingly. Jesus said so in John 10:11–18.

> I am the good shepherd. The good shepherd lays down his life for the sheep. He who is a hired hand and not a shepherd, who does not own the sheep, sees the wolf coming and leaves the sheep and flees, and the wolf snatches them and scatters them. He flees because he is a hired hand and cares nothing for the sheep. I am the good shepherd. I know my own and my own know me, just as the Father knows me and I know the Father; and I lay down my life for the sheep. And I have other sheep that are not of this fold. I must bring them also, and they will listen to my voice. So there will be one flock, one shepherd. For this reason the Father loves me, because I lay down my life that I may take it up again. No one takes it from me, but I lay it down of my own accord. I have authority to lay it down, and I have authority to take it up again. This charge I have received from my Father.[66]

This truth from the lips of Jesus can also be found in John 6:51, John 11:50–51, John 17:19, and John 18:14.

This parallels the predetermined plan and foreknowledge of God the Father (Acts 2:22–24). God the Father did not murder His own Son. Jesus Christ was a willing martyr who willingly submitted to God the Father's will in order to provide salvation for those God calls and to glorify the Father (John 17:1–5).

People have been demonizing God the Father, Son, and Holy Spirit since time began (Gen. 3:1–5). The accusations and recriminations may seem different with each generation, but they are born in the fallen heart of sinful man who rejects by nature the sinless God of salvation. Nothing less than God's sovereign grace can so save a person from this plight.

The Final Letter!

A man is accepted into a church for what he believes and he is turned out for what he knows.

—Samuel Clemens (Mark Twain)

A casual stroll through a lunatic asylum shows that faith proves nothing.

—Fredrick Nietzsche

It's a pity! You were afforded a chance to deal openly and honestly with the questions posed. You chose not to...not that I didn't expect such a response.

You sir are an intellectual coward. You failed and in so doing exposed the worthlessness of both your faith and your so-called god. As Robert Green Ingersoll has written, in Heretics and Heresies:

According to the theologians, God, the Father of us all, wrote a letter to his children. The children have always differed somewhat as to the meaning of this letter. In consequence of these honest differences, these brothers began to cut out each other's hearts. In every land, where this letter from God has been read, the children to whom and for whom it was written have been filled with hatred and malice. They have imprisoned and murdered each other, and the wives and children of each other. In the name of God every possible crime has been committed; every conceivable outrage has been perpetrated. Brave men, tender and loving women, beautiful girls, and prattling babes have been exterminated in the name of Jesus Christ.

For more than fifty generations the church has carried the black flag. Her vengeance has been measured only by her power. During all these years of infamy, no heretic has ever been forgiven. With the heart of a fiend she has hated. With the clutch of avarice she has grasped. With jaws of a dragon she has devoured. Pitiless as famine, merciless as fire, with the conscience of a serpent: such is the history of the Church of God.

Sadly, there is no hope for you. Either you are so delusional that you truly believe the idiocy you call a religion or you are so vile as to use it as a camouflage to fleece the ignorant. In either case, if there is a god, he shall "reward" you for your life choice. If there is no god, as is much more rational, then you are trapped within the prison of your own making. In either case, you have my pity.

Rest assured, I shall not pray for you as enough wasted effort has already been expended by man in that futility. But, I do hope someday it is not too late for you to realize how wasted your ideals have been. Farewell!

—The godslayer

How ironic for the pot to call the kettle black. Maybe I am being less than gracious. The godslayer calls me an "intellectual coward." Yet I have written what I am convinced is truth. I have not debated him in the forum he would enjoy, and for that I am a coward?

Who exactly is the coward? I would submit that my name and picture was affixed to each article that appeared in our local newspaper, which easily identified me as the author of my convictions. The godslayer has done no such thing in reciprocation. He has hid himself behind a pseudonym or alias, and has not revealed his address, when he has easy access to mine. Again, I ask, who is the coward?

As in previous chapters, let us not remain silent but rather answer this man and the issues he raises. Does he raise any concerns that prove problematic regarding the truthfulness of biblical Christianity?

Who exactly is Robert Green Ingersoll? Robert Green "Bob" Ingersoll (August 11, 1833—July 21, 1899) was a lawyer, a Civil War veteran, a political leader, and an orator of the United States during the Golden Age of free thought. He was known for his broad range of culture and his defense of agnosticism. He was nicknamed "The Great Agnostic."

Agnosticism is the worldview that the truth claims—especially claims about the existence or non-existence of God, as well as other religious claims—are unknown or unknowable. There may be a One True God, or many gods for that matter, but you can never know with certainty whether or not he exists.

I was curious regarding Mr. Ingersoll and what would make him doubt the existence of God, as I have already speculated about the godslayer. What I discovered was most fascinating and sad.

Robert Ingersoll was born and reared in a devoutly Christian household. His father, John Ingersoll, was a Congregationalist minister, a profound thinker in the opinion of some, an eloquent speaker, and one who accepted other people's views. It seems that father and son got along well. That could not be said of Rev. Ingersoll and his congregation.

Rev. Ingersoll's liberal views concerning life, living, and theology were a constant source of conflict between him and the church he pastored. He was often accused of being unbiblical. His ministerial career was, in fact, substantially brought to a close by a church trial, which occurred while he was pastor of the Congregational Church at Madison, Ohio, and at which his third wife appeared as prosecutor. Upon this occasion he was charged with stonewalling and unministerial conduct. The evidence that was produced was trivial and ridiculous, but the committee that heard it decided that though he had done "nothing inconsistent with his Christian character," he was "inconsistent with his ministerial character," and forbade him to preach in the future.

Pastor John went before the higher church authorities and was permitted to continue his pastoral ministry. However, he soon moved to Wisconsin, before eventually going to Illinois, where he died. The Madison trial occurred when young Robert was nine years old, and it was the unjust and bigoted treatment his father received that made him the enemy, first of Calvinism, and later of Christianity in its other forms.

The godslayer contends that he would pray for me, but since he contends there is no god, as is much more rational, then I am trapped within the prison of my own making. In either case, he pities me. He also hopes that one day I will realize how wasted my ideals have been.

If there is no god, as the godslayer contends is the more rational idea, then why are we having this conversation? Why does he expend so much energy on contesting with me, and I am sure other followers of Christ as well, regarding my holding to biblical truth? Why does this anger him so? Why does God anger him so?

Much like Mr. Ingersoll who he quotes, I still contend that it is because of some deep hurt for which the godslayer blames God. At some point in time, God did not measure up to or meet his expectations. It is because of those unmet expectations, whatever they were or are, that he holds God responsible. He blames God for not preventing something, or permitting something, to occur. I do not know what it may be, and the godslayer has not chosen to reveal it.

However, there is something underlying all this anger and hatred.

He may choose not to pray for me, for he believes that to be a futile gesture. But I will pray for him. Jesus commands me to do so. In the Sermon on the Mount Jesus said,

> You have heard that it was said, "You shall love your neighbor and hate your enemy." But I say to you, Love your enemies and pray for those who persecute you, so that you may be sons of your Father who is in heaven. For he makes his sun rise on the evil and on the good, and sends rain on the just and on the unjust. For if you love those who love you, what reward do you have? Do not even the tax collectors do the same? And if you greet only your brothers, what more are you doing than others? Do not even the Gentiles do the same? You therefore must be perfect, as your heavenly Father is perfect.[1]

Jesus initially quotes from Leviticus 19:18. It was a statement with which his audience would be familiar. The second part of his quote "hate your enemy" was an incorrect Pharisaical and scribal interpretation. Jesus applied the text differently.

Jesus's standard then and today is much higher. It is a standard to which God calls each follower of Jesus to fulfill. It is a standard that can only be accomplished through the power and assistance of the Holy Spirit who resides within each believer in Christ (Rom. 8:9).

Jesus taught that a believer's love for his neighbor extends to those neighbors who are his enemies (Matt. 5:44). We are to self-sacrificially love them and we are to pray for them. This is radically different from any other ethical norm that may be found within the world. Certainly, there are those who remain unconverted to Christ who treat people who love them quite well. This is not necessarily a universal reality but rather a general observation.

However, Christians are called to love and pray not only for those they love and who love them, but also to do the same for those who hate them. This is not a new concept but one recorded in Scripture (Prov. 25:21).

God's calling and standard is clear. It is restated by the Apostle Paul who writes, "To the contrary, if your enemy is hungry, feed him; if he is thirsty, give him something to drink; for by so doing you will heap burning coals on his head. Do not be overcome by evil, but overcome evil with good."[2]

It is exemplified by Stephen, the first martyr for Jesus. He exclaims, when he is about to die a martyrs death, "And as they were stoning Stephen, he called out, 'Lord Jesus, receive my spirit.' And falling to his knees he cried out with a loud voice, 'Lord, do not hold this sin against them.' And when he had said this, he fell asleep."[3] This is the standard Jesus calls me to display. I can do no less. I can do nothing else.

Perhaps one day I may meet my anonymous neighbor in person. Perhaps he may choose to reveal his identity and we can converse face-to-face instead of through the intermediary of the written page. Until then, the written page will have to suffice.

I pray for his soul. He has revealed enough to me to display a sadness and despair, which he seeks to mask with the veneer of anger, confused logic, and personal insults. I pray that in some way God will touch his heart and he will receive Jesus Christ as Savior and Lord. It may occur through this book.

I also wonder about those nameless and faceless millions who also hold on to the same anger the godslayer possesses. Do they know a follower of Jesus who is prepared to give an answer for the hope that is within them with gentleness and reverence? I pray so. It may be you!

What more can or should be said to the godslayer? I have endeavored to answer his questions and address his angry diatribes against the Lord and His followers. I have sought to truly and humbly understand who this individual is and what experiences he has encountered to bring him to the condition in which he currently exists.

However, no amount of logic or argument can ultimately regenerate the fallen and lost soul, which is my anonymous adversary. The salvation of this man, if this is ever to occur, will come about by a monergistic work of the Holy Spirit who brings new life and faith to the dead and faithless because of the person and work of Jesus Christ and God the Father's sovereign election. Yet I am responsible before God to give an answer to anyone who wants to know the reason for the hope or confidence, which is within me because of the gospel (1 Pet. 3:15). This has been our thesis and goal for this book.

Therefore, the gospel must remain our primary message. Everything flows from this central truth. Each and every answer to each and every question the godslayers in our lives pose revolves around the core message of Christianity: the gospel. The truth of the gospel must always shine forth and never be obscured by argumentativeness and efforts to prove oneself right and the other individual wrong. I am convinced that this remained the perspective of the Apostle Paul. In 1 Corinthians 2:1–5 he writes,

> And I, when I came to you, brothers, did not come proclaiming to you the testimony of God with lofty speech or wisdom. For I decided to know nothing among you except Jesus Christ and him crucified. And I was with you in weakness and in fear and much trembling, and my speech and my message were not in plausible words of wisdom, but in demonstration of the Spirit and of power, so that your faith might not rest in the wisdom of men but in the power of God.[4]

Paul comments upon the ministry God began through the apostle in the City of Corinth (Acts 18). Paul wanted the Corinthian church to remember that he was not a motivational speaker who sought to impress his audience with his rhetorical skills and ability to hold an audience's attention. The phrase "lofty speech" refers to high-sounding and pompous speech intending to impress. This was in keeping with the actors of the ancient Greek theater. It is a pattern many pastors and preachers have adopted to appeal to the current, contemporary culture.

Rather, Paul's focus was not himself but rather upon Jesus Christ and the message of the cross. Instead of being a motivational speaker, Paul was content and driven to be a herald of the eternal God and to communicate His eternal message. A herald is one responsible to deliver and communicate a message from his master. The content of the message is what is most important, not the messenger. The messenger must never become the focal point to the expense of the message. The messenger is simply the instrument by which the master's message is communicated. The messenger must never obscure, not misrepresent the master's message. The phrase "Jesus Christ and him crucified" refers to the substitutionary atonement Christ provides by His death on the cross (Rom. 3:21–26; Eph. 2:1–10; Acts 20:17–24; 2 Cor. 4:1–2; 2 Tim. 4:1–2). It is this fundamental message that consumed the apostle.

And lest anyone think the apostle brought forth this message by his own ability and strength of personality, he indicates that he communicated the gospel to these people with weakness and in fear and much trembling.

Weakness refers to a lack of confidence. Fear means a sense of impending danger. Trembling is the physical expression of shaking from fear.

Paul arrived in Corinth following his beating and imprisonment in Philippi (Acts 16:22–24) and his difficult experiences in Thessalonica, Berea, and Athens (Acts 17). He may have been physically sick upon arriving in Corinth. Regardless, his speaking would not include any theatrics or persuasive speech. Rather, his ministry would demonstrate the power of God in the man of God filled by the Spirit of God. What can compete with that? The purpose was that the Corinthian's faith and commitment to Christ would not be based upon the Apostle Paul, but rather upon the power of God.

My prayer for the godslayer is for the Holy Spirit to sovereignly move upon his soul and regenerate him unto saving faith in Christ. If that miracle is the result of this book, it will have been worth it, and then some.

Who are the godslayers in your life at this present time? Is it a relative, a parent, a friend or a coworker? Is it a high school teacher or coach you respect, but who at best is casually indifferent to your faith in Christ, or at worst is intensely belligerent?

Is it a college or university professor who belittles you in class for being a Christian? Perhaps it is your college dorm roommate? Maybe a fraternity brother or sister? What about your boss?

We encounter godslayers every day. We encounter men and women who are convinced in their spiritual blindness that they can see, and in their moral and ethical deafness that they can hear. They have for too long taken the offensive in challenging the truth and validity of biblical Christianity. It is time for followers of Jesus to do everything we can to prepare ourselves to not just give a defense for our faith, but to also graciously and firmly challenge the presuppositions of those who seek to refute the gospel and belittle our faith. May God be glorified in this endeavor!

Notes

Preface

1. Proverbs 16:3–4; 9

2. 1 Peter 3:13–17

3. J. Mack Styles, Evangelism: *How the Whole Church Speaks for Jesus* (Wheaton: Crossway, 2014), 18.

4. 1 Corinthians 3:5–9

1 The Biblical Evidences for God's Existence

1. Ravi Zacharias, *Beyond Opinion: Living the Faith We Defend* (Nashville: Thomas Nelson, 2007), 33.

2. Genesis 1:1

3. John MacArthur, *The Battle for the Beginning* (Nashville: Word Publishing Group 2001), 11.

4. Romans 1:18–22

5. Genesis 1:1

6. Leviticus 2:12; 23:10; Nehemiah 12:44

7. Numbers 18:12

8. Deuteronomy 33:21

9. Daniel 11:41

10. Genesis 31:13; 35:7

11. Psalm 42:9

12. Isaiah 12:2

13. Psalm 42:8

14. Psalm 57:3

15. Psalm 89:26; 102:24; 118:28

16. 2 Samuel 22:33

17. Psalm 18:32

18. Psalm 18:47

19. 2 Samuel 22:48

20. Isaiah 54:5

21. 1 Kings 20:28

22. Jeremiah 32:27

23. Isaiah 37:16

24. Nehemiah 2:4, 20

25. Genesis 24:7; 2 Chronicles 36:23

26. 2 Chronicles 20:6

27. Genesis 24:3; Deuteronomy 4:39; Joshua 2:11

28. Deuteronomy 10:17

29. Psalm 57:2

30. Isaiah 40:28

31. Isaiah 30:18

32. Isaiah 65:16

33. Jeremiah 10:10

34. 1 Samuel 6:20

35. Deuteronomy 5:23; 1 Kings 18:24

36. Psalm 68:7

37. Deuteronomy 8:15

38. Leviticus 20:24

39. Genesis 17:8

40. Genesis 26:24

41. Genesis 28:13

42. Exodus 3:6

43. Genesis 24:12

44. Jeremiah 23:23

45. 2 Kings 19:10

46. Deuteronomy 8:5

47. Genesis 48:15

48. Psalm 4:1

49. Psalm 59:17

50. Psalm 43:2

51. Psalm 116:5

52. Isaiah 43:1; Ezekiel 21:30; 35; 28:13, 15

53. Matthew 5:13–16

54. Ephesians 2:8–10

2 The Philosophical Arguments for God's Existence

1. Romans 1:18–23

2. Psalm 89:11

3. Psalm 90:1–2

4. Psalm 104:5–9

5. Acts 17:22–24

6. Hebrews 11:1–3

7. Psalm 104:10–24

8. Micah 6:6–8

9. Exodus 9:27

10. 2 Chronicles 12:6

11. Psalm 7:8–11

12. Psalm 116:5

13. Psalm 129:4

14. Psalm 145:17

15. Lamentations 1:18

16. Daniel 9:7

17. Daniel 9:14

18. Psalm 139:13–16

19. Isaiah 6:1–8

20. Irwin Lutzer, *Christ Among Other Gods* (Chicago: Moody Publishers, 1997), 132.

21. Paul Little, *Know why You Believe* (Chicago: Intervarsity Press, 2008), 47.

22. Matthew 12:38–40

23. Matthew 16:21; Matthew 20:17; Mark 8:31; 9:31; Luke 9:22; 18:31; 24:26; John 10:11, 15, 17–18

24. Psalm 2

25. Psalm 16:8–11

26. Isaiah 26:19

27. Isaiah 52:13

28. Isaiah 53:12

29. Acts 2:22–24

30. Acts 2:29–36

31. 1 Corinthians 15:12–19

32. 1 Corinthians 15:13

33. 1 Corinthians 15:14

34. 1 Corinthians 15:14b

35. 1 Corinthians 15:15

36. 1 Corinthians 15:17

37. 1 Corinthians 15:17b

38. 1 Corinthians 15:18

39. 1 Corinthians 15:19

40. Acts 4:2; 13:35; 17:18; 24:15; Philippians 1:21–23; 3:10–11; 2 Corinthians 5:1–8; Revelation 20:6

41. Don Carson, *The God Who is There* (Grand Rapids: Baker, 2010), 162–163.

42. Paul Little, *Know Why You Believe* (Chicago; Intervarsity Press, 2008), 52.

43. Ibid, 57.

3 The Evidences the Bible is the Word of God

1. Harold J. Greenlee, *An Introduction to New Testament Textual Criticism* (Grand Rapids: Baker, 1995), 54.

2. Isaiah 40:22.

3. Job 26:10

4. Proverbs 8:27

5. Job 26:10

6. Job 38:8, 11

7. Proverbs 8:27

8. Job 22:14

9. Isaiah 40:22

10. Job 26:7

11. 2 Samuel 22:16

12. Jonah 2:6

13. Genesis 15:5

14. Genesis 22:17

15. Genesis 26:4

16. Genesis 32:12

17. Deuteronomy 1:10

18. Isaiah 40:12

19. Jeremiah 33:22

20. Jeremiah 31:37

21. Hebrews 11:12

22. Genesis 7:1

23. Genesis 8:2

24. Proverbs 8:28

25. Job 26:8

26. Job 36:27–29

27. Job 37:16

28. Job 38:25–27
29. Palm 135:7
30. Ecclesiastes 1:6–7
31. Psalm 8:8
32. Genesis 1:20–31
33. Genesis 6:19
34. Deuteronomy 23:12–14
35. Genesis 17:9–14
36. Leviticus 17:11
37. Genesis 2:1–3
38. Psalm 33:6–9
39. Psalm 102:25–28
40. Romans 8:18–25
41. Hebrews 1:10–12
42. 2 Corinthians 5:17

4 The Evidences the God of the Bible Is the One True God

1. Exodus 20:1–6
2. Leviticus 19:1–4
3. Psalm 31:5

4. Psalm 96:1–5
5. Isaiah 45:5, 6, 18, 21–22
6. Isaiah 46:9–11
7. Isaiah 65:16
8. Jeremiah 10:10
9. John 3:33
10. John 7:18
11. John 7:28
12. John 8:26
13. John 17:3
14. Romans 3:4
15. 1 Thessalonians 1:9
16. 1 John 5:20
17. Revelation 3:7
18. Revelation 3:14
19. Revelation 6:10
20. Revelation 15:3
21. Revelation 16:5–7
22. Revelation 19:11
23. Psalm 19:1–6
24. Psalm 19:7–14

25. 1 Corinthians 2:6–16

26. Hebrews 1:1–4

27. Romans 1:18–32

28. Romans 1:20

29. Romans 1:21

30. Romans 1:22

31. Romans 1:23

32. Romans 1:24–27

33. Romans 1:28–32

34. Acts 15:11

35. Romans 3:21–28

36. Romans 5:15

37. Romans 8:28–30

38. 2 Corinthians 13:14

39. Galatians 2:15–21 (16–17)

40. Ephesians 2:1–10

41. Titus 3:1–7 (5–7)

42. 1 Peter 1:1–2

5 Why Reason and Revelation Alone Are Insufficient in Convincing an Atheist of God's Existence

1. Ezekiel 36:25–26

2. MacArthur Study Bible, *Commentary on Ezekiel* (Nashville: Thomas Nelson, 2006), 1178.

3. John 3:3

4. R. C. Sproul, Tabletalk: *Regeneration Precedes Faith* (Sanford: Ligonier. April, 2013. http://www.ligonier.org.

5. John 6:35–37

6. John 6:44

7. John 6:60–65

8. Romans 8:1–10

9. Ephesians 2:1–5

10. R.C. Sproul, *What is Reformed Theology* (Grand Rapids: Baker, 1997), 183.

11. Charles M. Horne, *Salvation* (Chicago: Moody Press, 1971), 53.

12. R.C. Sproul, *What is Reformed Theology* (Grand Rapids: Baker, 1997), 184.

13. Ibid, 186.

14. 1 Corinthians 1:18–31

15. 1 Corinthians 2:1–5

16. 1 Corinthians 2:6–13

17. 1 Corinthians 2:14–16

6 Letter One

1. Isaiah 40:21–23

2. Job 22:14

3. Job 26:10

4. Proverbs 8:27

5. Matthew 1:16

6. Luke 3:23

7. John 10:30

8. John 14:28

9. John 10:31–33

10. 1 Kings 4:26

11. 2 Chronicles 9:25

12. John MacArthur, *Rediscovering Expository Preaching* (Nashville: Thomas Nelson, 1992), 28.

13. MacArthur Study Bible, *How We Got The Bible* (Nashville: Thomas Nelson, 2006), xxi.

14. Bart Ehrman, *Mythicists* (National Public Radio), 2012.

15. Ibid.

16. Ibid.

17. Robert Gromacki, *New Testament Survey* (Grand Rapids: Baker, 1974), 95.

18. Ibid, 96.

19. John 13:23; 19:26; 20:2; 21:7; 21:20

20. John 18:15–16; 20:2; 21:1–2

21. Numbers 22:28

22. 2 Kings 6:1–7

23. R. C. Sproul, *Tabletalk: Are Miracles for Today?* (Sanford: Ligonier, June 2013), 59.

24. Leviticus 11:13–19

25. Genesis 1:2–25

26. Deuteronomy 6:4–6

27. Proverbs 4:20–23

28. Matthew 22:34–40

29. 2 Peter 3:1–9

30. Matthew 24:32–35

31. MacArthur Study Bible, *Commentary on Matthew* (Nashville: Thomas Nelson, 2006), 1408.

32. 1 John 4:7–12

33. Exodus 20:14

34. 1 Thessalonians 4:1–5

35. John Walvoord and Roy Zuck, *Bible Knowledge Commentary* (Chicago: Victor Books, 1983), 1:140.

36. Exodus 21:7–11

37. Exodus 21:1

38. John Walvoord and Roy Zuck, *Bible Knowledge Commentary* (Chicago: Victor Books, 1983), 1:141.

39. Ibid, 1:141.

40. Walter Kaiser, Jr., *Hard Sayings of the Bible* (Chicago: Intervarsity Press, 1996), 150.

41. Numbers 31:31–41

42. Psalm 137:9

43. Galatians 6:7–8

7 Letter Two

1. John 1:9–11

2. John 2:1–12

3. John 2:4

4. Ibid.

5. Craig S. Keener, *The IVP Bible Background Commentary* (Chicago: Intervarsity Press, 2012), 268.

6. John 2:13–22

7. John 2:19

8. John 2:22

9. John 20:24–25

10. John 20:26–29

11. John 5:1–17

12. John 6:1–15

13. John 6:22–35

14. John 6:26

15. John 6:30

16. John 9

17. John 11

18. John 11:45–46

19. Revelation 6:12–17

8 Letter Three

1. Isaiah 45:7

2. Harold Lindsell, *The Battle for the Bible* (Grand Rapids: Zondervan, 1978), 18.

3. 1 Corinthians 15:12–19

4. R. C. Sproul, *Necessary Blood* (Lancaster: Alliance of Confessing Evangelicals), www.alliancenet.org.

5. Isaiah 52:13–53:12

6. Howard Marshall, *New Bible Dictionary*: *Atonement* (Chicago: Intervarsity Press, 1996), 102.

7. John 3:16

8. 1 John 4:7–11

9. James Strong, *Strong's Exhaustive Concordance* (Nashville, Regal Publishers), Greek. 2435.

10. M. G. Easton, *Easton's Bible Dictionary: Propitiation* (Amazon Digital Services, Inc. 2009), 1,897.

11. Ephesians 2:1–9

9 Letter Four

1. Ravi Zacharias, *Beyond Opinion: Living the Faith We Defend* (Nashville: Thomas Nelson, 2007), 3.

2. Acts 20:35

3. John 21:25

4. John 7:38–39

5. Luke 7:38

6. Romans 5:1

7. Ezekiel 18:4

8. Romans 6:20–23

10 Letter Five

1. Ravi Zacharias, *Beyond Opinion: Living the Faith We Defend* (Nashville: Thomas Nelson, 2007), 4.

2. Ibid, 4.

3. Ibid, 5.

4. Ibid, 5.

5. Judges 21:15

6. 2 Peter 1:16–21

7. Simon Kistemaker, *New Testament Commentary: Peter and Jude* (Grand Rapids: Baker, 2002), 264.

8. Ibid, 264–265.

9. 1 Timothy 1:3–4

10. 1 Timothy 4:1–2

11. 2 Timothy 4:3–5

12. Titus 1:10–14

13. Ecclesiastes 1:9–10

14. John 18:37–38

15. John MacArthur, *The Battle for the Beginning* (Nashville: Word Publishing Group 2001), 62.

16. Wikipedia, *Dating Creation,* https://en.wikipedia.org.

17. Genesis 3:15

18. William J. Hendrickson: *The Gospel of Luke* (Grand Rapids: Baker Book House, 1978), 150.

19. John MacArthur, *God With Us: the Miracle of Christmas* (Grand Rapids: Zondervan, 1990), 5.

20. James Montgomery Boice, *The Christ of Christmas* (Philadelphia: P & R Publishing, 2009), 48.

21. Matthew 2:1–12

22. Matthew 2:1

23. Micah 5:2; Matthew 2:6

24. 1 Peter 3:13–15

25. Matthew 2:8

26. Matthew 2:9–10

27. Matthew 2:11

11 Letter Six

1. Exodus 19:18–25

2. MacArthur Study Bible, *Commentary on Exodus* (Nashville: Thomas Nelson, 2006), 123.

3. Exodus 24:12

4. Exodus 32:15

12 Letter Seven

1. James I. Packer, *Knowing God* (Chicago: Intervarsity Press, 1971), 122.

2. Karl Barth, *Church Dogmatics* (Westminster John Knox Press; 1st Authorized English translation under license from T&T Clark edition (November 1, 1994), 346.

3. Romans 3:9–20

4. 2 Corinthians 10:1–6

5. Ephesians 6:10–20

6. 1 Timothy 1:18

7. 2 Timothy 2:1–4

8. 1 John 5:18–19

9. Revelation 12:7–12

10. Job 5:6–7

11. Job 7:1–2

12. Job 14:1–2

13. Psalm 9:9–10

14. Psalm 22:10–11

15. Psalm 32:7

16. Psalm 46:1–3

17. Ecclesiastes 2:22–23
18. Luke 13:1–5
19. John 16:33
20. 1 Chronicles 29:10–13
21. Psalm 115:1–3
22. 1 Timothy 6:13–16
23. Revelation 4:11
24. Exodus 4:10–11
25. Deuteronomy 32:39
26. 1 Samuel 2:6–8
27. 2 Samuel 10:9–12
28. 2 Kings 17:24–25
29. 2 Samuel 12:15
30. Psalm 33:10–12
31. Psalm 103:15–19
32. Isaiah 14:24–27
33. Isaiah 46:8–11
34. Daniel 4:34–35
35. Amos 3:3–6
36. Matthew 10:28–29
37. Isaiah 45:5–7

38. Romans 8:28

39. Job 1:21

40. Job 2:10–11

41. 2 Corinthians 1:3–4

13 Letter Eight

1. Joel R. Beeke, Randall J. Pederson, *Meet the Puritans* (Reformation Heritage Books (February 1, 2007), xvii.

2. John 3:3

3. James I. Packer, *An Anglican to Remember* (St Antholin's Lectureship Charity 1996) 1–2.

4. *Mayflower Compact*, www.pilgrimhallmuseum.org.5.

5. Library of Congress, *Religion and the Founding of the American Republic,* http://www.loc.gov/exhibits/religion.

6. The Episcopal Church, *The Book of Common Prayer*, www.episcopalchurch.org.

7. The Massachusetts Constitution of 1780, www.heritage.org/.../massachusetts-constitution.

8. The United States Constitution, www.archives.gov/.../cons.

9. Library of Congress, *Religion and the Congress of the Confederation 1774–1789*, http://www.loc.gov/exhibits/religion.

10. The United States Constitution, www.archives.gov/.../cons.

11. Leviticus 19:34

12. The United States Constitution, www.archives.gov/.../cons.

13. Deuteronomy 17:15

14. The United States Constitution, www.archives.gov/.../cons.

15. Deuteronomy 17:6

16. The United States Constitution, www.archives.gov/.../cons.

17. Ezekiel 18:20

18. The United States Constitution, www.archives.gov/.../cons

19. Isaiah 33:22

20. Psalm 22:27–28

21. Daniel 4:34–37

22. Daniel 2:20–21

23. Romans 13:1

24. Proverbs 22:6

25. John 1:5

26. Proverbs 4:7

27. Micah 6:8

28. Psalm 19:1

29. Russell Kirk, *The American Cause* (Intercollegiate Studies Institute; 1 edition 2002), Loc 333.

30. Ibid, Loc 415.

14 Letter Nine

1. 1 Corinthians 2:14

2. 1 John 3:11–15

3. Matthew 5:11–12

4. John 15:18–25

5. Proverbs 26:4–5

6. Psalm 14:1

7. Proverbs 26:5

8. Matthew 12:38–40

9. Matthew 16:1–4

10. Luke 6:6–11

11. Romans 8:18–25

12. Luke 23:32–43

13. 2 Corinthians 12:1–3

14. Revelation 2:7

15 Letter Ten

1. Ephesians 2:1–3

2. Wikipedia, *I Heard the Bells on Christmas Day*, https://en.wikipedia.org/.

3. Henry Wadsworth Longfellow, *I Heard the Bells on Christmas Day*, http://www.hymnsandcarolsofchristmas.com/Poetry/christmas_bells.htm.

4. Psalm 19

5. Romans 3:9–20

6. Jonah 2:9

7. Hebrews 4:14–16

8. Psalm 27:1–5

9. Edward Mote, *The Solid Rock*, library.timelesstruths.org/music/The Solid Rock/.

10. Galatians 1:1–5

11. Galatians 1:3

12. Romans 5:6–8

13. Galatians 1:4

14. Galatians 3:13

15. 1 John 4:7–10

16. 1 John 2:1–2

17. Hebrews 2:14–18

18. Romans 3:25

19. Colossians 2:13–14

20. MacArthur Study Bible, *Commentary on Colossians* (Nashville: Thomas Nelson, 2006), 1803.

21. Galatians 3:10–14

22. Galatians 1:4

23. Galatians 1:5

24. Galatians 1:5

25. Genesis 3:14–15

26. Isaiah 7:13–14

27. Isaiah 9:1–2

28. Matthew 1:18–25

29. Luke 1:26–38

30. Genesis 12:3

31. Genesis 18:1–18

32. Genesis 22:18

33. Genesis 26:4–5

34. Genesis 28:13–14
35. Matthew 1:1
36. Galatians 3:16
37. Genesis 49:10
38. Numbers 24:17
39. Matthew 1:3
40. Mathew 2:2–3
41. Luke 3:23
42. Revelation 5:5
43. Psalm 89:27
44. Psalm 132:11
45. 2 Samuel 7:12–16
46. Jeremiah 23:5–6
47. Isaiah 11:1–2
48. Matthew 1:1
49. Luke 3:31–33
50. Luke 3:31
51. Micah 5:2
52. Matthew 2:1
53. Luke 2:1–7
54. John4:40–42

55. Deuteronomy 18:15–22.

56. Psalm 110:1–4

57. Hebrews 2:17–18

58. Hebrews 4:14–15

59. Hebrews 5:1–6

60. Hebrews 6:26–27

61. Psalm 2:1–12

62. Matthew 1:18–25

63. Luke 1:31–35

64. John 1:1–5

65. John 20:30–31

66. John 10:11–18

16 The Final Letter

1. Matthew 5:43–48

2. Romans 12:20–21

3. Acts 7:59–60

4. 1 Corinthians 2:1–5

CPSIA information can be obtained
at www.ICGtesting.com
Printed in the USA
FFOW01n2104201016
28646FF